Architecture in Space Structures

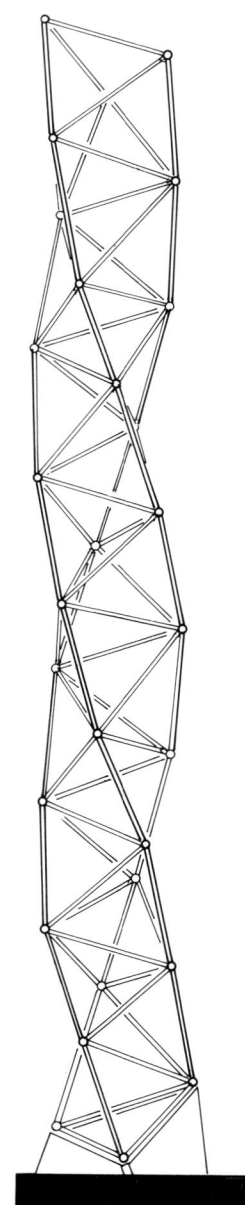

MICK EEKHOUT

Architecture in Space Structures

Uitgeverij 010 Publishers, Rotterdam

Copyright 1989 Mick Eekhout / Uitgeverij 010 Publishers

CIP

Eekhout, Mick

Architecture in Space Structures / Mick Eekhout
– Rotterdam: Uitgeverij 010 Publishers. – Ill.
Ook verschenen als proefschrift Delft, 1989.
– Met lit.opg. – Met samenvatting in het Nederlands.
ISBN 90-6450-080-0
SISO 711.3 UDC 72.011 NUGI 923
Trefw.: ruimtelijke constructies in de bouwkunst.

Vormgeving Rudo Hartman / Den Haag
Druk Tulp bv / Zwolle

Foreword

During the recent decade engineers and architects witnessed significant changes in their professions due to industrial and technological developments which had a far-reaching effect upon modern engineering, contemporary architecture and directly led to the birth of the High-Tech structures. Introductions of new building materials, improved constructional techniques and acceptance of new structural forms are responsible for the great interest now expressed all over the world in three-dimensional structures. Architects and many engineers discover that space structures not only offer them structural advantages but also produce striking simplicity of form leading to often unconventional but very pleasing appearance and visual beauty. Progressive architects talk nowadays of integration of structure with architecture and this is precisely what well-designed space structures achieve. The introduction and wide-spread use of high-speed electronic computers enables the designer to analyse even very complex frameworks with much greater accuracy than ever before and with a remarkable reduction in the time involved. The impact of industrialisation on prefabricated space structures has proved to be truly remarkable. During recent years a large number of scientific papers, treatises, monographs and books have been published in several languages, dealing with various aspects of the analysis, design and construction of space structures.

Many readers will agree that this book which they have now in front of them is unique and quite different from those already published. The author of this book entitled 'Architecture in Space Structures', deals with the aspects which are not covered in existing books. He is known as a designer of space structures built in the Netherlands and in many countries abroad. His approach in this book is based on his creative thinking and imaginative ideas.

Those who know the work of Mick Eekhout would give as the reason for his success the fact that the author presents in himself an unusual combination of a creative architect, shrewd structural engineer, progressive industrial designer and civil engineering contractor. There are very few people who can combine the characteristics of the above mentioned four professions. The author of this book is one of them.

Reading the book will reveal that the author possesses visible enthusiasm, scientific curiosity and readiness to experiment. It is a book which many architects and structural engineers will find really refreshingly different and directly useful in their own work.

Zygmunt Makowski
Emeritus Professor Civil Engineering
University of Surrey UK

Contents

Acknowledgement ... 7

Process

1 Space Structures in General

1 What are Space Structures? ... 11
2 Hypotheses on Architecture in Space Structures ... 11
3 Historical Development of Space Structures ... 12

2 Materials and Systems

1 Inspiring Materials ... 24
2 Structural Systems ... 28

3 Design Process of Spatial Structures

1 Architectural + Structural + Industrial Design ... 32
2 Design and Production in One Hand ... 35
3 Modelwork as a Design Tool ... 36
4 Creative Design, Research and Development ... 40
5 Marketing Aspects of Product Development ... 44
6 Production, Transport, Assembly and Erection ... 50
7 Application of Products in Projects ... 55

Products

4 Space Frame Structures

1 General Principles ... 73
2 Nodal Systems ... 83
3 Flat Space Frames ... 86
4 Stacked Space Frames ... 90
5 Macro Space Frames ... 94
6 Single Curved Space Frames ... 95
7 Dome Space Frames ... 98
8 Saddle Space Frames ... 103

5 Tensile Structures

1 Tensegrity Structures ... 105
2 Stretched Membranes ... 107
3 Spatially Guyed Structures ... 115

6 Integration of Structures and Cladding

1 Space Frames and Membranes ... 117
2 Space Frames and Metal Cladding ... 122
3 Space Frames and Glass Panels ... 124

Appendix

Evaluation of the Building Parties ... 132
Dutch Summary ... 137
Bibliography and Publications ... 141
Biography ... 143

Acknowledgement

In 1982 the author designed a number of prestressed membrane structures. At the time there was not yet an experienced tentmaker in the Netherlands who was willing to accurately manufacture the complex and irregular cutting pattern of membranes. However, this did not keep the author from trying to realise these attractively curved designs. The tents were designed and further developed with the manual model techniques of Frei Otto. Some clear space in the author's architects office was made and so the first tents were practically cut and welded on the drafting tables. At the end of that year a much larger space was needed to build the first export order: a tubular dome structure with a double suspended prestressed membrane for a swimming pool in Saudi Arabia. The neighbour, the Royal Delft Blue Pottery, offered to rent some space in one of their old and empty factory halls. This gave the opportunity to build the aluminium dome structure and the suspended membranes indoors and to test them.

Other structures were still sub-contracted out at the time, but were not made with the required quality in regard with exactness of size and coating. So after a while a number of machines were purchased and gradually a well-equipped laboratory was installed, with more and more production facilities.

The complicated stretched membranes made the author aware that a faster technical progression could be made by simultaneously designing and realising spatial structures. For this type of structures, an intensive relation with daily feedbacks between design and realisation became the author's personal and alternative way compared with the usual networks. In the history of modern architecture this 'Design + Build' attitude has only been followed by a few of the well-known designers. They illustrated what the force of personal commitment can mean for new developments. Normally new structural concepts are the result of the efforts in building teams performed by independent architects and structural engineers, working with independent contractors. The ad hoc character of these building teams make them not as appropriate for a more continuous building product development process compared with a team of architectural + structural + industrial designers in one company devoted to one type of product.

The step from architectural design to structural and industrial design and even to production, is not often made. The synergetic force of these four disciplines offered the author however all chances to realise those structures he was really interested in, while taking all responsibilities for the experimentation and the actual building. After seven years of continuous design, development and realisation of different types of space frames, domes, tents, tensegrities and glazed roof structures, the real pioneer organisation of the author's company, Octatube Space Structures bv, has gradually been changed into a professional management. So one of the aims of this book is to review the results of the initial pioneer period. Another aim is to illustrate the specialisation in space structures with a more basic design philosophy on the interaction of space structures and architecture, and to present the products and processes officially as an alternative to the normal routines of conceiving new concepts. Writing this book gave the opportunity to combine philosophies and technical information together in the form of a 'Process + Products' book, with all discussed and presented subjects linked in an orderly way. It also gave the opportunity to discover discrepancies, and to start new innovative projects at the same time as the book was written and as a consequence of the act of writing itself.

The topic of this dissertation the author owes actually to Jaap Oosterhoff who amended the original idea to write a book on 'the Relationship between Architecture and Structures' into the current one. For one year long he has read and discussed the texts very critically as a structural engineer and as a writer; the author owes him sincere thanks for the continuous interest in and encouragement of the work of his former student. Also Moshe Zwarts who accompanied the writing of the book from an architect-designer's point of view and who also agreed to the writing of this thesis not as a result of a theoretical study but as a result of the combined theory and practice of space structures as product development. This book would not have been possible without the support of Mrs Mieke Eekhout who enabled her husband to spend his spare time on writing the book in the midst of a very busy period of their lives, while she assisted with lay-out work and pictures. And last but not least without the enthusiastic support of the group of young architects, engineers, designers and craftsmen in the Octatube team, the shown projects would not have been built at all.

Process

Space Structures in General

Space structures are loadbearing structures applied in architecture that really make use of its three-dimensional action as a structure. As a spatial design feature space structures have a strong impact on the overall architecture. The major part of studies on space structures concerns the structural action. But as space structures are getting more popular to be applied in architecture, the time has come to give the view of a designer on this matter. Space structures can be defined in a few different ways: according to the involved aspects in architecture, in topology, in function, the psychological role and of course in the structural sense. No matter how confusing the word 'space structures' might be at first glance, the structural definition will be held. A number of hypotheses will be presented that will be worked out respectively in the succeeding chapters.

Space structures are known as structural schemes for building applications for approximately 200 years. The first iron skeleton dome was built in Paris in 1806. The first attempts to build space frames are known to be made by Alexander Graham Bell in 1907, although the real popularity of space frames only came in the 1950s and later when these structures were accepted as a means of design by architects. The stretched membranes were developed by Frei Otto from the 1950s and became popular in the 1960s.

As a whole the current use of space structures has been stimulated by a number of important developments, that will be dealt with separately:
1 The invention and further development of structural materials.
2 The striving for maximum use of structural materials.
3 Development of new structural 3-D schemes.
4 Development of structural analysis methods for statically indeterminate structures.
5 Functional requirements for roofstructures with large column free monospans.
6 Increased demand for square internal column grids in plan rather than rectangular grids in multispans.
7 The personal input and involvement of pioneers of three-dimensional structural design.
8 Acceptance of space structures by architects and integration of space structures as building components in their projects.

1 What are Space Structures?

The term 'space structures' or 'spatial structures' is used in the world of architecture and structural engineering to indicate loadbearing structures that require 3-dimensional space to act and to be stable. One could object that this description is in fact valid for all architectural structures. How would structures stand up in space unless they are stable in three dimensions? But the distinction is made between composed structures that are built up of 2-D elements and integral space structures where there is no further distinction to be made between smaller composing 2-D elements. An example of a composed structure is a trussed roof. Such a roof consists of separate flat trusses, vertical posts, purlins on top, windbracings in the wall planes and windbracings in the roof planes. This composed structure stands in space, but is composed of 2-D elements. One could say this total composition is a 2.5-D structure. This in contradiction with 'space structures', real 3-D structures, that cannot be analysed as composing elements acting separately. Yet the word 'space structures' normally confuses the public (and even professionals) slightly, because of the many implications of the prefix 'space'. This applies both to the Dutch word 'ruimte' in the indication 'ruimtelijke constructies' as to the English translation.

The description of 'space structures' can be seen from different points of view:

1 Structurally: Space structures are loadbearing structures that can be analysed as really 3-dimensional, and cannot be analysed in terms of cooperating 2-dimensional elements or planes. The word 'space structures' or 'spatial structures' is abbreviated from 'spatially stabilised structures' as an indication of their structural action.
2 Topologically: Space structures in architecture are the most space-bound structures in architecture: more space-bound than earth-bound: roof structures rather than floors.
3 Architectonically: Space structures are structures with a spacious impact, involving all three dimensions around the spectator. In reality the architectural attractiveness is the major cause for building space structures.
4 Literally: Space structures are structures in outer space, from outer space or connected with aeronautics.
5 Functionally: Space structures need space to act as a structure, are rather bulky and contain a large air volume like air-inflated structures.
6 Philosophically: Space structures tend to suggest a relationship between our terrestrial structures and aeronautical structures. There is a suggestion of a struggle with the laws of gravity and a relationship with the techniques of production derived from aeronautics. Or was it a helicopter view that made these structures possible? It lends its name from Space Age Science. (Almost Science Fiction becoming reality.) This last description might be too promising. Reality is more simple.

All these descriptions of space structures illustrate the usual confusion around the words. In this book the word 'space structures' or 'spatial structures' will be used in the primary structural sense, leaving the other descriptions only in the imagination of the reader to enrich the structural meaning.

This book will present the vision of a product-architect on all kind of design aspects of space structures. The aim was to write a broad overview rather than describe a deep specialism. The title 'Architecture in Space Structures' indicates the various design aspects of space structures with an inward-looking view. It is not a book on 'Space Structures in Architecture' which would mean an involvement or mutual radiation on the surrounding architecture, and would give a more extensive treatment of the buildings around the space structures. Architecture in the sense of the book is meant as the built environment; is not an opinion on the quality of these buildings, but rather used as a collection of all buildings with their relationships, from simple sheds to high quality Architecture. No comments will be given on Architecture in itself. Nor, for that matter, on Structural or Industrial Design. Architecture is an expression indicating the total aspects concerning the built environment, as a clear distinction from Structural and Industrial Design.

2 Hypotheses on Architecture in Space Structures

From experiences gained in the 1970s and 1980s by the author in designing and building Space Structures in Architecture, the author has deducted a number of hypotheses, concerning the process of designing space structures and a more general structural design philosophy. These hypotheses include the following:

1 The development of space structures is accelerated when the structural design is optimised simultaneously with architectural design and product development or industrial design. (See appendix 1)
2 The development of space structures is stimulated by a close relationship between design and building. New

systems prosper when design, development and research as the more intellectual activities are integrated with production, assembly and erection as the more economical activities in one company. (See par 3.2.)

3 The development of computer software and hardware has firmly stimulated the application of several types of statically indeterminate space structures. (See par 1.3)

4 The availability of computer aided design programs stimulates architecture students and young architects to design more on an abstract way; to pay less attention to the mechanical, technical and material side. The computer will defect the young architect in the ability to detail his/her designs, facilitating more the use of well-known materials and techniques than new ones. (See par 1.3)

5 A larger complexity and a higher price of a new substituting building element has a negative influence on the successfulness of its application when simple and cheaper alternatives are available on the building market. (See par 3.5)

6 Being frank and open about new technical information, intrigues architects and stimulates the application of new techniques. (See chapter 4,5 and 6)

7 The design and development of new products in the building industry composed of new materials and / or techniques, can ideally be done by a product-architect, combining the skills of an architect and an industrial designer. (See par 3.1)

8 Product development and product research in the building industry both benefit from a creative approach, combining broader and deeper know-hows. (See par 3.4)

9 In general the position of the architect has been reduced during the past centuries from the position of the master-builder in the middle ages to that of an artistic and overall designer of the scheme of a building. During the last decades this functional erosion process has not lost velocity. (See par 3.1)

10 The fragmentation in the building industry into distinct parties will not lead to new developments of techniques and products when these parties are not prepared to cooperate intensively. (See par 3.1)

11 During many centuries there has been a tension between an abstract (or material-denying) and a mechanical (or material-confirming) attitude towards architecture. In modern architecture abstract and mechanical tendencies co-exist. Even the design of structures can be performed either towards a mechanical or towards an abstract result. (See par 3.7)

12 Material shortage can lead to more ingenious structures than will be the case in times of low material costs: material luxury can lead designers to be less attentive, and seduce them to visually more boring structures. (See par 2.2)

13 The use of CAM-techniques will result in the flexible production of more custom-made or less production-standardised structural systems at only a slightly higher price than standard systems. CAM makes non-standard systems payable. (See par 1.3 / 3.6)

14 Scale models are very helpful and inspiring tools in the design stage to gain insight in the structural behaviour of space structures, especially when tensile elements are part of the structure. (See par 3.3)

In fact the hypotheses in this paragraph are a deduction of the main observations in the experience of the author, worked out in the paragraphs mentioned. Some hypotheses are the result of more general observations, and will not be illustrated particularly or extensively.

3 Historical Development of Space Structures

The 'prehistory' of space structures started when Bélanger and Brunet designed and built the Halle au Blé in Paris between 1806 and 1811 in the form of a hemispherical dome of cast iron elements. The first iron domes in England were built in 1815-1823 over the Royal Pavilion in Brighton in the famous flame form, and the greenhouse of Syon House covered by an iron dome was designed by Fowler in 1827. These dome structures more or less were translations of timber into cast iron. The statical scheme was simple, and in our eyes with insufficient stability. The domes of the Crystal Art Palace in the Botanical Garden of Glasgow by Kibble (1873) show by their twisted lines that the glass panels in putty contributed in a large extend to the torsional stability of the domes. Mainly due to the glass panel coverings, the glass houses were to become very popular in the nineteenth century, and were mainly built as serial produced buildings.

August Föppl (1854-1924) is generally recognised as one of the first scientists having introduced consequent research work concerning 3-D steel trusses. However, the first real attempts to design and realise metal space frames are known to have been made by Alexander Graham Bell (1847-1922). This scientist is generally known as the inventor of the telephone. But Bell has also been an universal genius engaged in different sciences: aerodynamics, aeronautics, shipbuilding, structural design, medical and electrotechnical sciences. In 1907 he was 60

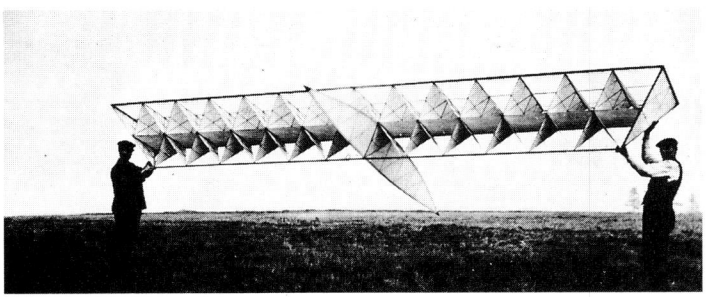

1 An areoplane wing composed of a timber space frame with cotton planes conceived as a regular spatial structural system by Alexander Graham Bell in 1907 introduces space frames to the public.

2 In the same year an outlook tower was built by A.G. Bell with steel nodes and bar elements, to watch the ongoing aeroplane experiments. Space structures are as old as the first flying machines.

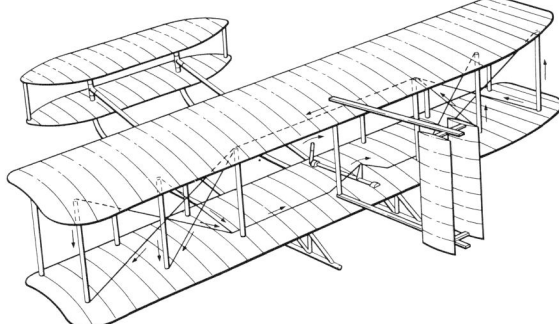

3 The famous Flyer III designed and built by Orville and Wilbur Wright, was the first aeroplane to fly in 1905. Its construction was largely determined by the 19th century experiments with spatial trusses.

years old, and lived in Canada. At that time much scientific research was focussed on the new aeronautical experiments. As we know, during the first years of this century, Orville and Wilbur Wright developed their flying machines in the USA. Their Flyer III became the first usable plane in the world in 1905. The model of this Flyer was very much influenced by the state of the art of the 19th-century knowledge of truss systems from the building industry. During the second half of the last century, a large number of interesting steel structures in buildings were conceived and built: bridges, exhibition halls, train stations, towers, and glass houses. (fig 3) Gustav Eiffel (1832-1923) was responsible for a considerable development of space truss elements he had made of separate open steel sections riveted to a whole. These elements were used in his Douro bridge in Oporto, (1877), his Truyière bridge in the French Massive (1880-1884) and his Eiffel Tower in Paris (1887-1889). At the same time Benjamin Baker and John Fowler were responsible for the design of the railbridge over the Firth of Forth near Edinburgh between 1882 and 1890. In this design cantilevering space trusses were used, for the first time in wrought steel and with tubular steel sections riveted together like boiler shafts. These steel structures in France and in the UK made the 1880s very important for steel structures in general, and actually formed the 'middle ages' for space structures. These works were realised about 20 years before Bell undertook his structural experiments. Especially the differences between earth-bound steel structures and flying structures, stimulated 3-dimensional thinking. As aeroplanes fly independent from any means of support, a different set of random conditions are applicable in the design of the overall structure of a plane: a flying structure must consist of a closed structural system capable both to take tensile and compressive stresses in its composing members due to all kinds of external loadings. Where buildings can be provided with additional fixings to the ground capable to get rid of horizontal or vertical compressive and tensile forces, aeroplanes must be designed as an entity of forces.

Although in structural engineering the space trusses developed by Eiffel, can be regarded as an assembly of 2-dimensional trusses, the early aeroplane designs showed explicitly that 2,5-D and 3-D entities had to be developed further, because the spatial stability had to be absolute. However, in the years directly after their successful flights with the Flyer III, the Wright brothers were discouraged to undertake further developments due to a lack of interest by the American government. In the years between 1905 and 1910 other pioneers also were fanatically experimenting new ideas and building new prototypes. It was in this ambience that Bell was stimulated to make a technical contribution. Two of his experiments have to be commemorated: a space frame outlook tower, and a space frame wing. He realised the outlook tower in the form of three intersecting space trusses in triangular cross section with a platform on top: fig 2. El Lissitzky would in the early 1920s make a similar scheme known as Lenin's Tribune. Bell's contribution was the first attempt to make 3-D space trusses with identical modular units of nodes and bars. Bell also constructed a multi-layered aeroplane wing model using identical steel nodes and bars, filled with cotton membranes to gain a large lifting area. (fig 1) The tower gave an excellent outlook in the sky for possible flying objects, but the wing proposal will have been too heavy ever to make a chance for taking off as a part of an aeroplane, even though the steel elements were connected by cotton membranes. At that time the aeroplane wing principle as we know it now, was not yet fully acknowledged. [1, 2]

So the first space frames coincided with the first successfull attempts in aviation technology. Be it that construction technology was lent from the building industry to aviation, whereas nowadays space aviation technologies are again adapted into the building industry. So space structures are sandwiched between developments in the aeronautical industry. The process of mutual influence has been changed in 80 years time, as Jan Kaplicky and David Nixon of Future Systems (Los Angeles) show[3] in their reasoning towards the use the available know-how of monocoque and semi-monocoque structures from airframes into the field of building construction. (fig 4) In later publications by Nixon and Kaplicky an even wider spin-off of aerospace technology for new concepts of lightweight structures is advocated.[4] These relations indicate that we can metaphorically use the word 'space' structures, with some justice.

The current use of space structures has known its popularity mainly in the post-war years. The public interest in space structures has been shifted in that period of time from shell structures, via stretched membranes, space trusses, inflatables to tensegrity structures, depending of various reasons. As a whole the current use of space structures has been stimulated by a number of important developments, that will be dealt with in this paragraph separately:

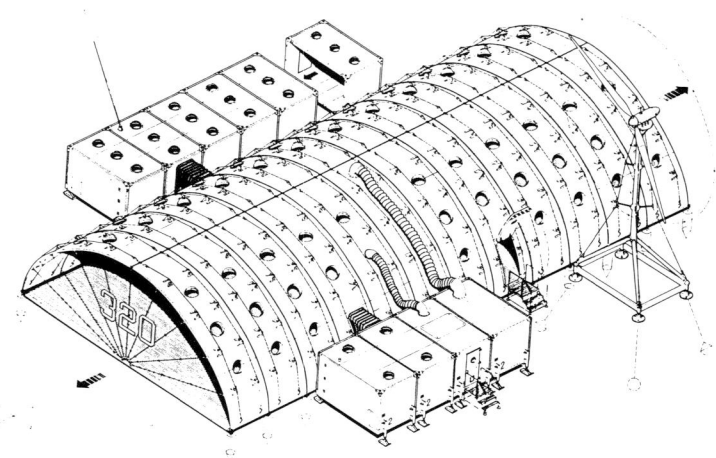

4 One of the many design proposals by David Nixon and Jan Kaplicky of Future Systems, Los Angeles, where they show a spin-off of the aeronautic experiments and progress the introduction of aeronautically proven structural components into architecture. Project 115 is an example of an industrialised unit Mark 3, 1983.

1 *Development of Structural Materials* The building materials suited for space structures like steel, aluminium and to a lesser extend also laminated timber, were invented in the last century and developed mainly before 1950. These materials are regarded to belong to the state-of-the-art.

Only the development of the various plastics, and of course refinements in the productions of the forementioned materials took place in the last 40 years. Steel and aluminium are relatively established building materials, that perhaps gained more popularity after 1950 by lower costprices due to large investments in the production facilities of the half products. This process was fruitful untill the material prices came within the reach, common in the building industry with its notorious tradition for substituting one material for another in the finished product on approximately the same price level.

The space structures designed and built by the author all use either steel or aluminium as structural material occasionally combined with plastics and glass. The inspiration derived from the virtues and properties of these materials for the designer of space structures are dealt with in Chapter 2, but are given in short:
• Steel as the most commonly used material for space structures, is well accepted in all its properties and is researched on in great depth. Most of the research results do not have an influence on design. Amongst these are the developments of high grade steel qualities, of welding in structures and of the effects by dynamic loadings. All of which have only a random effect on the use of steel

in space structures by designers.

- Aluminium is a less rigid material for structural purposes, but has advantages over steel in case of lightweight loadings and corrosion agressive atmospheres. Its material properties lead to another set of space structure systems, where form and geometry neutralise the lack of material rigidity, especially for the very design-sensitive glass-covered structures.
- Glass is only allowed in use by the building codes of most European countries as a non-structural material: only small bending moments are allowed to be taken, and no additional normal forces from external loadings like deadweight of other glass panels and wind/snow loading. The growing resistance of glass panels in regard to safety and vandalism, lead towards the use of heat-strengthened and laminated glass panels. These panels are so strong that an attempt seemed worth while to try to use glass panels as structural elements, replacing a part of the usual steel or aluminium elements. In Par 2.1. the properties are explained, and in Par 6.3 some experimental attempts are described.
- Plastics have known a positive and fast development as a structural material until 1973, when the oil prices went up dramatically and the prophesied plastics boom collapsed. As a structural material it was used in Glassfiber Reinforced Polyester shells, in the fabric material of stretched membranes and pneumatic structures. These inflatables since then also suffered from the high maintainance and energy costs, and are not very popular any more. GRP material has severely been restricted in use by fire regulations, and was occasionally replaced by Glassfiber Reinforced Cement (GRC), which does not have the same appealing structural properties. GRP is a good material solution for chemically agressive environments. Only in the fields of the stretched membrane materials some developments have taken place like the teflon- (or PTFE-)coated and silicone-coated glassfiber fabrics. These membranes can be combined with flexible pul-trusion bar elements to form small flexible membrane units with a simple manual erection.

2 *Maximum Material Use* Normally the most important requirement for load bearing structures in buildings is that they are built economically. The total cost-price is an addition sum of material, energy and labour prices. Energy and labour are added values in subsequent stages of production from raw materials to finished building elements. All three elements are subject to economical fluctuations in an uneven and hardly prophetisable pace. The actual costs of the three elements will differ in time and in location. In order to express

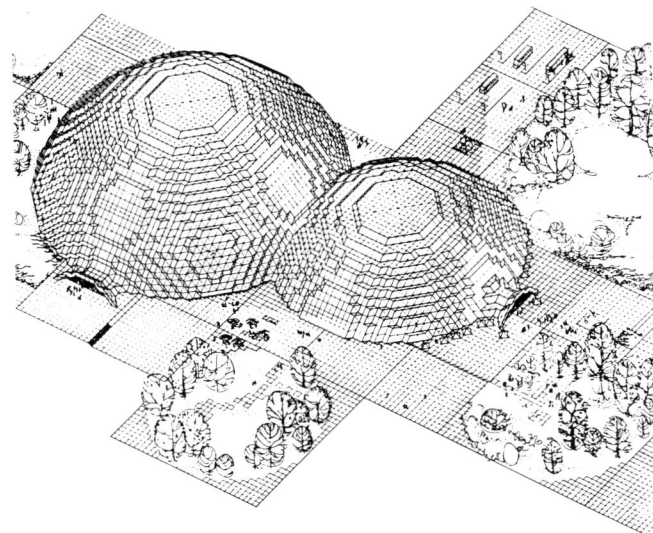

5 Design proposal for three dome structures by Max Mengeringhausen / MERO, composed of identical bar lengths and identical nodes in the early seventies.

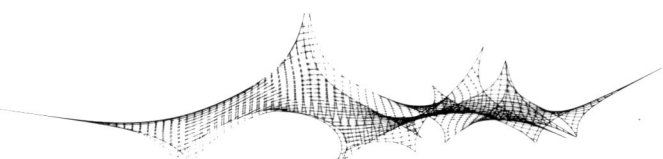

6 Computer graphics of the intermediate parts of the Munich Olympic Games '72 cable net structure by Gunther Behnish and Frei Otto. This work marks the change over from hand-made modelwork to computerwork.

one's opinion on the economy of a structure, the circumstantial data will have to be considered. But apart from the actual cost it is realistic to study the amounts of materials, labour and energy spent into a structure in absolute terms. In our time of growing abstrahism it is no wonder that several attempts have been made to approach the problem of the optimisation of the use of building material using various criteria. Richard Buckminster Fuller's statement was: 'you only need to weigh a building to know the state of technology it is built with'. Meaning that advanced technology resulted in less deadweight. For him building was an intellectual game.

Frei Otto displayed his theory on the 'Bic-value' of building materials as 'the ultimate length of a structural element able to suspend itself'. Otto's approach was based on theoretical tensile strengths of building materials, but not usable in more complicated situations when also compression forces and bending moments occur in a building element. Frei Otto's attitude was influenced by the post-war lack of material in the building industry. It would remain a driving force for him, although the economical circumstances would change in later years.[6]

Yet both approaches of Fuller and Otto encouraged the use of a minimal amount of material to result in maximum attainable effects, departing from high material costs and lower labour and energy costs. An opposite situation occurs when a designer is forced by the building economy to invest minimal energy and labour and maximum material input, in case material costs are low, but energy and labour are expensive. As the current economic situation is one of high labour costs and relative high energy, one might state that may be the countrary of Fuller's dictum is true: heavy structures require less labour and are more progressive in the current building economy, whether one likes it, or not. The actual choice between the optimisation of the three elements will be done on local conditions. The built result for the average bystander, however, displays only the optical result of having used a minimal amount of material, despite all the input in energy and labour that are history. The result is a visual manifestation in its own right. Nevertheless, while Fuller and Otto worked out their theories (early 1950s), the economical situation was in their right, and only changed afterwards. The development of space structures was enormously stimulated by the intellectual and more easy quantifiable approach of striving to use only a minimum of material that preferably was to be used in fully or with equally distributed stress situation. No wonder that Buckminster Fuller produced large amounts of inventions in different sciences, and took a considerable number of patents on building systems, most of them on the use of geodesic dome structures. Some of these patented building systems are still built all over the world nowadays, but mostly out of aesthetical design considerations, and not because of pure material use. Their prices are not low-cost any more.

Frei Otto pioneered the field of stretched membranes and inflatable structures from the early 1950s onto the mid 1970s, when developments were taken over by other sophisticatedly equipped and computer-related colleagues like Taiyo Kogyo in Japan, Walter Bird, David Geiger and Horst Berger in the US, Ove Arup and Ted Happold in the UK. Worldwide speaking, stretched membrane structures are regarded as new architypes, and have found applications as umbrella or parasol roof structures, especially for sport stadia, and outdoor coverings in warm climates.

Of all the space structural systems, space frames are the ones with the largest reserve capacity against changing loadings (prestressed elements can also take a certain amount of compression forces). This means that not the same optimalisation has taken place as in stretched membranes. Yet compared with two-dimensional steel trusses for example, the resulting deadweight can show considerable savings: reductions of 15 to 30% are quite often reached. But, again, this does not implicate that the resulting structure always is cheaper.

Space frames are originally a combination of an industrial concept and a structural concept. The former refers to the work of Konrad Wachsmann and Max Mengeringhausen. The latter refers more to the work of Zygmunt Makowski. The structural concept being that all elements should be sized to the structural function and that by two or three way grid systems external loadings result in low but equal stresses in the individual elements: optimal use of material in the members. The characteristics of space frames are treated in full extent in Chapter 4.

Conclusion from these considerations is that the development of space structures was enormously stimulated in times of high material costs, but now, in 1989, is more interesting for architects as a design phenomenon than a structural or economical must. Like the adaption to the new 19th century iron, steel and glass building techniques occured quite slowly in architecture, the same can be said of the adaption of space structures by architects: acceptations began only in the 1960s, long after most of the technical developments took place.

3 *New 3-Dimensional Structural Schemes* In this century three basic types of usable space structures have been developed, classified by the author as: membrane-like, truss-like and shell-like structures. This subdivision of space structures and their combinations, will be treated more extensively in par 2.2.

4 *Computer Analysis Programs* The development of fast working computer programs has actually enabled space structures to be built. As space structures usually are statically indeterminate and hence complex to analyse, the development of computer programs enabled these structures to be realised on a large scale. These computer programs follow the same method of calculation as usually done by hand but only in fractions of the time. An illustration of this is the comparison between the time in which the statical analysis of one of the first Dutch space frames, the Amstel-halls of the Rai complex in Amsterdam were performed by hand in 1966, and a statical analysis which nowadays is estimated to take only two weeks complete with input and output

writing. Structural engineer Hans Enserink of the architects- and engineers office DBSV in Rotterdam estimated the time consumption in 1966 on 2 months for 2 engineers (surface area 11.130 m²). So the computer developments have had a considerable influence in preparation time.

Structural analysis programs usually are based on the finite element method. A widely spread computer program in use at the TU Delft since 1960 is the ICES-Strudl program, running on IBM main frames at the Computer Centre of the University. Since the development of micro-computers, however, smaller programs have been developed that often also appeared to be more flexible in use. At Octatube's a special program has been developed according to the same finite element principles as ICES, but running on ATARI micro computers, connecting the possiblity of in-house use of 2,5-Dimensional graphical presentation and statical analysis. The program is called SPACE-CAD, and has shortened the average speed of structural project analysis by 50 % in 2 years time. The next step in the development after the spatial drafting program with the statical analysis part will be the connection with and further development of a detail drafting program giving exact sizes of the composing elements of the structure. Number and size should be exact enough to result in actual shop drawings for the factory. At this moment there is no such a low-cost computer program at Octatube's available, but in co-operation with Ludwig van Wilder of the TU Delft his detail program has been used for some projects with stayed skylight structures.

The last and ultimate step will be the listing of the detailed size data to feed equally automised sawing, cutting and drilling machines. In the company, these last two phases have not been realised yet, remaining in the goals for the coming time and will not be treated in greater detail. However, the author estimates that one of the most influential impulses from the use of computer technologies is the calculation of the composition of geometrical elements that are used to build a space structure. In regular structures these composing bar and node elements are similar. Interests of the author lead to an emphasis on geometrically irregular space structures that are composed of elements with different lengths, different spatial angles etc. It is in fact the engineering of these irregular space structures that could be stimulated economically when the composing elements are engineered by computer and when the engineered elements are manufactured by computer-assisted techniques. In which case the amount of involved human engineering is minimised, as is the error factor. Computer Aided Engineering and Computer Aided Manufacturing promise to enable the realisation of non-standard space structures for cost prices only slightly higher than completely standard. This attitude is believed to make a more meaningful progressive step forward than exploiting computer techniques to reach the minimum budget standard structures as a goal.

Generally one can conclude that of all human energy spent in the space structures realised by the author, one third is spent in engineering, one third in manufacturing and one third in assembly on site. This relatively large amount of engineering energy is caused by the consequences of frequent developments and experimenting. But in itself (where possible) computer techniques can be a means to reduce the involved manhours in engineering, or to dedicate these manhours to the more intellectually demanding and rewarding design and development work.

Space structures are lightweight structures. Due to their relatively easy handling they are ideal for international trading. At this moment the know-how and manufacturing occurs mainly in the western countries. It is to be foreseen, however, that before the end of the century, some production facilities will be transplanted to the low-cost labour countries and distribution starts from these points to the rest of the world. Apart from different labour costs, new tax barriers play a role here. Also computer techniques play a peculiar role. In this respect the warning of the state of affairs at for example the Gaastra Sails Company from Sneek, NL, is illustrative. Sails for yachts always were made by master-sailmakers. Starting in the 1970s the sails were optimised by means of a computer program developed at the TU Delft, on the department of shipbuilding, that was applicable to 80 % of the standard sails. The know-how was (be it somewhat restricted) made cognitive, and by sending over one small computer-disk to Hong Kong, the begin was made of a Hong Kong based production unit, that ended last year in the bankruptcy of the original Gaastra Sails Company in Sneek.

5 Larger Mono-Spans In generally with space structure excellent proposals can be set to make large spans over single spaces using only a modest deadweight, usually a smaller deadweight compared with structures composed of 2-dimensional structural elements. Certain types of factories, exhibition halls, sporting halls sporting arenas and stadiums ask for large single (of mono-) spans. Both with space frames, stretched membranes, inflatables and dome structures, large free spans are possible.

7 Perspective view of an office building in Como, Italy, by Piano and Rogers, realised in 1973. A one storey office room, sandwiched between floor and space frame roof structure, and a glass-walled pedestrian bridge.

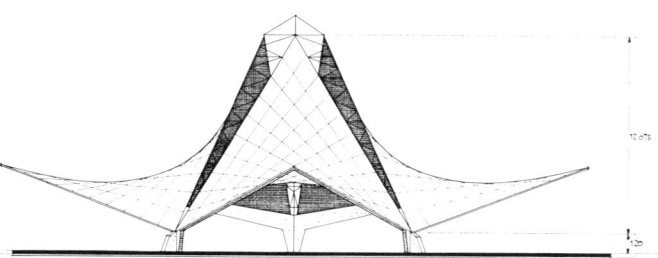

8 A drawing of the triple hyperbolic paraboloidal shell structure of reinforced concrete realised as the San Vincente de Paul chapel in Monterry, Mexico, in 1961, by structural designer Felix Candela. A structural composition of shells and glass skylights.

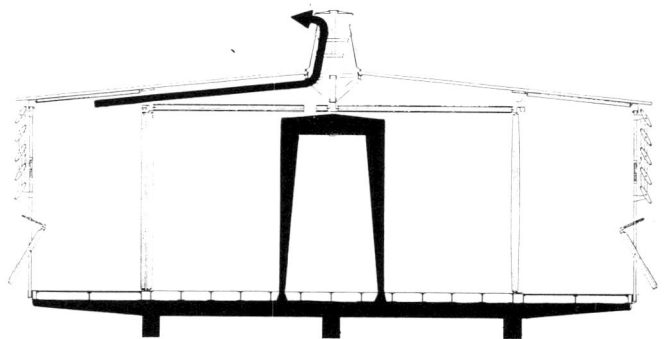

9 A schematic composition of a tropical house, designed and realised by Jean Prouvé, showing the integration of a loadbearing structure, claddings and glazing structures with a natural ventilation flow.

10 Richard Buckminster Fuller during one of his extensive (and exhaustive) lectures on space frame and geodesic structures he still gave as a 80-year-old scientist all over the world.

6 Square Column Grids For warehouses and factories a tendency towards greater mobility of the factory or storage lay-out in future and the modest investments of the building shed compared with an ever growing investment in machines and automation, leads to the adaption of the building shed to its function instead of the machinery to the building. After all, factories are more or less 'currogated sheets around machines'. Space frames are ideally suited for a two-way span and quite easily column grids in square or almost square plans can be obtained of 30 x 30 m or 24 x 36 m, with modest tube sizes. Often these square grids are combined with the request for a certain flexibilty of overhead loadings that still can be suspended underneath the space frame as the space frame has a capacity to spread local loads over a larger surface area by the intensive connections between the individual bars and nodes composing the space frame.

7 The Personal Engagement of Structural Designers An early first impressive influence from the building industry on the author was when he went, as a 10 year old boy, with his father, a Dutch greenhouse contractor, to a building site to make preparations for a temporary greenhouse on the Floriade Garden Exhibition of 1960 in Rotterdam. Greenhouses form a special item in the building industry because they are perfectly optimised both in function, technique and costing. They form completely standardised structures that indeed are sold for super competitive prices: the current square meter price of an average greenhouse is about dfl 50.=, while factories cost dfl 500.= and offices or houses dfl 1000.= as a rough indication. No wonder that Eekhout Sr always told his son not to design too expensively, but rather to be keen on weight and labour. The greenhouse industry marks every kilogram weight, and is, as a result, the largest exporting building industry from the Netherlands. This was perhaps the kind of industrialisation Konrad Wachsmann had in mind when he wrote his 'Wendepunkt im Bauen'.[1] Of course greenhouses have everything to do with plants and hardly with human beings, let alone with the well-being of humans. Hence the general technical requirements for greenhouses are less sophisticated in terms of strength, rigidity, safety against glass breakage and solar control. But nevertheless, the industrial approach behind greenhouse building appeared unconsciously as a starting point in the career of the author. The professional development of the author was further influenced by a number of designers of structures:

Frei Otto (1925) The first impressive impact during the professional education of the author came from Frei Otto. Starting with his lecture in Delft on 17.10.69, followed in times of complete study freedom during the student-revolution years in 1969/70, student Eekhout went to work in the Institut für leichte Flächentragwerke in Stuttgart-Vaihingen, where at that time about 70 other students, graduated architects and structural engineers were very busy preparing the scale models for the Munich Olympic Games cable net roofs. The Institute acted as a bee-hive, an international centre for architecture and new technology. And indeed, after a few years most of these designers flew back to their homeland (50 different countries). They were inspired by the work of Frei Otto, and their own experiences in these projects, each of them in an individual way. They created a world wide new technology network started by Frei Otto.

At the time a very strong difference in attitude was felt between the German as the rather theoretical but very basic approach, and the Anglo-Saxon, as the more pragmatic and less thorough approach.[5, 6, 7, 8] As usual, the Dutch way was somewhere in the middle: talking initially more about possibilities than about problems, and stimulated by theory and practice. Partly it was the curious mix of theoretical research combined with the realised projects, that generated a very enthousiastic atmosphere around Frei Otto. Partly it was the presence of so many young and devoted designers, eager to learn and to develop a whole new set of technology tools for the building industry and for architecture.

Renzo Piano (1937) A similar enthousiastic atmosphere was experienced by the author as a working student during the summer of 1970 in the studio of Renzo Piano in Genova. At the time he had a small architects office and had strong interests in new materials, techniques and applications. Piano's attitude was then presented as being very scientific in his systematic approach towards design but with more of a personal flavour. Frei Otto devoted himself completely to tensile structures at the time. Renzo Piano remained more an architect-artist in heart and soul, who liked to work with new materials and techniques. Piano tried to fit in these techniques more and better as an architect, while Frei Otto could be characterised as the man who took one structural element and developed it fully within the scope of a complete design made by his colleague architects.[9] Because of statements Renzo Piano made in a lecture on 17.10.69 in Delft, an impression was settled that the design methods Piano used were objective and scientific. However, it was only during a discussion on the 'Lightweight Structures in Architecture' Conference in Sydney in 1986, that the author realised that the design methods of Piano had changed from very scientific with a personal statement, into very personal, and artistic with a light scientific influence. Piano has the great gift to make a more intuitive combination of materials and techniques, and when these techniques fail yet: he simply develops them. The designs of Piano and the new route every new project seems to lead for the interested outsider, have given Piano a prominent place in architecture as one of the very few to develop new techniques, forms, material applications and combinations, and to apply them in projects of high architectural quality (fig 7). An outstanding mixture of project-architect and product-architect.

Felix Candela (1910) Though Candela belongs to an elder generation than Otto and Piano, and his work is no longer actual, yet his hypar shells in Mexico are still very impressive. He did more than unite architecture and structures in his designs. In order purely to get his ideas realised he was forced to be both architect, structural engineer and contractor in a number of his projects: he took complete responsibility for the realisation. In other projects he only acted as the structural engineer and contractor.[10] The mixture of designing + building is not unusual in Mexico and South America. Candela was forced to take up the profession of contractor, because no contractor was prepared at the time to take the risks of these complicated and unknown hyparbolic paraboloidal structures. Candela retired from professional life after the completion of the Mexico Olympic Games stadium in 1968, that in a way could be regarded as an apotheosis of his work. (fig 8) Since Candela retired, the development of hypar shells almost stopped, apart from the work of Castaño who builds space frame hypars.

So private persons are really able to stimulate and keep a development going. Their personal involvement can mean the start and the very end of a new technology.

Jean Prouvé (1901-1984) The discussions with Jean Prouvé were very tiring, due to the author's lack of the French language, still he has been an inspiring example for the author in three ways:
1 He combined design and experiment with production and real building activities, and started as a producer, eager to be a project-architect.
2 He worked from deformable sheet material like steel and aluminium up to complete building systems.
3 He combined in his work load bearing structures with non-structural cladding structures.[11, 12]

The cunning move by a commercial organisation that expelled him from his own company by buying shares from his labourers without his knowledge, is a good warning to stay commercially alert, and to combine creativity with a sound business administration. (fig 9)

Richard Buckminster Fuller (1895-1981)
This genial scientist has invented and teached until the very end of his life. At the age of 80 he still gave seminars worldwide. Although his work is much more sided than geodetics alone, geodetic domes and tensegrity systems would not have been in existance without his inventions and those of his pupils.[13] He did not care about what people thought about him, but besieged the world with all of his sometimes crazy ideas. Only a couple of years ago the author had the privilege to compete with his design company Fuller and Sadao for a sport stadium in Penang, Malaysia. (fig 10)

Zygmunt Makowski (1922) The very active civil engineer, who was responsable for the first 747 jumbo jet hangar in London Heathrow in the early seventies, setting an example for large span space frames, and who was and still is a major source of information and inspiration for space frame structures in the entire world. (fig 11) He retired from Surrey University in 1987. Looking back, his personal advice for the student Eekhout in 1972, not to go directly into too much theoretical work, but rather build and publish later on, has been literally followed up. However, at that time there was clearly a different attitude as to the supposed role of architecture and architects involved in space structures: there still was the professional gap between the engineer and the architect, that nowadays gradually has been closed.[14 to 17]

Max Mengeringhausen (1903-1988) Could be regarded as the 'Godfather' of space frame structures as he invented his famous Mero system almost fifty years ago. (1942). It was the first commercially succesfull space frame system ever.[18, 19] His system is the most widely used space frame in the world nowadays. Max Mengeringhausen was

11 Zygmunt Makowski, one of the leading scientists on space frames, personally testing one of his space structures: a combination of theoretical and practical research in his Space Structures Research Laboratory in Surrey.

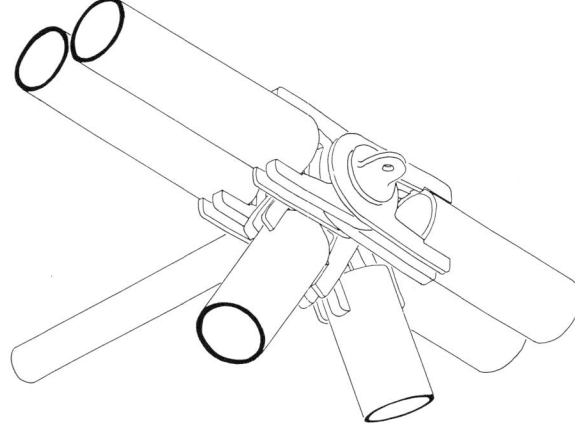

12 Design proposal by Konrad Wachsmann for a connection joint for a large span space frame structure in 1944.

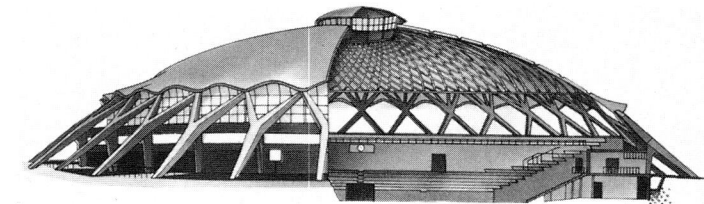

13 The small sport stadium in Rome designed and built by Pier Luigi Nervi in prefabricated reinforced concrete.

the perfect example of a scientist who also succeeded in exploiting his invention. (fig 5) The name 'Mero' is almost synonymous with Space Structures for many architects all over the world.

Pier Luigi Nervi (1891-1979) Nervi only worked with reinforced concrete as his structural material. His way of realising new structures can be seen as an inspiring example: innovative designs of new structural systems and material application only can be built when the originator really is an addict: Nervi worked sometimes as an architect, structural engineer and as a main-contractor (often, but not always at the same time). But his main interest and ability was structural design.[20, 21] In this way he followed the same path as Candela did. (fig 13)

Konrad Wachsmann (1901-1980) This more theoretical designer and developer was not lucky enough to realise many of his projects and inventions. His writings were very inspiring and illustrative for the approach towards industrialisation during the fifties and sixties. He was a rigorous advocate of the hard line in mass-production, understandable and logical in his time. A starting point to change closed industrial systems to open systems, but nevertheless very important. (fig 12)

Of course a possible list of interesting structural designers is more extensive than mentioned. But other structural designers have not been influential on the work of the author in such a direct way. The above list of inspiring structural designers shows that the interest in 3-dimensional structural design is strongly internationally orientated. Structural design is applicable all over the world; the actual application, however, is strongly influenced by local circumstances of technical, economical, climatological and traditional architectural nature. In case local products are interesting, they should be published on the same scale. The Dutch are convicted to follow international developments and to import foreign designs and developments and to adapt them to local conditions. But some Dutch Designs are worthwhile to export in return.

The influence of forementioned structural designers is partly due to their direct designs, but even more so they inspired the author by their methods of working, their commitment and the subsequent success in the times and circumstances they worked in. Times and environments can rapidly change, and so will the results of their work and the appraisal thereof, but their general attitude is more timeless. This is also why an ever changing set of buildings or other products of related structural engineering are inspiring for a structural designer. Structural design is universal, yet the circumstances leading to the design of structures in every project can be very different. Also the conditions under which new designs have to be made are again different. It is no wonder that architectural and structural designers also have been inspired by fresh examples from outside their direct professional fields, like the architect Le Corbusier was inspired by the ocean liners and grain silos. Architects sometimes are inspired only by the outlook of such a design: only the looks and not the systems are studied. Structural designers should also be inspired by the way peculiar design conditions led to the designed result.

Buildings are usually known by the name of the designer, mostly the architect and only occasionally the structural engineer. Designers of towers, bridges, cranes and offshore islands, ships, yachts, aeroplanes, cars, trains, motors, machines etc are more anonymous. Still these designs can be a source of inspiration. Usually these designs are the result of a teamwork co-operation, effectuated rather in larger corporations that are more anonymous than small private designers offices: the company's interest overrules the personal interests.

8 Integration of Space Structures in Architecture The general acceptance of visual structures as a main component in architecture, and of three-dimensional structures in particular, is depending on the attitude of the project-architect towards structures as a visual expression in the design of the building, and more generally towards technology in his architecture, on the type of dialogue between project-architect and product-architect acting as a (structural) co-designer in this case. Reference is given to Par 3.7 where a number of cases will illustrate experiences from 1982 to 1989 in the approach, quality and openness of discussion between project-architect and product-architect. In general it is fair to state that Dutch architects designing in different architectural styles are willing to enter into an open discussion with the product-architect to allow him to co-design the structural part of their overall design. This can be seen as an influence of the popularisation of High-Tech architecture, be it in case of for example space frames not necessarily in an overwhelming form. In both England and in Germany the situation is experienced as similar, while in countries with a larger tradition of more conventional building materials, the architect usually tends to be less open for discussion. (Belgium, France). Nevertheless, experiences show that a discussion between a project-architect open for information and allowing for a partial co-designership in his overall scheme, follows a general schedule in places all over the world. Architects all over the world react similarly in these discussions.

An example is the presentation of a proposal for the design of a mosque dome for the Labuan State Mosque in Malaysia. The space frame proposal was derived within the overall form prescribed by the architect, and by purely designing a very detailled spatially curved dome and eight curved lower surfaces, the drawing clearly showed the spaciousness of the proposal plus the technical confidence in the techniques of space frames. The drawing was made in Delft, travelled 10.000 km, was unfolded in front of the architect and needed no further explanation: it prooved that the language of a drawing was stronger than words, even for two designers from completely different cultural backgrounds. (fig 14) Although the architect was very enthusiastic, the proposal came too late to stop the contractor from building an in-situ cast concrete shell structure.

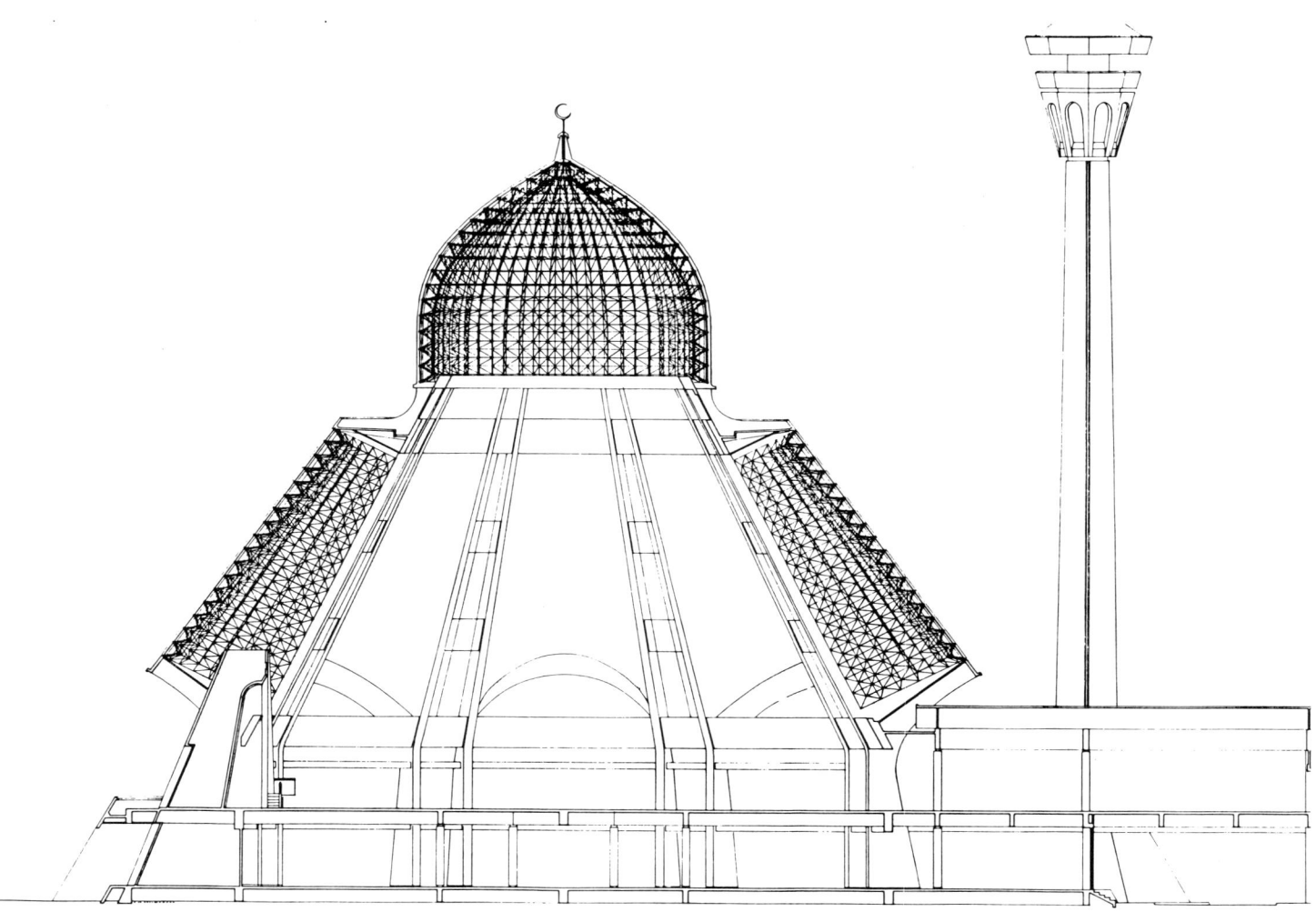

14 Design proposal by the author (1985) as a space frame structure in a mosque dome and eight diverging cylindrical barrel vaults for the Labuan State Mosque in Malaysia.

2 Materials and Systems

The three main ingredients with which a structural designer has to materialise his design concepts are:
- Materials
- Production Techniques
- Structural Systems

These three items are employed to realise, but also have an influence on ideas and concepts before they will be regarded as definitive. There is a clear interaction. It is within this reciprocity that the project-architect finds a part of his inspiration to visualise his building concepts. The product-architect finds an even deeper inspiration from the material properties, the production techniques and the structural systems he employs. Architects are by tradition very familiar with traditional building materials like timber, brickwork, reinforced concrete and rolled steel; in general there is less knowledge on lightweight steel, aluminium, strenghtened glass and plastics. These materials and their applications in building products have been developed mainly in organisations that seriously protect (or at least select) the newly gained information from outsiders' eyes. Materials, techniques and systems are vital for architects in order to design adequate systems and applications. Sometimes the study of the properties of materials can bring the designer a step further. Materials science is generally seen by designers as a mathematical and rather dull subject. But freed from the algebraic approach, the actual meaning of properties of single materials or combined materials can lead to specific discoveries.

The possibilities from production techniques that are different in metal, glass or flexible membranes are basic for the understanding of the design potentials. In this book there will be no listing of production techniques in themselves as impressive basic developments compared with the state-of-the-art did not occur in the Octatube factory. Reference is made to paragraph 3.2. and 3.6. where some dissentient aspects are illustrated.

The availability of certain materials (with suitable production techniques) can inspire one to use an adequate structural scheme. The interest of the author in new materials is primarily generated by the desire to realise structural schemes and forms. The survey given on materials and structural systems is necessarily highly selective and can be seen as a personal choice of inspiring components. A consequence of the use of building components made of new materials is the prefabrication character, that changes the building process from pouring and stacking into assembling and eventual dismantling after use. All the described new materials can be prefabricated in a workshop or in a factory, and are not processed on site, but only connected usually by bolting techniques. So these are all prefab materials as distinct from the site materials.

The importance of the study of statical systems was of course the basis for the oeuvre of the author.

1 Inspiring Materials

The Dutch windmills, as they were developed during the 16th and 17th century and have been in use until the beginning of this century, were functioning for either draining the Dutch polders or for all kinds of industrial purposes like grinding corn, sawing timber, squeezing palm-oil etc. For centuries these mills provided a specifically Dutch means of energy for those activities. The structure of the mill was a loadbearing timber frame or a brickwork tower shaft, with a completely timber machinery, connecting the production elements in the lower part of the mill via the central axis up to the energy generating wings. The different components of this timber machinery have been optimised during four centuries until the elements with a different function were made from different timber material. The central vertical axis used to be made of strong and torsion resistant oakwood, while the tooth elements on the friction wheels were made of self-greasing and tough olive wood. A similar use of different types of timber was exploited during the same centuries in shipbuilding: elements with a different function within the whole assembly were made of different sorts of timber.

Properties of new materials should be viewed in the same light. Within the composition of the entire spatial structure, the different composing elements having a different function are made from suitable, and hence maybe different, materials. This paragraph treats the material properties concerning their use in spatial structures, so only those properties are taken into account that are specifically interesting for those structures, and from a designer's point of view. The author does not pretend to be a material scientist but is mainly interested in the cause-and-effect between materials and techniques. Studying material properties by the author was inspired by the lectures of Professor Dick Dicke who taught Applied Mechanics at the Architecture Department of the TU Delft in the seventies. He requested his students sometimes to analyse the possibilities of an imaginary building material with random properties: a non-existing material that led to specifically designed structural concepts. He used his lectures to sharpen the imagination of his students, and to free them from too well known combinations of material properties.

For a good comparison the material properties of both steel and aluminium will be treated simultaneously, but combined with the properties of glass and plastics because these materials are used in combined structural designs. These properties will be dealt with in a broad

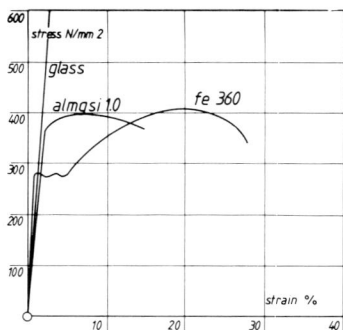

15 Strain-stress table of steel, aluminium and glass.

way, so as to understand the consequent directives for use in the design of space structures and structures with claddings. The given values for materials whose properties can be chemical influences in alloys, are only the average values found in the consulted literature, where no exact corresponding figures could be found.[22, 23, 24]

1 *Young's Modulus of Elasticity*   The stiffness of materials is expressed in Young's Modulus of Elasticity: 'E' being the quotient of stress 's' and strain 'e'. E describes the elastic flexibility for the material as such. The flexibility or stiffness of a given structure will thus depend upon the Young's Modulus of the material plus the flexibility of connections between the material elements plus that of the geometrical overall shape of the structure. E-values in N/mm2 are:
- Steel 210.000
- Aluminium 67.000 to 73.000
- Ordinary Glass 73.000 to 75.000
- Heat-Strengthened Glass 73.000 to 75.000
- GRP (glassfiber reinf. pol.) 5.000 to 50.000
- PMMA (acrylate) 2.500 to 3.500
- PC (polycarbonate) 2.300

A remarkable difference is seen between the E-glass, E-acrylate and E-polycarbonate: PC is about as rigid as PMMA, but glass is 3 times as rigid as PC on its turn. This deformability of the transparent plastics indicates that it can hardly be utilised in the form of flat sheets, but preferably in a shell-like form, whereby the form stiffens up the weakness of the sheet material. The material itself is very well utilised when a dual/triple wall sheet is used. Heat-strengthened glass and tempered glass have the same E as normal glass. In applications where E is important (on bending or buckling), heat-strengthened glass does not offer any advantages above normal glass.

E-values for glassfiber and polyester fabrics for use in membranes are hard to give as they are greatly influenced by the form of the weave material. Yet building stretched membranes from these two materials, shows that the E-value of glassfiber weave is about 2.5 times as high as polyester weave, meaning that polyester elongates at the pretension stage and in the rupture stage 2.5

times as much as glassfiber fabric. For production people this means that glassfiber membranes have to be cut 2.5 times as accurately as polyester because there will be less possibilities of straining wrinkles away. This is an important influence by material technology on production.

The large variety of E in GRP (tenfold) in rigid panels or structures is due to the large variety of the glassfiber fibers, weaves or fabrics, and the polyester.

2 Tensile Strength The permissible tensile strengths in N/mm2 of the different building materials are given as follows:
- High tensile steel 520 to 1.500
- Mild steel (Fe 360) 360
- Cast nodular iron 400 to 800
- Pure Aluminium 60 to 70
- Alu alloy AlMgSio.5 215
- Alu alloy AlMg3 230
- Cast alu G-AlMg3 170
- Ordinary Glass 40
- Heat-Strengthened Glass 200
- PMMA 70 to 110
- PC 60 to 100
- GRP 80 to 500

There is no direct relationship between the tensile strength and compression strength because of various complications by element form and buckling.

Ordinary glass and heat-strengthened glass differ about 5 times in tensile strengths, so in applications where tension or tension/bending stresses are decisive, strengthened glass is preferable. Reversedly, structures of glass are more optimal in the material sense when the glass panels are acting under tension, and not under compression. Avoiding micro-cracks leads, however, to the conclusion that compression surpresses cracks and compression works better than tension.

The nodular cast-iron quality GN50 does not have bad strength properties compared to steel. The strain at rupture is, however, 3 times smaller. This brings us to the importance of the stress/strain diagrams of the different materials. In principle 3 basic diagrams are possible: (fig 15)
- Materials with an explicit flow route and tough behaviour, by which virtue a redistribution of forces in the structure is possible (Fe 360); The safety factor between flow stresses and permissible stresses can be as little as 1.5.
- Materials without an explicit flow route but with a tough behaviour. When the safety of the flow route has disappeared, there will have to be a proper ratio between rupture and the 0.2 % strain value, preferably about 2. For example aluminium alloys.
- Materials without an explicit flow route and with a brittle behaviour, so without an inherent 'warning' system, where only a larger safety factor will ensure safe working stresses. For example heat-strengthened glass with a safety factor 4.

Generally there is also a considerable difference between rolled steel and cast steel or nodular iron, or extruded aluminium and cast aluminium, in that the rolled or extruded materials have a longer flow route, and deform before breaking, while cast products rupture with less deformation. Cast iron still has a small deformation, whereas cast aluminium (depending on its chemical alloy) has no noticeable deformation at rupture, so is even more brittle. Again a larger safety factor is used in this case for this aluminium alloy compared with steel / iron. The daily practice of space frame nodal design shows that given a certain cast nodal form with the same dimensions, the steel / iron model has a higher permissible strength. The nodular iron spheres of Tuball deform before rupture, when they rupture at all, while the aluminium nodes crack and tensile bars tend to tear out a complete cheek of the sphere.

Tensile strengths of glassfiber and polyester fabrics for use in membranes are hard to give as they are measured in another way than the voluminous materials, and are depending on the type of weave, the weight and the straightness of the yarns. In general experiences show that the tensile strengths of these two materials do not differ more that 10 to 20 %, so in practice they are very similar in strength, but not in elongation. (See 1)

3 Brittleness   This property is very important for the use of glass as a structural material. The weakness of glass as a structural material (and to a far lesser extend also brittle cast metals like some aluminium alloys), is caused by brittleness. Very generally put, there are two fracture mechanisms competing to break a material: Plastic Flow and Brittle Cracking. The material will succumb to whatever mechanism is weaker. If it yields before it cracks, it is ductile. If it cracks before it yields, it is brittle. The potentiality of both forms of failure is always present in most materials. Yielding is a safety property, spontaneous cracking is an undesirable property for a structural material. Since we are interested to see in how far glass could be used as a structural material, the failure mechanism for glass can be seen as follows. Glass is cooled during fabrication so fast that the molecules do not have time to sort themselves out into crystals. So cooled glass is a solidified liquid, not a crystallized solid.

However, the tendency into crystallization is present, and given time, glass will crystallize. This is known as devitrification. It involves shrinkages, the glass is often weakened, and sometimes falls into pieces during the process. It will always fracture in the same brittle way. In fact, if we want to prevent the glass from cracking, we have to put it under compression. This can be done by heating the glass panels again, and chilling the two outsides of the hot glass panels during fabrication very rapidly, so that the two outsides form with the core a tension + compression mechanism. When the outer surfaces are cooled, they solidify, while the core is still hot (700 C). The shrinking during cooling of the core causes the outside skins to be compressed, while the central core will remain under tension. So the outside skin of heat-strengthened glass is under compression, the core under tension. This is a mechanism to avoid surface cracks, but also hides internal cracks. The mechanism is the same for nodular iron and cast aluminium: the outside surface can be very smooth, while irregularities can be hidden inside the material.

After strengthening the outcome is a glass panel with higher tensile strengths, also a higher impact strength. Great care has to be taken that the glass surface is not scratched by a sharp tool, because then it will crack into thousands of small bits. Try to bring glass panels out of the reach of vandals. Or sharp glass hammers are a safety tool to break out of an all glass cage. (See Par 6.3 for use in the Glass Music Box in Amsterdam).

In heat-strengthened glass panels possible cracks are avoided by the compression mechanism. Making connections (holes) in the glass can, consequently, be done best by a pretensioning type of bolt connection: in that case not the hole edges are loaded on flush, (with the inherent danger of enlarging the micro-cracks around the bolt hole by drilling), but the pretensioning bolt will compress the two outside metal rings or components on the glass where the mutual friction will bring over the connection force. The friction force can be enheightened by grinding or blasting the surface around the bolt hole. A flush-type connection will have to contain an intermediate material between bolt and glass hole to avoid local toptensions in the hole, from which micro cracks can cause serious cracks. But another idea might be to fill in the irregular left-over spaces in the holes between the outsides of the holes and the bolts by liquid epoxy, in order to get a firm abrasion connection. The type of connection will decide on the vulnerability of the irregularity of the bolt shaft and the bolt hole.

The maximum compression forces for ordinary and heat-strengthened glass both are 800 to 1000 N/mm2, quite high compared with the values of 40 to 200 N/mm2 respectively for maximum tensile forces.

On scale of the glass panels, a possible compression (normal) force introduces the danger of buckling the panel so that the largest commercially available panel thicknesses (12, 15 or 19 mm) will have to be used, and these glass panels are quite expensive per volume. The danger of second order buckling (from a curved element position) is even greater when using heat-strengthened glass panels which cannot be produced completely flat. It would be better then to load the glass panels under tensile (normal) force in stead of compression: that is to suspend rather that to stack them. Further reference is given to par 6.3, where a number of experimental all-glass structures are explained.

4 *Creep* This is the continuing deformation of the material in time under constant load, usually decreasing (in time) in magnitude. Aluminium is quite sensitive to creep. Steel does not suffer from creep. But most non-metals like the plastics are very sensitive to creep. For a designer it means in the first place that using creep-sensitive materials, automatically the design has to allow for creep. It is advised to use minimal loadings and hence minimal internal stresses in the materials, so that the effects of creep are less noticeable. But there will be a limit as to the price of low-loaded structural materials. Another consequence is using structural forms where the effects of creep are not noticeable: for example non-rectilinear forms, but rather curved designs, where deformation is not notizable: domes and cylindrical forms. Structures suffering from creep should be covered by elements or materials that can adapt itself to the deformations because of this creep. Creep in glass and heat-strengthened glass is nil, but for PC and PMMA is fairly high (although no exact figures are known).

Polyester weave has a larger creep deformation than glassfiber weave, meaning that prestressed membranes in polyester regularly need post-tensioning, and glassfiber membranes need less maintenance care.

Creep in aluminium depends on the working stress, time and temperature: above 100-150 C there is a noticeable influence. This is extremely important when export designs are to be made for desert climates for example in black anodised aluminium. On the other hand, aluminium has the peculiar property that the 0.2% strain-value, and also the working stresses improve when the temperature drops far below zero. As a result of this property, aluminium domes are very suited as a structure in the Arctic or in the Alps. It is also one of the reasons why aeroplanes are built in aluminium: at an altitude of 10.000 m the average temperature can be -50 C. So aluminium is an ideal structural material to build with in cold climates.

5 *Thermal Conduction Coefficient* The respective values in W/mK for the materials are:
- Steel 40-50
- Aluminium 200
- Glass 0.80
- PC 0.07 to 0.21
- PMMA 0.12 to 0.19
- GRP 0.12 to 0.72

This shows how problematic aluminium can be during manufacturing (fast spreading of high temperatures during machining or welding) and during erection in extreme weather (danger of fingers freezing onto the aluminium surface, or burning fingertips on sun-heated black anodised aluminium elements). Glass does conduct less heat, but combined with the brittleness effect can cause surprises when some parts of the glass panels are covered (for example by metal strips) and other parts are completely exposed: the danger of thermal breakage. This is an ever present danger for aluminium/glass skylight structures, especially when the glass is heat-absorbing like some tinted glass types are more vulnerable for thermal breakage around the edges, or for shadowed and exposed surfaces. This does not occur in such a magnitude with the solid transparent plastics because of their more favourable flow route.

6 *Temperature Elongation* This temperature elongation is important for the mutual differences between structural and cladding materials, and between co-operating materials in structural or cladding components. The values in m/mK are:
- Steel Fe 360 12×10^{-6}
- Aluminium (AlMgS 0.5) 24×10^{-6}
- Glass (all types) 9×10^{-6}
- GRP 50×10^{-6}
- PC 65×10^{-6}
- PMMA 70×10^{-6}

There will be trouble in material combinations when the temperature elongation values differ too much. The solid plastics elongate 7 times as much as glass. There also is a large difference between metals and solid transparent plastics, that no doubt cause problems in regard to permanent watertightness in joints of aluminium or steel mullions and plastic panels. One simply needs intermediate elements to allow for the mutual movements. When considering the materials for a curtain wall, the combination (stainless steel) steel strips + glass causes less problems than the combination aluminium + glass or aluminium + PC or PMMA.

7 *Deadweight in kN/m³*:
- Steel 78
- Aluminium 27
- Glass 25
- GRP 12 to 17.5
- PC 12
- PMMA 12

8 *Behaviour at High Temperatures* As a very rough working rule the maximum workable temperature for most metals is half the melting temperature in degrees Kelvin. (That is to say at that temperature structures will fail). The workable temperatures in degr Celcius:
- Steel 550 C
- Aluminium 250 C
- Ordinary glass 60-100 C
- Heat-strengthened glass 270 C
- PC 115 C
- PMMA 80 C
- GRP 200 C
- PVC-coated polyester 80 C
- PTFE-coated glassfiber 250 C

These figures have some importance, as aluminium structures fail at a temperature of 250 C , while steel holds up to 550 C. That is to say these are the temperatures where the flow / 0.2% strainstresses are far below the normal values, so that already a failure mechanism has been initiated. For aluminium there are two ways out: paint the structure in fire-retarding foaming paint, or choose a space frame that has an enormous reserve capacity to spread and re-distribute internal forces around the spot with the overstressed bars. The multiple statical indeterminacy of space frames helps efficiently in this case. Also in case a fire-resistance of 30 minutes is required for steel space frames, this redistribution mechanism convinces the local authorities. But this leads more from materials to structural systems.

A consequence of the different values for the two membrane materials is again found in the use of these stretched membranes in the Middle East. Surface temperatures can be as high as 100 C. Building with PVC-coated polyester membrane fabric is not advised as the material softens and bonds itself with sanddust, so that a bright white tent can get the appearance of a concrete bunker after one hot sandstorm. PTFE-coated material will stay smooth and non-sticky. In fact this material is even supplied as beige and bleaches after a few weeks sun exposure.

9 Corrosion Sensitivity The different structural materials all have distinct resistances against chemical attacks, be it from outside or from special chemically aggressive inside climates, as for example becomes clear in several industrial climates, swimming pools and sewage wastewater disposal plants. Steel needs protection against corrosion, which can be met (by hot dip galvanisation), maybe combined with an additional coating on top. Aluminium corrosion is dependent upon the chemical alloy. There are seawater resistant alloys, sulphor-acid-resistant alloys for wastewater coverings, but the usual alloys that 20 years ago were recommended as having bare exposure without permanent corrosion, will now have to be coated or anodised additionally even in the outside climate. The danger of pit-corrosion is recently recognised in badly treated aluminium surfaces. The best chemical resistances are offered by glass and by the plastic materials. In this respect the concept of prestressed membranes suspended under metal dome skeletons (like in figs 157 to 161) was developed: as aluminium (but even worse galvanised and coated steel) is more sensitive to the highly acid and humid atmosphere of wastewater treatment plants than PVC and GRP, the concept was chosen to have a chemically resistant envelope, stabilised on the outside by a metal space frame. Even the PVC-coated polyester membrane fabrics offered quite a long lifetime (20 years). As a cladding material also GRP panels in very thin and prestressed form were developed. The advantage of the larger prefabricated prestressed membranes of PVC-coated polyester - and of course even better, PTFE-coated glassfiber - is their complete water- and gastightness.

2 Structural Systems

Space structures are structurally characterised by the 3-dimensional internal action of forces under an external loading, not in one plane (2-D), and not in an assembly of flat planes (2.5-D) but in space (3-D). This spatial action is an indispensable fact. There are a number of different types of space structures that can be divided under the main categories as follows:

1 Membranes / Membrane-like Structures ('Membranes')
- stretched membranes M
- prestressed cablenet structures Cn
- pneumatic structures P

2 Spatial Truss-like Structures ('Trusses')
- space frames Sf
- tensegrity structures T
- spatial guyed structures Sg

3 Shell-like Structures ('Shells')
- cylindrical shells C
- dome shells D
- saddle shaped shells Ss

These categories are all spatial structures, but have quite different characteristics that will become apparent in design, fabrication and building. Their basic elements are different in the first place because there are other structural principles involved.

Membranes and Membrane-like Structures In all spatial membrane structures the real structure is formed by a relative thin surface, able only to take tension forces. The flexible membrane can not resist compression forces as a membrane material, and is stabilised by pretensioning the membrane. This can be performed in two ways: either by introducing normal forces in the plane of the membrane (e.g. by cables pulling outward), or by an overpressure perpendicular to the plane of the membrane (e.g. by air pressure). In both cases the prestressed structural system produces even with these flexible membranes stable and fairly rigid structures. Prestressed membranes and cablenet structures have the same structural set-up, only the scale of forces and the used thickness of fabric weave or cable net is different.

For theoretical completeness the category of pure compression structures has to be mentioned that however is not the domain of the author and will be neglected in this book. They are seen as reversed tensile structures.

Spatial Truss-like Structures All structural systems in the Truss-like group have in common that external loadings are taken by a system of linear structural elements (bars) that can only take normal forces: either compression; both compression and tension; or only tensile forces. Normally no bending moments are carried by these elements. External loadings are taken over a certain span by an assembly of interconnected tensile and compressive linear elements. Spatial truss-like structures can be divided into systems that are adequate for single and for multiple loading cases. Multiple loadings (like upward and downward directed loadings) result in elements that can take both tension and compression. All elements will be able to take the calculated maximum compression and tensile forces in its position, are dimensioned on the maximum buckling forces and hence are made of profiled elements. Single loaded systems are

16 Morphological chart of possible combinations of the nine types of spatial structure that have been experimented with from 1982 until 1989.

mainly dimensioned on one single loading case, can result in distinct tensile and compression elements. Other loadings, or loadings from different directions are in this case taken after the introduction of extra pretension forces in the tensile elements. Pretensioned elements can take compression by reduction of pretension. Such is the case in spatially guyed structures where pretension is either deliberately made, or is produced as a result of the application of extra deadweight in order to resist expected upward loadings that the structure normally cannot take. Tensegrity structures form a unique group of structures in which the compression elements are never directly connected with each other, only indirectly by means of cables. Compression forces in the cables have to be taken by an extra pretension, which of course influences the entire structural system.

Shell-like structures Real shells are usually made of continuous material like reinforced concrete, laminated timber, or reinforced plastics. Although these materials are relatively thin (but thicker than the tensile surfaces) they still possess a certain rigidity against local bending moments. Also they are able to resist shear forces in the surface of the structure. The spatial curvature in the surface produces normal stresses instead of bending stresses. Although theoretically both folded plate structures (like prismatic folded plates and pyramidal folded plates) and gently curved surfaces (like single curved shells, rotation shells and anticlastical shells) are possible, the curved shell structures are more inviting for experimenting with different types of structures. Inspired by the structural action of shell structures, a group of truss-like structures in the form of shells can be envisaged that also could be called 'shell-like'.

Combinations Apart from the nine main categories of space structural forms, clustered under the three groups of spatial 'Membranes', 'Trusses' and 'Shells', also combinations of these categories can be built. These combinations can be envisaged on three levels:

- Firstly on a direct level. That is to say a direct combination of two systems. For example a (truss-like) space frame in the form of a dome shell.
- Secondly on an indirect level: combining two separate systems, composed together, like space frame with a tensegrity structure as two separate elements in one design.
- Thirdly on a sub-level: the combination of a main space structural system with another structural system as a cladding system: like a space frame structure with a secondary stretched membrane covering.

These combinations in two dimensions are shown in fig 16. It is only during the writing of this book that the author realised that a minor part of the possible combinations have yet been realised, and that more and interesting future combination possibilities can be explored. The morphological chart shows a number of designed and realised combinations on different levels, mixed together.

1   Pneu + Membrane / Energy Express / Tilburg
2   Pneu + Cablenet / Reinforced Iglo / Hebrides
3   Space frame + Membrane / Pavilion EVD / Osaka
4   Space frame + Cablenet / stadium / Kuala Lumpur
5   Space frame + Pneu / Petrol Station / Birmingham
6   Tensegrity + Membrane / Hemweg / Amsterdam
7   Space frame + Tensegrity / Nederl. 1870 / Diemen
8   Space frame + Guyed str. / Stadium / Singapore
9   Cylinder + Membrane / Tennis Hall / Rome
10 Space frame + Cylinder / Arcade / Amsterdam
11 Dome + Membrane / Tent dome / Jeddah
12 Dome + Pneu / Science Park / Rotterdam
13 Space frame + Dome / Orchard Blvd / Singapore
14 Tensegrity + Dome / Exhibition Dome / Sevilla
15 Saddle + Space frame / Circustheater / Zandvoort

These examples are represented in fig 17 and will be explained in the book under the various chapters.

Structural Systems

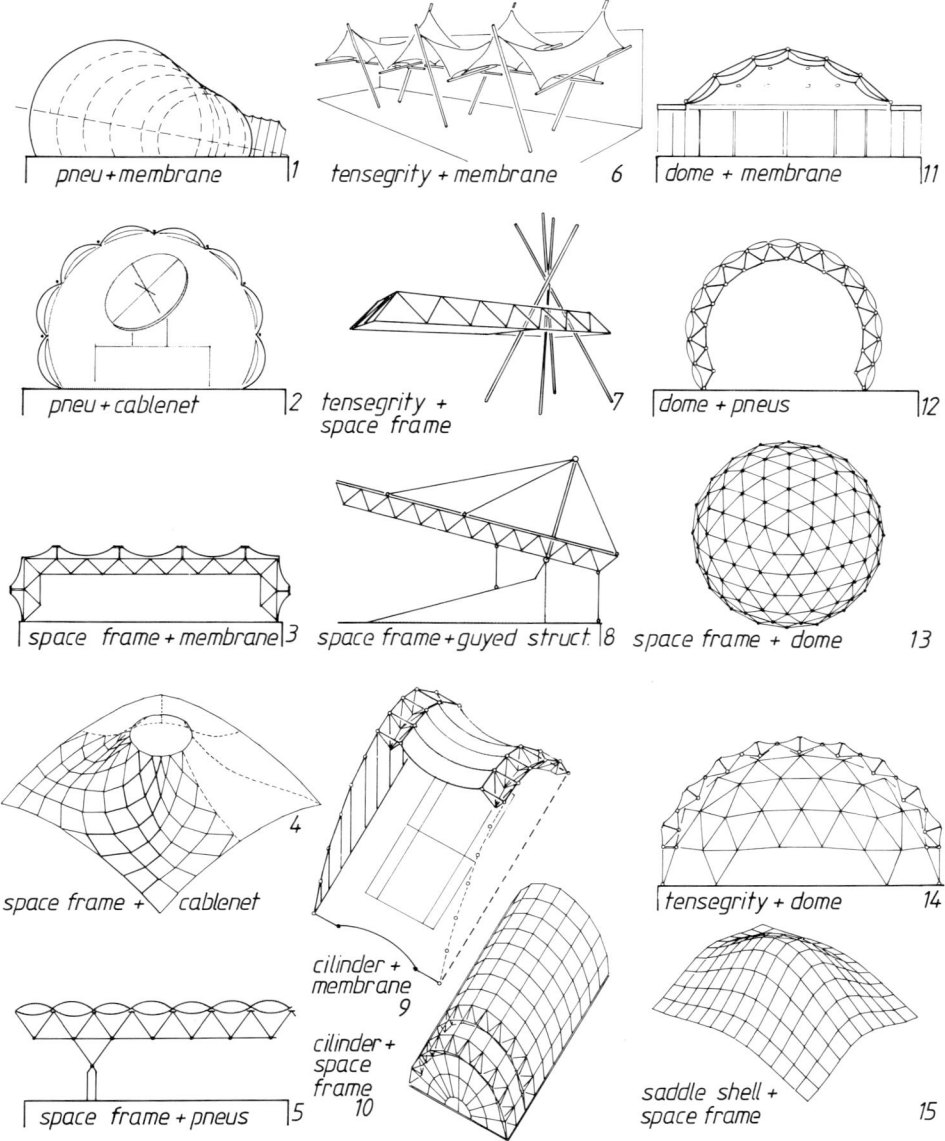

17 Design schemes indicating the different combinations of the nine basic types of spatial structures.

17.1 Pneu + Membrane: The Energy Express travelling exposition in 1983 consisted of an inflatable in the form of an old-fashioned light bulb, scale 300 to 1, combined with a stretched membrane as an entrance porch, prestressed over steel arches. This structure has been built.

17.2 Pneu + Cablenet: A proposal to make an air-inflated pneumatic 3/4 radar dome for civil aviation on the Hebrides, reinforced by polyester cables running along great circles. The cable net was envisaged to reinforce the membrane material against the high wind, snow and ice loadings, and when iced up it could reinforce the ice layer so that the static overpressure would be redundant. Not built.

17.3 Space Frame + Membrane: A design of a pavilion for the Dutch Export Promotion Board in Osaka 1989, co-designed with architect Frans Prins, consisting of a space frame in portal section, covered with stretched membrane elements on the roof and the two short sides, while the longitudinal elevations are glazed with guyed glass frame elements, as described in Par 6.3. Built in March 1989.

17.4 Space Frame + Cable Net: A design proposal for a single layered space frame reinforced by the pretensioning action much like that of a prestressed cable net structure but with a larger local rigidity, plus the opportunity to fix the cladding in an easy method. The resulting structural system was believed to be somewhere in the middle between space frames and cable net structures.

17.5 Space Frame + Pneu: A design for a petrol station in Birmingham consisting of a flat regular space frame with air-inflated cushions the size of the single modules, attached to the upper chord members.

17.6 Tensegrity + Membrane: Design perspective of the tensegrity structure with prestressed membranes as infill elements in Amsterdam. See Par 3.7.12.

17.7 Space Frame + Tensegrity: Perspective of an entrance element for an office building in Diemen NL, composed of a 'floating' space frame stabilised in space by 4 independent tensegrity poles piercing through the frame. Stabilisation by guy rods. Realised autumn 1988. See par 5.1.

17.8 Space Frame + Guyed Structure: A proposal for the Yishun indoor stadium in Singapore where a large span flat space frame is supported by guy cables from surrounding masts 1986. Design not realised.

17.9 Cylinder + Membrane: A cylindrical space frame, spanning approximately 40 m, formed by delta trusses centered 18 m, and stabilised by delta trusses covered with a prestressed membrane covering: a 1984 project for a tennis hall in Delft, not realised.

17.10 Space Frame + Cylinder: Single layered tennis hall proposal in Rome 1987, consisting of a single layered space frame in triangular configuration, which is reinforced every 18 m by a delta truss. The structural arched form is used to obtain a relative lightweight space frame.

17.11 Dome + Membrane: Aluminium triangulated single layered space frame dome with a double suspended membrane as a swimming pool covering in Jeddah 1982. See 3.7.14.

17.12 Dome + Pneu: Proposal for a 70 m three-quarter sphere as a double layered rectangulated space frame covered by a system of air inflated cushion elements with three walls. The outer two walls have aluminium reflective stripes, so that inflation and deflation of the outer and inner chamber could result in daylight penetration or reflection. Projected in Rotterdam 1988.

17.13 Space Frame + Dome: A 19 m diameter semi-spherical dome-form structure in a single layered space frame with triangulated sandwich panels for a planetarium in Dwingelo. March 1989.

17.14 Tensegrity + Dome: A shallow 70 m diameter dome proposal for the covering of an indoor exhibition area in Sevilla. The space frame is single layered, composed of hexagonal 'bicycle wheel' elements with tensegrity poles as central stabilisation. See fig 133.

17.15 Saddle Shell + Space Frame: Saddle shaped roof elements in the form of a single layered space frame. Circus Theater, Zandvoort, See fig 128.

3 Design Process of Spatial Structures

The will to realise non-conventional space structures has encouraged the author to experiment during a period of seven years (1982 - 89) with a different process of Design, Development, Research and Application compared with the usual processes. From these experiences a few remarkable observations can be made:
- In the design process the three disciplines of Architectural, Structural and Industrial Design co-operate inseparately;
- In the design process both very established drafting and model techniques are used, as well as more advanced computer aided design techniques;
- The initial development of new designs and systems is stimulated effectively by the presence of a well equipped laboratory;
- By working as an application-designer / product-architect and a producer, the author is able to present ideas as well as to guarantee their realisation for agreed prices to clients and project-architects;
- The very realisation of the designed space structures is performed in one company, with its own staff and personnel, giving fast feedbacks on realised designs, (and sometimes just-in-time management to prevent errors);
- During the development of new systems of space structures, for future architectural applications, the marketing side of the process is studied simultaneously with the technical development;
- As a result of the constant efforts to improve the designs with new materials, spatial and structural concepts, engineering, fabrication and assembly methods, and their application to the buildings of client-architects, the quality of the space structure product is hopefully continuously heightened, thus contributing to an enheightened quality of the total architectural environment;
- From the experiences shown in this book a strong recommendation follows to stimulate students in the field of development of new structural building components to study simultaneously a mixed program containing both architectural, structural and industrial design aspects in order to become product-architects;
- The introduction of product-architects into building research will result in more Creative Research and Development.

1 Architectural + Structural + Industrial Design

The presented designs and realisations of space structures are the result of a synergetic process of Architectural, Structural and Industrial Design. Synergetic means that the result is more than the sum of the composing parts. The very close co-operation of these three disciplines produce better and faster results than probably would have been possible when these three disciplines were cooperating from independent positions. In order to explain this process, a clear distinction will have to be made between the design of two different types of structures:
- Custom-built structures
- Structural systems

Custom-built structures are normally designed for a specific application, under specific conditions and usually by the project-engineer, directly in discussion with the project architect. But also space structures can be designed for one project only, designed by the product-architect in direct dialogue with the architect and engineer of the project. Custom-built structures in the category of spatial structures are:
- Invention and first application of a space frame
- Space frame systems made for specific demands
- Dome structures
- Membrane structures
- Shell structures
- Tensegrity structures

Space structure systems that have been conceived as a general system, are designed, developed and optimised as an industrial product. Their very existence can be developed according to a list of requirements larger and more general than just one application would require. A system has more possibilities to offer than will be used in a specific application. It is therefor over-designed. As this usually costs money, the development of a system has to be very carefully performed, also because possible mistakes or expensive solutions of many parts and aspects of the system can ruin the economical future of the system, or shorten its life-cycle. Therefore the design and development of a space structure system usually needs more attention than an ad-hoc solution. On the other hand it will not fit so perfectly on every application as a specially tailored structure would do. In order to adequately process a product like a space structure system, the development process will resemble that of other industrial products. (fig 28) The popular form of spatial structural systems are:

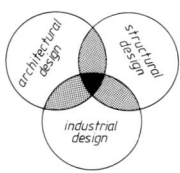

18 The synergetic co-operation between Architectural, Structural and Industrial Design leads to Product Architecture.

- Space frame systems;
- Dome structures;
- Cylindrical structures.

In order to develop a good system, it is advisable to stress the importance of an input from industrial design especially the product care and the marketing care. So for systems of space structures, the three disciplines of Architectural, Structural and Industrial Design are working together closely during development. The specific task of each of these disciplines in the design and developments process are:

Architectural Design   The architectural discipline knows about the problems of implantation of a space structure into an overall scheme, from the level of the architectural concept to the level of structural and architectural details. This discipline also is aware of the degrees of freedom the system has to offer in order to fit into most buildings. Assuming that most of the applications of space structures in architecture form only a minor part of the overall concept, the structural system has to be adapted to very different conditions in each application: overall size, module, structural height, covering system of purlins, gutters, cladding in different materials in wall areas, roof areas and even on floor areas, and transparent glass coverings. Also colour and colour-contrast , the graphical outcome of the grid choice of space frames, the design of columns and wall supports etc.

The architect will appreciate an architecturally educated view on the implantation of the structure that automatically thinks well ahead of him, discovering discrepancies so that even an inexperienced architect can have a space frame application. For the more complex applications, there is a remarkable tendency amongst client-architects to leave all further detailing to the producing specialist. There is a general shift of activities from the project-architects office to the specialists office. Space structure techniques usually are complex and worth a specialist's task. But consequently, by only judging the result, the client-architect often looses the lead in developing his material language. This transition of activities from the project-architects office to the specialists engineering office, has large consequences for the

Architecture in Space Structures

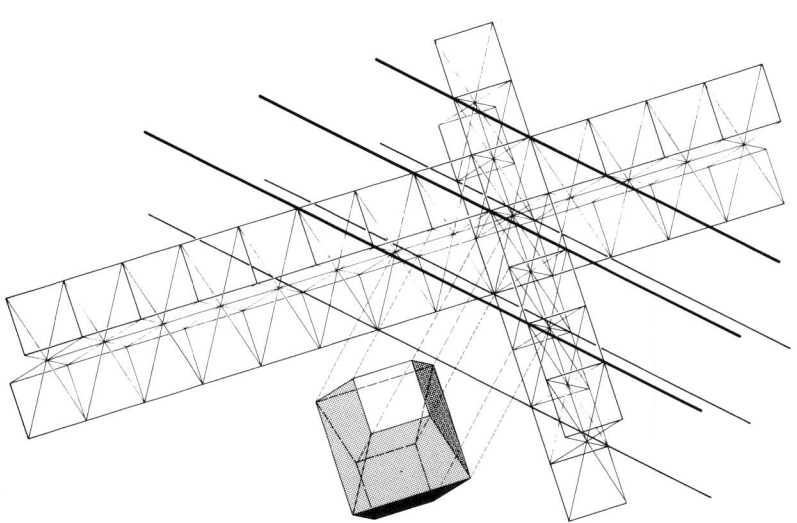

19 Schematic elements of a triple layered three way space frame proposal for a new Fokker factory in Schiphol (NL) for the cancelled project MDF 100 in 1984: Two intersecting X-trusses with diagonally crossing main chord members. The maximum air volume incorporated is shown by the exploded snub octahedron. Total size 200 × 135 m, divided in bays of 90 and 45 m, with crane loads suspended from the roof structures of 80 tonnes.

profession of the independent architect, and is caused by the following tendencies in the profession:
- Firstly: the position of the architect is gradually reduced to overall design and overall 3-D management, leaving much detail design work and drawings in the new materials and building techniques to advisors and specialist-producers. He is forced to do so because of the growing complexity of the building process.
- Secondly: the education of architects should also be focused on new materials: there is ample know-how about the traditional building materials and techniques, but less about new ones. The specialist industries are not willing to supply the missing information, either. At the best the Schools of Architecture offer an updated overview of the current catalogue of existing building products, without any know-how in depth about the design and development of these products. Less effort is placed on the possible future developments that will take place on the field of building products. Moshe Zwarts is the only professor engaged with product development on the Architecture departments of TU Delft and Eindhoven. Architects are evolving from producers of traditional building products to consumers of new technical products.
- Thirdly: this lack of understanding of the material side of the building process is encouraged by a current interest among young architects towards a very abstract way of designing buildings. To see a building only as a complex of abstract elements coincides with a minor interest to design new structural and industrial techniques needed for a durable building. Too much abstraction with less proper technical know-how will leave the architect only in the position of the design artist, enabling contractors and specialists to gain more power in the process. As a former independent architect, the author regards this process as a regrettable devaluation of the architectural profession, although his current specialist position has been firmly derived in the same process.

Structural Design   The first and most important function of space structures is to carry external loads via forces in its composing members over the free spaces to the foundations. Because of the usage of minimal material in space structures compared with conventional 2-dimensional structures, space structures have been the domain of research and development of structural engineers who studied isolated aspects in great depth.

Compared with research studies of other structural designers, the author has put the emphasis of the structural design task on the applications of existing statical systems, methods of analysis and structural forms bringing these techniques from an experimental phase into standard day-to-day use. In some cases, however, different structural systems have been designed in combinations that were not known to have been experimented with at all or in particular. For example:
- Tensegrity structures with internally prestressed membranes.
- Skeleton dome structures with suspended stretched membranes.
- Space frames with omitted upper chord layers, substituted by a compressed stressed skin of plate materials (sandwich/metal panels or glass panels).
- Tensegrity elements as integrated parts of a larger structure;
- Hybrid systems of triangular or 'delta' space trusses.
- Flat space frame with suspended prestressed elements;
- Cantilevering flat space frames over spaces between existing buildings with suspended 'curtain walls' all around to avoid additional loading on existing roofs;
- Semi-cylindrically curved space frames supported on 4 corners and acting as a shell structure;
- Prestressed single layered saddle shaped space frame;
- A flat space frame held in space by an independently stabilised tensegrity structure not visually connected;
- An inflatable structure on the Hebrides reinforced by

a cable net that (when iced and snowed up) could be regarded as a reinforced iglo, and deflated.

In all the abovementioned cases (treated in greater extension in the last 3 chapters), it was the very application that led to a special combination of in themselves already existing structural techniques. Sometimes a certain amount of creativity was introduced into the structural design, producing a new system application.

Industrial Design   The industrial designer takes care of two aspects in the process of design and building of space structures:
- Product development
- Product marketing care

Developing the product and optimising it in detail in regard with production, assembly and erection, and the adaptability to other requirements of architectural detailing and cladding. Initially as a separate and more theoretical development process, and subsequently as the development of the system in practice during the applications, project by project, and the feedback afterwards. (see schemes in fig 28) Step by step, until the product is evolved to complete maturity. Product marketing care means all aspects regarding the marketing analysis, marketing plan, marketing mix, and product-marketing plan. These aspects are treated in greater length in paragraph 3.5. Characteristic for the marketing approach of the design and development of space structures is that the first development of the Octatube system took 10 years of slow development from the initiating final studies at the TU Delft in 1973 during the time of the private architects office to 1983, maintaining a low marketing profile. The second space frame system, Tuball, took about two years, with a more intensive marketing assistance. The average design and development time of a new product is now scheduled at about one year with full support. Marketing is an efficiency tool, and gives ample indications which directions are most profitable in scientific or financial respect. Also, possible hobby-like diversions of highly theoretical research are ruthlessly dissuaded. Needless to say that the natural mutual professional disagreements that in practice exist between the professions concerned are normally discussed in the open in building team meetings. In case of the author's organisation these disagreements are discussed in-house, sometimes with the same energy level. But usually there are faster feedbacks when things don't work out as they are planned. At the end of internal disagreements there is sometimes the final decision to be made by the author choosing between his position as a product-architect and as a company director.

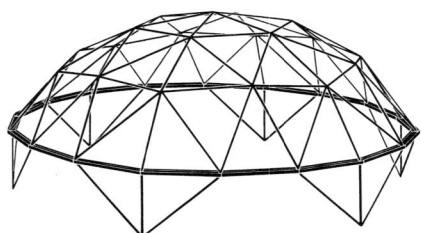

20 Perspective drawing of a sewage waste water tank covering composed of a lamella-type single layered dome (divided into six parts), resting on six foundation points. Design 1981. If built on an existing reinforced concrete basin, no large horizontal forces are expected.

Product-Architecture   The above described synergetic combination of know-how from the profession of Architectural, Structural and Industrial Design could be given a new and more general name: 'Product-Architecture', indicating the concern for building products of different kind, but always on purpose designed and developed for application in architecture. The designer who is able to combine the different professional know-hows will be called product-architect:
- The author's integrated approach for the design and development of space structures is characterised by this term, but also for example climate installations for use in architecture, that could be designed and developed in a similar way as space structures, deserve the same approach. Also glass skylights, curtain wall systems, internal wall partitioning systems etc. could be developed in the same synergetic method, and could possibly upgrade the state-of-the-art.

The experiences of the author show that such an approach is worth while following up in other products. In fact from this practice a strong recommendation follows for the University of Technology of Delft to start a separate study-discipline around 'Product-Architecture', with preferably closest links to the faculty of Architecture, and linked with Civil Engineering and Industrial Design.

It would fulfill three purposes:
- Stimulate the design and development of new building products or the innovation of existing products in a creative way, so that hopefully also the quality of the built environment is heightened.
- To make the building industry as a whole less conservative, to raise the quality of its production.
- To give a great number of future architects and industrial designers a proper education for the function which they will get anyway.

Dutch industrial designer Rogier de la Rive Box has

characterised this synergetic way of working thus: 'bridging gaps seems to divert borders'.

(Appendix 'Evaluation of the Building Parties' gives a more general analysis for possible cooperation for building product development.)

2 Design and Production in One Hand

The space structures designed and realised between 1982 and 1989 have been stimulated by simultaneous Design and Production. As can be read from the motivation given in the acknowledgement of this book, material production was originally drawn into the architect's office to realise experimental structures that either no Dutch company wanted to quote for, or made these experiments impossible when they quoted. So the first production was done to enable the designer to regain the status of the old 'master-builder' who once was the leader of the total building organisation and had the right to decide upon worthwhile building materials and techniques.

Gradually this relationship 'Design + Production' has been changed. Once a design has been made, developed and realised as an experimental prototype (this usually is a contracted building or building component already), the very experimental phase is almost over. After an evaluation of the first prototype, some changes can be introduced for the second application, which usually is seen as a duplicate-with-minor-alterations. The third and further applications are regarded more or less as a standard product already, and mainly are conducted by the experiences of the in-house-engineering staff. This is usually how far 'mass-production' in the building industry will go. ('Zero'-series are usually not permitted.) Only very occasionally is there an opportunity to get a separate contract for experimental design and development work. And as the projects for subsidised experimental design and developing work have been very scarce, the financial means for experimenting is mainly provided by the positive financial results of standard work: as a privatised 'tax' system for experiments. So, in 1982 self-confidence was the major driving force behind the integration of Design + Production, while in 1989 there is an equilibrium of standard production with experimental developments. Company profits (and sometimes even more) are directly utilised to enable the constant stream of experimental designs and developments. And the experiments in their turn profile the company.

21 Inside view of the full size laboratory cum factory of Octatube in Delft. Ample free space to test + assembly mock-up structures, and to allow a flexible production machinery lay out. 4 t overhead crane is suspended from the space frame directly.

One could wonder whether the integration of production into design is fruitful for other designers to step into. The integration of design into production is a common practice for many contractors. But even apart from the quality obtained, it weakens the position of the architect in the building process. Is the combination of Design + Production as practised by the author an example to be followed or is it just the one deviation that underlines the general rule of split-up competences? Thinking and doing result mostly in different attitudes, characterised by the different professions with their habits. Often smart ideas are not realised because producing parties do not see the advantages or simply are not prepared to take the risk and the responsibility. One of the negative sides of combining design and production is that in practice there is a double risk compared with normal contracts: the first risk is the involvement in presenting a new idea or design, and the second risk is quoting for this design that has never been realised before. And hardly anybody wants to risk his neck twice. In this respect the process of working with separate design and production contracts is more convenient for most parties involved except, then, for the building industry as a whole because the number of experiments and resulting new ideas will be restricted. The building industry is still commonly regarded as a rather traditional industry. In the circles of industrial designers the practice of joint Design + Production is more common. This is possible because their products involve usually a smaller scale and financing: like furniture, fashion or ornaments. Also sculptors have done it for centuries. But in the building industry it is an exception to the rule: architects never dare to practise it. Sometimes architects take the responsibility for the overall contracting and building organisation, dealing directly with many sub-contractors and organising the building process just as they propagate it. In most of these cases, however, the actuating motive will be to have a tighter financial control, more than a quality control. A typical example is the practice of the Delft architects office Cepezed.

But hardly any architects are known to specialise in the field of the building component products. Most architects will regard this field being too far from their intellectual activities. Some of them will even regard it as a step down on the social ladder. Also the required management and the capital investment to manufacture building component products is quite large, and architects usually are not accustomed to invest large amounts of capital in building materials and equipment, nor do they want to be too directly responsible for a large money flow and to take too many risks. Moreover, the distinct pattern of functions in the Dutch building industry does not allow an architect to act as a contractor or as a producer without losing his independent role of main advisor of his clients. Architects who want to enter the field of product-development for the building industry will probably at the end have to choose between being a project-architect or a product-architect cum producer.

Designing with a Laboratory at Hand

Apart from more general considerations on the subject, it is very stimulating for a designer to have an extensive laboratory at hand where new ideas can be realised immediately after emergence. The daily relationship with materials he can physically take in his hands and the techniques that can continuously be checked in each following application, cause new ideas and brainwaves to emerge, that would not have occurred in a more theoretical designer office situation. The oeuvre of Jean Prouvé forms an example of the fruitful co-operation of Production + Design brought in practice from the early experiments of Prouvé as a steel-construction craftsman who was inspired by the deformability properties of the materials at hand and by the results he could get with it. The current trend amongst young architects to admire the visual results of Prouve's work and to make inspired copies in his way of design, ignores the roots of his way of design: namely inspiration from production. Inspiration only from the visual results could very well prove to be trendy, while inspiration from the method of combining design and production has a more general value and

is not specifically restricted to the same designs or industry. Designers brought into this production-bound situation will have to realise that the non-committal way of making designs and drawings in the normal designers office practice of many architects, many structural engineers and industrial designers, disappears directly. This could be a frightening future for many a designer, who normally enjoys the economical buffer of the client and the main-contractor between his concepts and its realisation. At the same time drawings with a lack of exact data commonly produced in architects offices (with references like 'to be measured on site' or 'as to specialists detail') will have to be replaced by very accurate detailed and dimensioned drawings for both design and production purposes. This heightened responsibility is never valued as such except when things go wrong: at that time all parties in the building process sweep their own floor, and will try to blame the other party. It is clear that the party that takes more responsibility at the end is rewarded with a higher social respect and function, but apparently at the costs of more risks. The conclusion from the forementioned arguments is that before an architect enters the field of the production of building components, he will weigh the enlarged possibilities against the enlarged risks. The combination of Design + Production is then only worthwhile when it enables him to realise his experimental ideas and designs. When experiments are over, there is only the balance between normal company risks and profit, which is technically not very interesting for a designer. Basically, designers are more interested in design and realisation of these designs, and are personally less concerned when experimental designs go over into standard production, independent of the interests of the company as a whole.

3   Modelwork as a Design Tool

Apart from the brainstorm synthesis on product-design and product-development, that normally is very personally coloured, (but can be directed by competent marketing data) the tools of communication used in the design and development phase for spatial structures need to be commemorated. In the practical experience of the author both the modelwork and computerwork can work as a stimulation on the development of new techniques, besides the more commonly used sketches, drawings and also statical analysis by hand. The computerwork as described in par 1.3.4, is still in full development, and not a particular speciality of the author. Modelwork, however, can be described more as a result of the particular per-

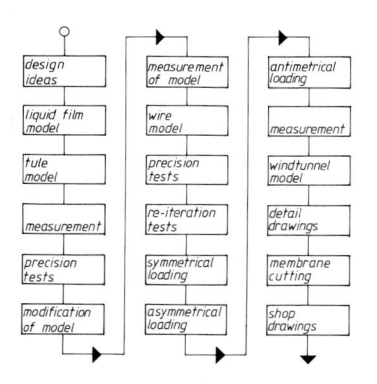

22 Flow diagram of the main activities from initial idea leading to the shop drawings of a prestressed cable net or membrane structure purely by modelwork; developed by Frei Otto and his students in the sixties, and still suited for small one-off projects.

sonal experiences. In the world of architecture, structural engineering and industrial design the denomination of the different model techniques are not corresponding. For that reason the most commonly used names for modelwork are given:
- small scale structural models (model material)
- detail models (real/fake material)
- visual mock-ups (real/fake material)
- production prototypes (real material)
- performance mock-ups (real material)

Even the advanced technology of the computer, offers usually an insufficient spatial insight in designs of space structures. However, because of the lack of 3-D insight of many clients in the first place, and because of the spatial complexity of many space structure designs in the second place, and thirdly because of the need for complete presentation by the designers, models will always stay a very convincing tool. Presentation models serve another purpose than design models. Design models are used to examine a certain hypothesis. In this paragraph the emphasis is on design and development models. Presentation models are not treated.

Small Scale Models Making models is a first step to gain knowledge on unknown material properties, techniques and structural systems. In small scale models usually only the structural system is represented, so the complete 3-D geometry can be checked, and the statical behaviour. Rigid space frame models and the more flexible membrane or guyed models both have their own properties. Space frame scale models usually are soldered in the laboratory. For models with stressed membranes the tension in the stressed membranes or cablenets on scale can be felt by sensitive fingertips, or sometimes even by tuning the model. For scale models on 1 : 5 to 1 : 20 scale for prestressed membranes and tensegrity structures (where the co-operation between form and tension is very close), often was experienced that models give a better simulation of structural reality under prestressing and external loading stage than the best ad-vanced computer programs could do. Models are still indispensable.

Model Sequence for Prestressed Membranes Based on the experiences of the author as a student when working at the Institute of Lightweight Structures of Frei Otto in Stuttgart in 1970, the adjacent linear sequence still is valid for a pure 3-dimensional design and development scheme for stressed membranes. The process activity flow diagram in fig 22 is based upon the cable net designs of Frei Otto. The flow diagram shows how elaborate the design process of stressed membranes is, where the warped surfaces have to be optimised in regard to geometry and stress analysis in a number of phases. Since the 1970s a further development has taken place mainly in the UK and USA to simulate the optimisation of the warped surfaces by computer programs but these programs are not freely available for designers. Hence in case of realising occasionally a design of a stressed membrane, the average designer still can make use of the above flow diagram. The complete set of activities is described in detail in the magazine Zodiac 21, 1972.[7]

Small Scale Tensegrity Models In fact, during the structural design phase of the tensegrity structure for the Hemweg Electricity Board Amsterdam, in 1983, the author experienced that largely due to the large displacements of the designed tensegrity structure, the usual computer program ICES STRUDL, or any equivalent finite element program was not able to react on these large displacements and give an improved geometry-stress position. (fig 23) Structural engineer Minos de Jonge had to retry each iteration until the equilibrium was found between the geometry and pretension in all tensile elements, respectively the change in tensile and compression stresses due to the different external loading cases. The total period of this computer work including the interpretation and correction took about two months. The complete computer analysis work was done on the IBM machines of the Computer Centre of the TU Delft. It would have given both structural engineer Minos de Jonge and the author as the architectural and overall designer in cooperation with artist Loes van der Horst a better and faster insight into just fabricating a 1 to 10 scale model, made of steel tube masts, steel cables and even turnbuckles with a few strain gauges to measure the different stresses under different loadings. In fact we did not do so because of our high faith in computerwork. The suitablity of the modelwork method became very clear during the actual installation where

23 Competition design model of the Hemweg tensegrity in 1982 on scale 1 to 20, with aluminium masts, thin cables with turnbuckles and stretched white membrane.

24 Full scale visual mock-up of a space frame system, designed by Frans de la Haye, to be built for Shell Nederland in large series. Prototype was only meant for visual approval of the system (1986).

25 Production mock-up for the Serangoon Gardens barrel vaults in Singapore 1985 to check the overall geometry, size of components, glass detailing, gutters and the performance of the electrically operated sun screens.

26 Performance tests by TNO Delft for static and dynamic over- and underpressure combined with water spray tests for watertightness of a skylight system for the Raffles City Complex skylights in Singapore 1984.

both the geometry of the complete structure as well as the correct pretension had to be carefully established on site. Because of the multiple statical indeterminacy (caused by the frequent interconnection of the 13 different tubes in space, connected by in total 105 cables) the smallest change in geometry caused an immediate change in geometry and in stress distribution in a great number of adjoining cables, and of cause also in the compression elements. The total erection process consumed only one day, but the prestressing process to a satisfactory situation comparable with the prestress situation of the computer, took 3 full weeks, performed by highly schooled engineering staff, too. After this erection sequence was finalised, we realised that an eventual 1/10 model would not only have given a fair insight into the internal stress distribution, but also a better simulation of the erection process itself. The second tensegrity designed by the author as structural designer, in co-design with the artist Krijn Giezen, and also calculated by structural engineer Minos de Jonge posed less of a problem as this design was more elementary and had less degrees of freedom in the struc-tural design. Yet we found that the 1/20 model of this structure, made by the two co-designers displayed a very comprehensive stress distribution, easy to influence by the turnbuckles on scale 1/20: the intelligent designer easily observes that even the smallest deformations have large and sometimes unexpected impacts. The real outcome was a process of understanding of structural behaviour, more direct than the most advanced computer program. It was only after this project that at the department of Civil Engineering on the TU Delft, Karin Laglas made her graduation work on the computer analysis of tensegrity structures, developing a more responsive computer program that works more satisfactorily.

Full Scale Detail Models   During the later phases of development of the product like phase 3 and 4 of the development schemes (fig 28) full scale models will have to be built in real material or in a substitution that only represents the form, to evaluate the suppositions taken in the earlier design phases, to actualise the real production problems and to test the reaction of the market on the designed model. Taking these very form models in hand, looking at them and getting accustomed to the real scale, often inspires different arguments than before, in the more theoretically oriented phases. Problems concerning production, handling, assembly and installation as well as functional performance can be checked when form models are used in the definitive material. Often a positive feed-back can be the result.

Full Scale Mock-ups   In order to check the functional performance of at least a part of the assembled structure, real scale build-ups of different components are very useful: either to test the total visual appearance, the structural behaviour by full scale tests, or to perform windtightness and watertightness tests for products that include cladding components. All these assemblies are called mock-ups in project specifications of buildings. Especially the development of products with a complex character, with an assembly of different components can be influenced positively by using mock-up tests for the benefit of the designer and producer in case of pure product-development. Clients, on the other hand, might ask for full scale mock-ups in order to give a final approval to the visual and functional performance of the product application, usually requested in specification.

Visual Mock-up   An example of such a stimulus for product-development was the building of a (full scale) mock-up for a lattice truss space frame with a completely new nodal system, designed by industrial designer Frans de la Haye for Shell Nederland and executed in 1986.(fig 24) The size of the mock-up was 4.8 x 4.8 m, and 3.6 m high, and only a part of the real Shell petrol canopy 20 x 24 m in size. The mock-up was welded in steel components, while the real structure should be a bolted one. The mock-up served only a visual purpose. The prototype showed a firmness of dimension of the structural components, deducted from the chosen statical scheme and the new and exclusive Shell-nodal system on the one hand, while on the other hand it inspired new ideas of manufacturing larger elements than usual in space frames, and the complicated assembly methods, in relation with the universal use of the structural units. This mock-up was made just after a first full scale (visual) model of a single joint was approved by Shell. Later the development of the intended new type of canopy for Shell petrol stations, lead to a first application in 1987, in Rotterdam by Kloos-Hollandia, waiting for a full series of applications by Hollandia and Octatube in close cooperation. At the moment of writing this book the project is postponed, in favour of laminated timber.

Production Prototype (Serangoon)   Two other models are worth while mentioning: the first more a visual and functional production prototype for Serangoon, the other a pure performance mock-up for the Raffles City atrium skylights, both in Singapore. As part of the rapid design and development of the barrelvaulted atrium structure for Serangoon Gardens Country Club in Singapore, as described in more detail in paragraph 3.7.3 a full scale prototype was built of a complete span width and 3 modules of 1.7 m in length to test the geometrical assumptions of production, the application of the glass panels on top of the space frame, including the watertightness seams, and also the performance of an interior sun screen, operated automatically on two electrical motors. This last item was tested during 3 full months every 5 minutes running in and out. The testing revealed two weak spots in the total assembly: too thin tubes with insufficient torsion stability, that had to be replaced from thin aluminium (2.5 mm) into thick wall tubes (5 mm) and at last into thick walled steel tubes (5 mm) that at last gave enough stability, and did not cause a deformation in the sunscreen itself that appeared by wrinkles in the screen fabric and by deformation of an intermediate straight area between two adjacent screens. (fig 25) Apart from functional information used for production feed-back, the Singaporean client, the architect and the structural engineer examined the prototype in the factory before they gave approval to commence production.

Performance Mock-up (Raffles City)   The mock-up made for the roof and wall glazing of the Raffles City Complex in Singapore (fig 26) in 1985 performed at the premises of the the research institute TNO in Delft was prescribed in the contract specifications made by I.M.Pei architects of New York. The skylight and curtain wall specialist of I.M.Pei's is Fritz Sulzer, a former student of Konrad Wachsmann. The aim of the mock-up testing was to get a certificate of technical behaviour of this specially designed and developed glazing system. The initial design was made in standard extrusion profiles, from the catalogue of Kawneer, Germany. Because of the high and new requirements for the extrusions, most of the standard ones were replaced during the one year long development period by a set of 17 new and only 2 existing Kawneer extrusions. The functioning of the developed skylight system in respect of the watertightness and windtightness had to be tested under changing conditions of dynamic and static overpressure and underpressure, combined with rainwatertests. For this aim a small part of the total (approximately 3000 m2) glazed area was erected on a connecting part of the supporting space frame. The space frame itself was not tested structurally, only used for detail and coating approval. Yet for the space frame the mock up also proved to be a benefit because some geometrical mistakes became apparent that were not recognized before. The mock-up was built in a closed box in which static overpressure and underpressure could be generated by means of a compressor, while the dynamic overpressure outside was produced by 4 big axial ventilators (aeroplane propellors) rented from a Belgian institute and built in a custom made steel frame. Water was sprayed on the mock-up by fire hoses. The result was a special combination of wind loadings and water attacks that due to the wind loadings even went vertically upward. This situation, according to the architects' specification (based on wind-tunnel tests), was in accordance with reality because the skylights' glazing was only the covering of the lower atriums on the 5th floor of a complex surrounded by 4 skyscrapers of hotels and offices of about 70 stories high. Due to the size of the mock-up (6 m wide, 8 m high and 5 m deep), the mock-up could not be built inside the usual testing halls of TNO in Delft. So an outside location was chosen with minimal annoyance for the surrounding buildings by the wind generators. Alas the screw anchors used for fixing the foundation damaged a sub-soil waterpipe that accidently seemed to be routed under the structure and the tests were hindered by severe frost, snow and ice as the testing was scheduled in December 85 and February 86. So in a nutshell the normal problems of a real building site were experienced as well, but unfortunately more the Dutch winter conditions than the Singapore climate. It took two series of tests to get the required technical certificate, because in the first run due to the low temperatures the silicon sealing was not applied properly, and some detail connections had to be changed.

Production Prototypes   There is a slight confusion in terms used for models in architecture, in structural design and engineering and in industrial design. In accordance with industrial design habits, a prototype is a first built product, on full scale, and working in its definitive function. However, this description does only apply to small scale (i.e. scale of industrial design) products, but not to large scale structures. In larger structures the prototypes unfortunately (for the feedback) almost always are the built structures themselves. When the term 'prototype' does not refer to a macro-scale structure, but to a micro-scale part, reference is for example taken to the separate nodes and bars of which the entire space frame structure is composed. In which case the prototype is made of the real material, and in principle meant to function like the end result. So single element prototypes can be tested, and researched on tensile testing. Performance 'prototypes' or mock-ups are used for testing the behaviour of the assembly of a number of prototype elements together, like in the reality of a space frame composed of a small number of bars and nodes. The given descriptions show how useful modelwork in its various stages can be as a tool for improving the design, development research and production process.

4   Creative Design, Research and Development

This paragraph describes in generalized terms the results of the process of Design, Research and Development experienced in the space structures shown in this book. They are deliberately generalised because their use has proven them to be applicable for a much larger scope.

Creative Thinking in General   In all processes of Design, Research and Development, it is good to realise that true Creative Thinking which is the basis of these processes, generally will consist of 5 subsequent phases: (see scheme 27)

1 First Insight   In the early stadium of first insight the problem is simply recognised to exist and the intention is made to solve it. The formulation of the problem is often a very critical stadium in the process of Creative Thinking as it can easily send the complete process into the wrong direction. A mystified problem definition might cause many return loops in order to start all over again after having discovered to be on the wrong trail caused by an inexact problem description. In architecture it is a well known feature that the activity of describing the list of requirements by the client is a very

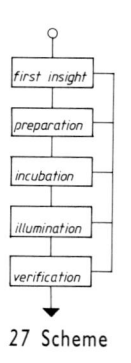

27 Scheme

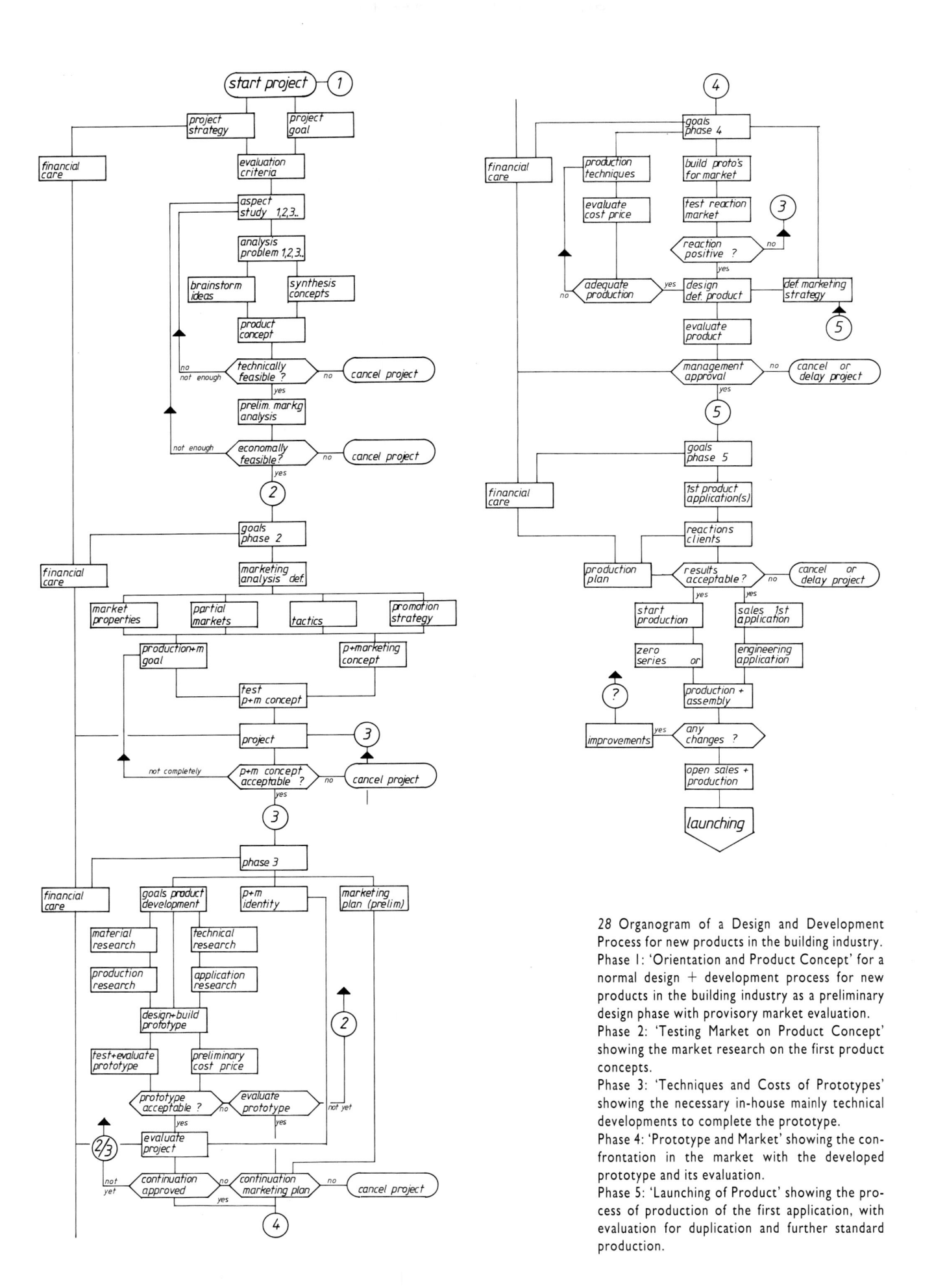

28 Organogram of a Design and Development Process for new products in the building industry.
Phase 1: 'Orientation and Product Concept' for a normal design + development process for new products in the building industry as a preliminary design phase with provisory market evaluation.
Phase 2: 'Testing Market on Product Concept' showing the market research on the first product concepts.
Phase 3: 'Techniques and Costs of Prototypes' showing the necessary in-house mainly technical developments to complete the prototype.
Phase 4: 'Prototype and Market' showing the confrontation in the market with the developed prototype and its evaluation.
Phase 5: 'Launching of Product' showing the process of production of the first application, with evaluation for duplication and further standard production.

critical phase on which the complete design will be based, which too often is not realised by the client.

2 Preparation In the stadium of preparation much conscious effort is involved to develop an idea for solving the problem. There may be much coming and going between the first two stadia as the problem is re-formulated or even redefined. Yet this period involves hard work. Trying to analyse the problem means trying to get a grip on the problem. The problem is preferably cut into smaller pieces that are first solved separately, and then tried to be combined.

3 Incubation It is always followed by a period of incubation which involves no apparent effort and indicates a stalemate, a sort of mental block to come any further. Often it takes a certain distance from the problem process, 'a fresh view', an evasion from problem blindness, to come any further. There are always problems that are so complicated that requirements contradict each other and no apparent solution can be found. After a while one gets bored, one does not actually see the problem in its right proportions. In this phase an outsider could help out, sometimes by his specialist advice, but sometimes by ignorant remarks, that however can inspire again, leading to the next phase.

4 Illumination All of a sudden there is a sudden emergence of an idea or an illumination which can be explained as an apotheosis of an unconscious effort to reorganise and reexamine all previous thoughts, be it with a certain distance. By withdrawing from the subject one is able to come with a fresh view and approach which often might prove to be more productive than the initial conceived development. In that way incubation and illumination always are seen to appear after each other. Sometimes these illuminations occur during car driving on long distances, when a person's mind is set at ease and all considerations can be put against each other.

5 Verification Once The Idea has emerged, there will be a conscious process of verification to test and to develop the idea further into full maturity, and to check whether the solution is an answer to all problems. Once the idea is born, a new energy stream in the process is introduced that feeds the very laboursome last phase: the working out of the solution. The process has to be experieced by the full design and development staff. When the staff is only allowed to work in the last verification phase, the staff will miss the internal drive to prove the idea. Although, generally speaking, the linear sequence of the 5 different phases seems to be a normal routine, the respective lengths of the different phases can vary greatly according to the person in charge, the problem at hand and the available technology. Solving problems in the first and rather abstract phase of a process may more often lead to 'eurekas' than the pure technical problems from a later phase. Conceptual ideas are abstracted and (mostly over-) simplified, while technical ideas tend to coincide with long periods of heavy work with only small injections of sparkling suggestions. Technical problems sometimes are made just too complicated. But between conceptual and technical processes there is no essential difference in creative thinking.

Design in General   A definition of design is impossible to give in this short paragraph without the danger of ridiculing the education and practice of designers in many disciplines. Yet one attempt is worth while noting: 'Design is a material or an immaterial solution for a given problem in given circumstances with given means, performed in a creative way'. Design is an act or a series of activities that has common features described in the process of creative thinking and applies both for immaterial designs like writing a book or a computer program as for material designs with the aid of materials and techniques.

The question which confuses many young designers is where design starts in the first place, but also where it ends. Is design only regarded as the few brainwave phases in the total development, or reaches the process of design as far as the completion of the product or the building? Depending of the personal occupation the design process meant by a designer might be the same process as the development process by a product-developer. Usually design adds more creativity and over-value to the process than pure development. How far should the interest of a designer go? Designers with an architectural background are more or less indoctrinated that they are only seen as a designer when they are engaged in the conceptual design phase, thus in the initial phase. They are apt to think that spending energy in other phases is not worth while for them. Industrial designers have a different view and regard the development work before and after this conceptual phase as rewarding and essential to the total process. The central question is in fact how determined is the designer to influence all phases of the product process?

In the opinion of the author design is connected with all aspects of product development onto the very last phase of application, as this phase very often gives enough feedback to start all over again with some aspects of the design, and because this phase also provides information and motivation to improve the design of other products and buildings. So, Design, Research, Development and Application are inseparable, and are all worth the involvement of the designer.

Research and Development   Although R + D or 'Research + Development' is often referred to in industry as one activity, a better explanation is to regard the whole process from birth to maturity of a product as 'Development'. 'Design' is the most creative component of 'Development', while 'Research' represents the more technical component. The total process of overall development of a new product for the building industry is visualised in the organisational schemes of fig 28 in five subsequent phases. Especially for designers with a graphical insight these schemes show the mutual relationships between the separate activities. For the author these schemes have proved to be a valuable asset in trying to organise the development of a new type of product. During well over 15 years these schemes have been adapted and improved continuously to the present general form. These schemes are quite universal and apply in principle to designs and developments of different products: like a car, an aeroplane, an industrial building, a building component, or to some extent, also a book, and a design process for students. Of course there will be differences in interpretation in the schemes for each type of product, and usually some small adaptations of the schemes are necessary. In the schemes the five different phases are:

1 Orientation and Product Concept
2 Testing Market on Product Concept
3 Techniques and Costs Prototypes
4 Prototype and Market
5 Launching Definitive Product

Only the first phase can be regarded as a sketch design. Phase 3 is definitive design, technical research and further development. In phase 4 and 5 adaptations are made in regard to production, the first application, and the start of the definitive production and further applications. These schemes are product-development orientated, but give also the relative importance of the respective activities of architectural, structural and industrial design, fitting in the whole process, when at least these distinctions in some process-steps can be made. The marketing aspects mentioned in these schemes are treated in paragraph 3.5. The schemes are believed to be self-explanatory.

In order to launch a strong and creative new product, the separate activities of Design, Development and Research should have strong interrelationships. The process around the product itself can be seen separately from the application of the product in buildings, connected by a feedback relation of more general requirements.

For 'open' building products where a number of characteristics can be influenced by the project-architect, the process of application of the product in a building design deserves an analysis of its own. The resulting method of working will be different for each type of product, but will not be treated in this book. The results of the design, development and research processes of different products have resulted in space structures realised by the author, and are presented in the last 3 chapters.

One of the general themes in the work of the author is to aim for 'Creative Research + Development' in order to get the best products. Designers have to cooperate with technicians. This brings us back to the role of the architect in the building process and the way architects are usually involved in R + D. Although project-architects will maintain that they are also involved in a process of R + D in the building process, this results in a slightly different approach than the one leading towards an industrialised product. Firstly, the actual R + D done by projects-architects concerns mostly the topology of building elements, that is to say the positioning of these building elements in space. They are less concerned with properties, technical behaviour and repetitive use for other buildings, by themselves or by one of their colleague architects. Because of the mutual competition between architects and the public character of their work, they will regard the copying of the results of their design and R + D as unauthorised, but also quite inevitable. Wanting to publish for more work and keeping one's own secrets simply does not go very well together in an open society as the building industry. In order to copy designs one simply has to subscribe to the leading architectural magazines, with preferably foreign examples for more design inspiration. Secondly, the education and experience of architects limits their R + D often to the more traditional building materials and building techniques.

An example are the very well designed building furniture elements of the architect Herman Hertzberger in his own buildings. Very well-detailed elements like balcony parapets and table lamps are made of traditional materials with traditional techniques. Such elements fulfil their function in his buildings very well, but cannot be seen isolated from his own buildings as possible components to be used by other architects. This might display an opinion of the architect Herman Hertzberger, but it leaves a chance for his very well designed, researched and developed building components, that could sell very well in the building market. On the other hand, when Herman Hertzberger would realise that his products were to be applied in projects of other architects, his designs should be developed further into more sophisticated products in aspects of material properties, production technical performances and cost. So for more general applications, the complete given organisational schemes have to be worked through. In the opinion of the author R + D is a part of the activities of a joint team of different disciplines, either working together from independent positions, but preferably within one organisation, and even better a team composed of designers who are able to cover more than one discipline (as advocated in par 3.1: product-architects). Specific tasks like the technical research on material properties or the behaviour of building components under loadings of different kinds, are performed for example by material or structural engineers, but always closely commented on and held alive and creative by their architectural and industrial colleagues. The purpose of this cooperation is to reduce the gap between design and research and to have both aspects benefit from each other's impulses. Design has benefited from scientific impulses during the recent decades, so maybe research could - in its turn - benefit from creative impulses.

Also the particular technical research tasks that are regarded in the respective university departments as their own domain, have only the limited function in the development process of a product as appears from the schemes: they are very important, but only a rather small activity in the total process of product development. In addition to this, the majority of the technical research is regarded by designers as too specialised for them to be involved competently. There is a missing link between conventional research as performed in the building research laboratories and the creative research by designers. Dutch research institutes like TNO in Delft are nowadays realising more and more that there is an extensive market for research institutes to be covered called 'Creative Research + Development', when the fees would be adapted to designers standards. Compared with conventional research activities applicable in the building industry, at best ending in performance certificates, these new creative R + D projects introduce positive results by the mixture of the know-how potentials of the research institutes and pure creativity. It might also indicate that the potentials for the Research and Development market serving private and smaller companies without an in-house R + D department, and covered by the semi-professional Technical University faculties of Architecture, Civil Engineering and Industrial Design in Delft and Eindhoven, will go beyond the limitations of these separate faculties, so the mutual contacts and relationships between these faculties will have to be frequented.

5 Marketing Aspects of Product Development

In the building industry the mechanism of price setting mainly depends upon tendering/subtendering with a large scale competition effect. In these types of markets substitute products are difficult to introduce. When the quality of the building product is described in the specifications, the price level competition is ruthless. There are two ways out. The first way is to design new products or systems with a level of quality beyond competition. The second one is a larger scale route: more turnover, more product against lower prices but a reasonable totalised profit. This paragraph deals with the marketing consequences of building products for a wider circle of application than just one building with one client as is the custom in the building industry. The consequent approach is halfway between the consumers market where products are pushed through the market and the industrial market where products are exactly demanded by clients. Yet, people in the building industry tend to regard personal contacts and obtaining contracts thereof, as the main marketing technique. Surely for sub-contractors or specialist-producers a more systematic insight into marketing possibilities can give a better logistic support, as they will be the ones who are continuously developing new products for the building industry.

This paragraph has been written from the point of view of the marketing of building products, and more general than space structures alone. As the information collected for the specific space structure designs of the author are vital for the company, there will not be any publication on this matter. The marketing development of a product has to run parallel to the technical development. In fact marketing aspects and technical aspects are supplementing each other in the development process.[25, 26, 27, 28]

Large Failure Risk According to the American marketing advisors Booz, Allen & Hamilton it is realistic to estimate the failure risk of a new product even with good marketing preparation at 80%. Looking on all new products introduced on the market this failure risk might even be as high as 98 %.[25] That is to say only two out of a hundred new products will survive. (fig 30) This rule is applicable to the consumers market, but in a lesser extent also to industrial products for buildings and architecture when the product should have a reasonable life cycle, longer than just one building.

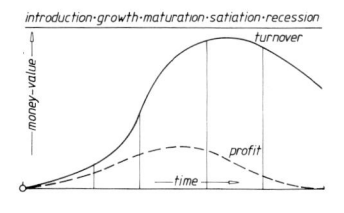

29 Scheme of average Product Life Cycle showing growing and decreasing turnovers and an average profit curve which is maximal during maturation. A wise company policy is to have a range of products with overlapping Product Life Cycles so that overall profitability is assured.

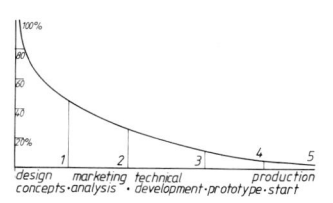

30 Death rate of new products according to Booz, Allen and Hamilton, applied to the five design and development phases of fig 28, showing the small number of successful products and the loss of the large number of less successful ideas. The good luck to develop a successful product is normally surrounded by the bad luck of less successful ones. So the fear from this curve causes stopping at first instance and ensures many a conservative company management policy in regard to product development.

Product Life Cycle As to the product itself, it is essential to realise that each product has only a restricted life cycle. The different stages in a lifetime of a product are:
- Introduction
- Growth
- Maturation
- Satiation
- Recession

This restricted product life cycle displayed in fig 29, resembles that of an organism: products are born, develop themselves into maturity and finally die.

When the speed in which new techniques are developed or existing techniques are innovated, accelerates, the life cycles of the newer products tend to be shorter. This applies absolutely to the consumers market, but also the industrial market of the building industry cannot distract itself from these undulations. Theoretically one could experience a catching-up in case the average life cycle of products becomes shorter out of marketing competition reasons than the time necessary to develop a new product. In which case a newly developed product is launched in a market that is already decreasing. The importance of a correct and timely social and technical forecast is proven here. Accepting the existence of limited lifecycles of building products, means remaining alert for changes that can influence these cycles: both from the product (supply) side and from the client (demand) side. The result for a company as a whole is that the different current products all have life cycles of different lengths and are in different phases of development within the life cycle. A wise company policy is to try to have the maturation phases (being the most profitable) of the different products as a continuation of each other. The company has to influence this total addition of life cycles into a manageable direction. Marketing analysis is one of the possible tools for it. Life cycles apply to products, but of course also to services rendered: for example to a method of design, to an architectural style, even to the popularity of architects in society, but also to different types of space structures. Space frames will probably have a limited life cycle, too. Apart from natural causes like tendencies in the market and being overtaken by new and better products, the disappearance of a large number of products can also be due to bad marketing policy:
- Not performing preliminary marketing studies
- Strategic failures during launching.
- Not being adapted to realistic market needs.
- Over- or underestimation of the competition.
- Bad coordination between R+D, sales and production.
- Too fast introduction on the market, etc.

The introduction of a new building product can only be successful when the product is an excellent answer to the needs of a client. A study of technical product design always has to be accompanied by respective marketing studies, when a product is designed for the open market. As the building industry always has been used to mainly produce buildings upon request of clients, there was not much need in the past for a wider marketing analyses. Only the introduction of building components designed and manufactured as an industrial product introduces the need for a wider marketing survey than one single contract meeting. It is on this point that a clear distinction between contractors building with traditional materials (concrete, brickwork and timberwork) has to be made, and specialist-producers responsible for industrially manufactured building components. Traditional materials are transported as half products, and could eventually be used for another building if the contract is cancelled. The materials are rather flexible in application. Most new building products made of non-traditional materials are completely finished building components, and can hardly be used in another building if the contract is cancelled. So they need a more extensive marketing as the flexibility of application is smaller.

This paragraph has been written in the form of a recipe for the marketing of new industrial products in the building industry in general. The author has had practical experience with many of the presented marketing aspects for a number of products ranging from space frames, tent structures, domes, mobile structural frames, exhibition stands, skylights and metal cladding systems for use and application in architecture. This experience shows that without a thorough marketing plan, without patience to overcome the pioneer time and without products that inspire colleague-architects to apply these products in their overall designs, and last but not least without capital to invest and staff with a full support, nobody should start to hope for a chance of two out of hundred.

Marketing Analysis The primary function of the marketing analysis is to find a correct market for the product/service or to find a suitable product/service for the market demands with the optimal use of the present personal abilities, capital and equipment. As will be shown in this paragraph, the relationship between an existing market and supply on that market by new products, can be interpreted as an act of self-fulfilling prophecy. Only focusing on an existing market means that future possibilities will not be envisaged. And designers can be annoyed by a short-sightedness of marketing people who completely lack any future vision. Like the Dutch industrial designer Frans de la Haye stated bluntly: 'marketing is blackmail'. But marketing people are to determined score on the short term. Yet, a complete lack of long term vision as often exists in the building industry can be even more disastrous. But there is no doubt about the discrepancies between the designing and marketing disciplines.

The aim of marketing analysis is to gain information about facts in history and future, to track possible trends and to indicate a direction for short-term planning fitting into the long-term strategy of the producing company. The development scheme in 5 phases as shown in fig 28 is also used as a guideline for the marketing aspects of this product development. Refences are taken to the respective phases of these pictograms. The marketing analysis is a combination of the preliminary product/marketing analysis of phase 1: 'Orientation and Product Concept'; the 'Definitive Product / Marketing Analysis' in phase 2; and the testing out of prototypes on the market described in phase 4: 'Prototype and Market'. Marketing activities, in order to launch a new building product, have to run parallel to the technical product development. When this is not realised (for example in situations like at the universities sometimes is the case), the resulting product can be a complete misser, and is never heard of later.

Although the two aspects of product- and market-related studies are treated in different chapters, the pictograms also indicate that in a well-prepared development these two aspects are almost inseparable. The aspects of marketing in this paragraph 3.5 ought to be seen as complimentary to the technical product design and development dealt with in the other paragraphs of this book.

The marketing analysis can be divided into two major parts: Market Exploration and Product Qualities.

The market exploration is engaged in identification of clients; numerical estimation; analysis of market size; is the market growing or contracting? Which distribution channels? What are the market characteristics? Is the market to be divided into partial markets, with specific characteristics? Is there any reason to disqualify some partial markets? On this moment the so called 'Pareto-rule' might be applicable: when a certain part of the market with a small size (say 20%) is responsible for a large amount of complicated requirements in the design - say 80% -, then leave that partial market or allow it to your competitors. Or is it the reverse Pareto-rule that enables specialist-producers like the author to distinct their somewhat experimentally flavoured production from other standard productions? In that way the production of the author is anti-Pareto! Estimation of competition, the number of companies involved and their respective market share, their prices, respective qualities and promotion possibilities; the strengths and weaknesses of the competition; the properties, advantages and disadvantages of their products by a competitive value-analysis. The emphasis on the earlier part of the marketing analysis will depend more on the market information than on the actual product qualities, that can be listed as follows: functional needs to be satisfied by the product, seen from the point of view of the clients; with their preference and attitude towards quality and price level of the product. After the technical design phases and building of the first prototype the confrontation of the market with the prototype and eventual alterations in the product will mean a further refinement of the product. In this paragraph the importance of product qualities will not be worked out any further; the results are actually given in the last three chapters of this book.

Literature research is a theoretical method to find the potential magnitude and importance of the market. Developments in the choice pattern of clients are important. Which factors are decisive for the choice? Via questionnaires and personal discussions the motivations and preferences of the clients, the strength of the competition and their pricing could be analysed in a complete marketing overview. Literature gives a clue about information from the past; a future forecast, however, is of far more importance. So the marketing analysis should also estimate the preferences and motivations of clients on products never experienced before. Also a listing has to be made of product properties that clients like and dislike. In practice the use of literature research is only of minor importance, as the collected data often are not complete. Marketing analysis also involves the effectiveness of various forms of advertisement and the strength of the competition, so no time and energy are wasted by fighting a too strong competitor or advertising for nonexisting clients. Marketing evaluation of products is the basis for a sound product policy of a company. This evaluation includes an investigation of the opinion of the client, discovering the image of the product and an analysis of the total product range of the company. Usually it does not take too much effort to discover if the client is satisfied with a certain product, but it takes a more impressive view of the opinion of the client to analyse which image the client has formed of the product.

Marketing Plan   A marketing plan of a product usually is short-term directed, but has to fit into the medium-term and long-term company policy. It has to render an account of the following 7 items:
• Sales Forecast   The forecast of the expected sales is based upon the data of the marketing analysis. In the building industry this forecast used to be based upon a personal presentiment, or a break-even turnover. However, there are techniques of predicting turnovers keeping in mind all factors that can possibly influence the sales in the near future. A correct forecast is a base for the choice of production techniques connected with the expiry effect (or expected life cycle of the product), for costprice calculations and for sales strategy.
• Sales Strategy   Selection of clients, sales, distribution channels, selection of product and product ranges, sales methods. On the basis of the results of the marketing analysis an estimation will be made of which clients will probably buy the product. The plan also will have to include transport and shipping, storing in stock and on site, the phases of pre-assembly, real assembly on site and erection or installation. The final quality of the building product should also reflect the time, energy, and know-how invested in the product.
• Pricing   Fixation of sales price of the product. Decisions have to be taken in regard to margins for overhead costs and development costs. A distinct feeling for the reaction of the market is necessary, as is an elementary knowledge of economy. On the one hand marketing will lead to the satisfaction of the client, on the other hand the producing company will have to be continued. The earning capacity of the launched product will have to be subtantially larger than the costs made during the development phase of the product. (fig 29)
• Advertisement and Sales Promotion   Planning of advertisement and sales support are very important. Designs of advertisements, documentation and other promotion material will have to be made. For engineering products emphasis has to be put on reliability and technical behaviour, adapted to demanding clients.
• Presentation   The marketing plan has to provide for ideal and physical presentation of the product, of prototypes models, samples, and demonstrations or testings. For engineering products more technical and academical information has to be distributed in the form of lectures, articles in professional magazines etc, in order to help project-architects to design the possible applications in their total building. Planning the introduction on the market, indicating and detailing the relation with advertising and promotion.
• Organisation   When a product is developed in an existing company, most probably a part of its structure will have to be adapted and reorganised, taking into account technical-organisational aspects, the economical-financial and social-human implications of the changes in the existing structure. As the social level is increasing, a continuous reflection to adapt the organisation to external stimuli, is absolutely neccesary.
• Estimates   Budget estimates of expenditures and revenues are a numerical proof for the plausibility of the recommendations listed in the marketing plan, acting as a detailed background.

Properties of an Industrial Market   The building industry market distinguishes itself from the usual consumers market by the durability of the product, the method of choosing a product and the nature and abilities of the client. Opposed to the consumers market the building market is a real industrial market, with the following properties:
• Products usually are building components or building elements, fitting into a larger product (the building) by assembly and erection;
• The product is bought for a specific purpose in the building industry: for example the primary function of space structures is to form roof structures.
• The product is bought by other organisations via quotations and tenders. Main contractors may buy on price, but usually architects will finally decide, more on quality and appearance of the offered product.

- The industrial marketing research is concerned with the needs of the building industry (to be seen as the collective of principals, architects, structural engineers and main contractors), keeping in mind the goals of the building industry.
- On the industrial product market, clients usually are experts. They will base their decisions on quality and other objective criteria of primary function; secondary functions can sometimes influence the final choice.
- The product is usually bought in large quantities by a limited number of clients. This causes a different sales and promotion strategy compared with the consumers market.

The marketing analysis of building products is hindered by the fact that clients do not form a homogeneous group of buyers. During the preliminary and definitive stages of the marketing analysis, also the relation product and producing company has to be evaluated. The company has to answer the following questions:
- Are there enough financial resources to take the risk of developing a new product?
- How accessible are the half products that will be the elements for manufacture of the product? Is the market of these elements monopolised or competitive?
- Does the new product require investments, or can it be fabricated on the existing equipment?
- Is the production lay-out of the factory suitable for the new product? What restrictions will coincide with eventual expansion?
- Are patents applied for, or is there a design protection and a registered trade mark?
- Will the company's reputation based on former products in the past and in the present be advantageous or disadvantageous for the marketing of the product?
- Is there enough labour force with the required skill and quality awareness available?
- Is the organisational competence sufficient?

When the producing company has agreed in principle on the above described consequences to take the new product into production, during the definitive evaluation of the product in the company more explicit discussions will be raised in the specific departments of the company. A listing will have to be made of the relevant factors for each department. On the other hand each of the departments will make a list of requirements that absolutely will have to be fulfilled before the product is accepted in the department. Each factor will be given an award as an indication of the importance. The results of the different departments will lead to a conclusive document. This management game can be detailed by multiplying the overall importance with the weight of each factor, giving each department a certain number of points. This could be a base on which to conclude whether the product will be successful or not.

Sales Forecast   There are a number of reasons to make an accurate sales forecast:
- Drafting of a sales budget and estimation of rentability; opening possibilities for investments on short to long term;
- As a base for the management information system of the company: profitability of the new product, accuracy of sales promotion, effect of price changes and necessity of advertisements;
- Planning of production and distribution schemes with special attention for buffer stocks when prices of elements will raise and just-in-time management when they have risen;
- When continuously adapted to the actual situation it spreads a pattern of behaviour of clients which is general management information.

Both internal and external factors will have to be taken into account. Amongst the external factors belong the influences of governmental interventions: import and export limitations or duties, for example American, Saudi or Malaysian protectionism and the open common European market from 1992. Sensibility for strikes of production or shipping personnel. (UK) Limitations in credit facilities, insurance premiums, political instability in the world and regional limitations of trade and shippings at war. World market prices on elements, half products and energy. Artificial, political or natural scantiness of elements displaying larger fluctuations than the building industry itself. Fundamental changes in the market like high industrial investments, growing numbers of a specific type of building; size and seriousness of international competition; anticipation of their product range improvement. Availability of replacement products. Payment terms in principle and in detail, guarantees of payments, letters of credit against bid bonds, performance bonds and warranty bonds.

The Internal Factors are: production capacity in total, but also regarding the optimal division of different products in the total production facility is important. In the short term the factory will probably not be adapted to the changing needs of the market. So the available labour force, machinery and capital have the greatest influence on the sales prognosis. When the right sort of people in the factory are not available, nor the capital to invest in element supplies, products in stock or products installed, or only paid on a retarded scheme, sales will automatically be restricted.

Optimism and self-confidence of the management team is important. This can be expressed in the willingness to invest in materials, to experiment in new products, to undertake more promotional activities and more research and development. Especially architects can be convinced with proper and efficient visual promotional material. For an outsider there seem more reasons to confirm the relative inactivity in the field of technological advancements in the building industry, but at the same time there are ample opportunities for a positive management team to improve products and initiate new ones in just that industry because of its slowness.

And last but not least the quality and service the company displays in her products. Bad quality, wrongly or retardedly executed installations and slenderly attended after-sales service are long term reminders. Also changes in pricing, willingly provoked or not, have an influence on sales figures, although less than in a consumers market when one considers that time and time again new clients will use the products, more than a regular small group of repeated clients. A completely different picture appears in export, when in a country one company is appointed as sole representative or sole agent, being a continuous client. In that case some internal factors become external.

Marketing Mix   The successful marketing is a result of a careful combination of different methods, known as the products own Marketing Mix, of which the elements ought to be analysed to show the effectiveness of each component and of the entity as a 'Mix'. The most important ingredients are shown in figure 31: Product Design, System Image, Advertisement, Personal Sales, Sales Promotion, Distribution Channels, Pricing and After Sales. The Marketing Mix of Octatube space frames shows an engineering product: much emphasis will be given to the reliability of the producer: in nearly all cases he will be held solely responsible for both the application design and comment on the design of the project-architect, the statical analysis, the production. But also for the assembly on site and the installation, as these two last aspects both are an integral part of the legal product responsibility. In the space frame mix, distribution is in practically all cases direct from factory to client, via the main contractor. Promotion, advertisement and personal sales are all bundled in a very limited commercial advertisement campaign and an extensive information stream on professional and academical level, based upon experience, design capacities and will-

31 The marketing mix of new products

ingness to experiment more frequently and more extensively than is the custom in the building industry. Two other aspects: 'Product Design' and 'System Image' work out differently for the two main space frame systems Octatube and Tuball. (par 4.2) Octatube is industrial looking, simple and elegant on a distance, but sometimes rather laboursome in detail. Space frames of this type often are compared with conventional structures, as they seemingly have a comparable degree of technology. Tuball, on the other hand, is the antithesis of this system: no direct connectors are shown, the system in all its components looks more abstract and is easily regarded as an architectural phenomenon, rather than a result of structural engineering functioning. The applications are smaller, the system is more expensive, but are very often tightly interwoven with the most interesting parts of buildings.

Marketing Concepts for Building Products
These marketing activities must be related to the company as a whole. This can be clarified by the term 'Marketing Concept'. Often there is a confusion with two contradictory terms: 'Production Concept' and 'Consumption Concept'. These terms can be clarified as follows:
• Production-directedness for producing companies is self-evident. The producer decides what he will produce, how and how much. Often without problems, that only appear when a competitor manufactures a product more suited for the needs of the client. This sometimes applies to import-products from technologically advanced countries.
• Sales-directedness is the other extreme. The company (one only has to think of main contractors in the building industry) tries in all aspects to fullfil the wishes of the client. All kind of products with all kind of specifications are made, largely due to the availability of an army of specialists and sub-contractors without regular contracts. There is a large assortment and a large competition effect. Marketing is not invented to impose silence upon the competition.
A number of indications show that both concepts do not work in the building industry entirely like they used to do. The problem is not any more how to produce more with less material because material is scarce, but rather

the general surplus of products and services. Project architects can choose from a wide variety of products; the number of simultaneous architectural styles using different products increases. In a former market situation price reduction could have been a suitable answer. The larger extent of scientific research will give a more fundamental answer. Technology and research have become more powerful weapons than pure price reduction. The competition will increase. The research for newer and better products makes the apparatus more and more expensive. More investments are required in order to keep a stream of mature products. All these investments have to be based on future sales potentials.

6 Production, Transport, Assembly and Erection

All lightweight space structures designed and produced by the author have a number of properties in common that make them more suitable for serial production, semi-automated production, or possible completely automated production, for transport and shipping in standard containers, simple assembly on site and ground level, and erection by mobile cranes.

Production   Working with steel and aluminium as the primary structural materials means first of all remarkable differences for the production preparation phase, actually being a part of the engineering: the preparation of shop drawings. Engineering is understood as the total of all office activities of development and research of new systems, and of application of a system in a building: (comment on) the design of the application in the building, lay out, topology, geometry, etc, statical analysis, detail analysis, proposal drawings, working drawings and shop drawings, and finally assembly drawings. All engineering activities of metal structures are definitively different from other structures because of the structural build-up of many very small components: a possible dimensional mistake often is repeated in a large number of identical items, possibly with disastrous financial effects.

The cutting and machining of the separate bar and nodal elements of a space frame system can be performed at a length accuracy of 0.5 mm per element. Alas the hot dip galvanising process and the powder coating process don't have such tightly controlled thickness accuracies: a reason why the total lengths of assembled elements must be checked in a mock-up regularly, in order

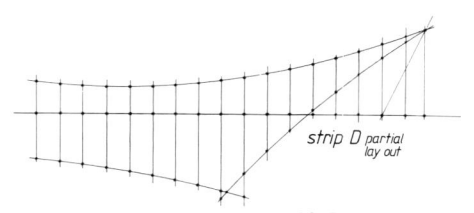

32 Partial cutting pattern of membrane strips for the Veronica tent structure 1982.

to prevent an additional treatment of the elements after coating. Inaccuracies in a space frame can lead to 2 problems:
• An unexpected sag might occur in the free spanning space frame when the upper chord members do not have the required overlength over the lower chord members. Its consequences are evident: negative rainwater draining when there are no extra purlins in a positively curved roofplane. In some cases this can lead to collapse of the entire roof. Another consequence is the bad view. Structurally there may not be a direct problem as long as the water can drain off by means of an additional layer of positively cambered purlins.
• Running out of line of the foundation anchors. This problem arises sometimes in practice. Even more often, however, not caused by inaccurate lengths of metal frame members but rather due to the inherent inaccuracy of reinforced concrete work. For example in the Tuball space frame over the atrium of the Esso Benelux main office in Breda (designed by architect Kraaijvanger) the total length of the space frame of 51 m was measured as 8 mm plus over a multitude of 45 modules, thus 90 elements in all. The problems on site were however caused by the placing of the anchors in the precast concrete elements, and by the positioning of the precast concrete elements, giving inaccuracies of 40 mm plus in total. The differences in the accuracy of steelwork and concrete are not always of this magnitude, but differ considerably. Problems between space frames and concrete substructures always show in the positioning of the anchors.

Apart from accuracy, a second requirement is valid for the design process: designers and draftsmen absolutely must have a complete 3-dimensional insight, as space structures are composed of small elements of slender dimension, each manufactured or assembled from standard sections and nodes or specially profiled sections coinciding in non-perpendicular angles.

The production process of space structures is not very different from usual production processes in the metal industry, apart from the dimensional accuracy and the visually high degree of finish : a degree more like interior finish quality than steel structures quality.

Two other aspects needs to be commemorated: the production process of space frames could be excellently automated in the case of standard elements. The production of standard and non-standard space frames asks for a development into the direction of flexible production, managed by CAM-operated machines. At that time hopefully the price of the non-standard product will almost be equal to the price of the standard one.

Production of Stretched Membranes

Another remarkable aspect of the production process concerns the production of membranes. As this was, strictly speaking, the original reason for the author to start his production facilities, the special nature of this process needs some explanation. The initial steps of the production process are described in paragraph 3.3 in the design and development process of stretched membranes. The last phases of the flow diagram in fig 22 indicate that from quite sizable models (preferably scale 1 to 10) the exact strip sizes are obtained by dividing the total curved surface into a number of strips in scale in the proper stress direction with warp and weft direction. These strips have always a hollow side form, when stretched on a flat surface. The local curvature of the membrane influences the possible width of the membrane. A large radius of curvature means that wider strips are possible, while a smaller radius is responsible for more slender strips. The membrane material (PVC-coated polyester fabric) is available on a width of 2 m or 2.6 m. The average strip width might be taken as half of that size, but at spots of small curvature near the tops of masts, the widths might only be 100 mm or 200 mm! The usual model technique is to prepare strips of estimated size in millimeter paper, provide this element with a central linear axis and cross axes at a regular distance for example of 300 or 500 mm. The strips are taped on the surface and will partly overlap each other. The overlapping areas will be decided, divided and drawn in ink on the strip. Now the individual strips have received the central axis, the hollow sides and an equally accurate upper and lower side. The accuracy of this model technique scale 1 to 10 can be measured with a marking gauge to a accuracy of 0.05 mm, so 0.5 mm in reality, which is more than accurate enough as during the subsequent process of cutting and welding errors can be made of 1 to 5 mm, and the membrane material can be stretched to overcome these errors. The next step after scaling the exact sized from the model strips is enlarging these sizes on real scale, and bringing them over to either paper cutting pattern moulds or the membrane material directly, taking oversizes for sleeves and welds into account. The membrane material is cut by hand with a knife or scissors, but can of course be mechanized in a procedure of a cutting table with an overhead cutting machine, working in the same principles as a drafting machine or an overhead crane: taking data of X and Y direction in longitudinal and cross direction, and cutting accordingly, fed by CAM data. (fig 32) The individually cut membrane strips are taken together and with an overlap of 30 to 50 mm the seams are high-frequently welded, preferably with a short electrode (300 mm) when curvatures are steep and a longer one (500 to 1000 mm) when curvatures are slight. High-frequency welding machines are commonly available for the welding and melting of PVC materials and other thermoplastic foils. Actually, during welding, the PVC on both sides of the polyester fabric is melted together around the two separate layers of polyester weave. The shear stresses of the PVC on the polyester weave give at a seam of minimal 30 mm, and with only minor weft angles a stronger seam than the original material. For simple straight seams there are rolling hot air melting machines that have a much larger velocity than high frequency welding. After the welding together, and when the last and most difficult closing seam has been finished, PVC transparent garden hoses of 20 mm are inserted into the edge seams of the membrane through which the stainless steel of galvanised steel cables are fed and fixed. These tubes function to protect the membrane material from friction of the hard steel cable during tensioning, and allowing a separate adjustment of cable and membrane (compare stretching arm and sleeves of shirt and jacket).

The erection of a prefabricated membrane structure manufactured by the forementioned method is a process that has the peculiar moment of a total surprise effect when the membrane is stressed: the membrane is usually provided with ample rectification possibilities in the form of turn-buckles, and it is the combination of certain extensions that will produce a perfectly smooth surface. Often a wrinkled surface only spontaneously disappears when the correct turn-buckle formula (or ratio) is reached. For the designer who works hard to get his design smooth, it is a supreme reward. Again it is the very accuracy, the required personal devotion, but also the labour-intensiveness that makes this process hardly popular for an average factory management to strive at, and for individual craftsmen to perform. Only real 'membrane-addicts' will have enough patience for the job. This elaborate process is one of the major causes of the relatively small popularity of prestressed membranes.

33 Erection photograph of an aluminium macro sized space frame structure consisting of four tetrahedrons with rib lengths of 6 m, with one continuous suspended prestressed PVC-coated polyester membrane for outdoor television broadcasting purposes, erected in Delft 1987.

34 Picture of the assembly at ground level of the first Octacube space frame structure in 1975 (two years after initial design of the system in the final studies of the author), consisting of RHS-profiles in square or diagonal geometry. Node size 220 x 220 mm was later enlarged to 250 x 250 mm for ease of assembly. Designed frame was 24 x 33 m, as a small truck garage warehouse in Loosduinen. To be regarded as the first Octatube prototype application.

Prefabrication But speaking about space structures in general, the materials steel, aluminium, glass and plastics are excellently suitable for pre-fabrication. All manufacturing activities will be performed before shipping to site, even conservation and coating. The more sensitive products like aluminium coated space frame elements will be transported to site wrapped in plastic hoses per bar element, only to be removed after the handing over of the structure. This degree of pre-fabrication has a great influence on the degree of engineering in the first place. A normal labour investment in an average space structure project requires one third engineering labour costs, one third production labour costs and one third site assembly labour costs. If all parts of a total assembly have been properly engineered and produced, the erection itself is only a question of bolting like a 'Meccano' system.

The used materials and the used systems lead toward a dry method of assembly on the site, so that the eternal doom governing the building industry of rainy, cold and windy weather, or dry and hot days that complicate the exactness and progression of the building process, is partly avoided. Only partly, because assembly of a roof usually takes place under the bare sky and still suffers from climatological influences, but less so than using conventional materials. For example in the severe Dutch winter of 86-87 during a two months period all building activities out in the open air were stopped except the assembly of space frames that still continued as long as the air-compression tubes were not frozen by internal condensation. Assembly of aluminium components in temperatures below zero had to be done with gloves on in order to avoid the freezing of fingertips and hands on the aluminium elements. Once all the composing elements have arrived on the building site in knocked-down position, the assembly can of course be performed by a local crew, eventually assisted by professional supervisors. This applies to the Dutch situation sometimes (assembly of the structure of the Quintus sporting hall by members of the sporting club, see fig 113), but even more for export situations.

As space structures usually have modest deadweights and the individual components are quite small the individual components are bundled and crated and can easily be transported by truck for small distances and in a standard 6 m or 12 m container for longer distances. The total capacity in weight limit (20 tons) will not be used to the full usually, (apart from heavyweight steel space frames), the volume is more decisive for the usage of the container, apart from the vulnerability of some materials. Shipping glass panels only means shipping weight. Even tent structures are rather bulky in volume and not in weight. Space structures are because of that reason the most transportable structures for architectural applications existing.

Transportable Laminated Timber Space Frames Reasoning the other way around has brought the author to a timber export space frame idea, during a discussion with a Dutch laminated timber specialist, Henk Bosch, and Stephan Polonyi. Since space frames can be containerised and shipped over the world for modest costs, we could look into the possibility of developing a laminated timber space frame. The total product could be built up of Dutch know-how concerning space frames and lamination techniques, while the timber material could be prepared in Malaysia or Thailand, where excellent hardwood timber qualities are available. The harvested trees should be replanted on a scale similar to the replanting schemes in the Scandinavian countries. When the central production units could be positioned in Malaysia, the total Far East could be the potential market, including Japan and Australia. The length of the space frame members is restricted to the internal size of the containers: 2.4 m wide and 5.8 m or 11.8 m length. The ideal length of the timber elements should be 2.4 m or 2.9 m. With these elements possible spans can be made in flat roof elements of 30 to 50 m span, in semi-cylindrical form 30 to 100 m and in spherical form of 40 to 120 m. The idea couples high-grade Western technology with excellent Eastern inland timber, produced with an improved quality. A marketing analysis is currently being set up around this idea, speeded up by the hear-say that the Japanese already had bought the total harvest of trees on the Indonesian Island of Celebes!

CAM-Production for Open Building Systems One of the problems of prefabrication is of course a relative high capital investment in production facilities. The prefabrication of plate elements is even more costly than that of linear elements. One of the consequences of these costs is that the panel producing factories usually will concentrate on mass production in order to avoid too high cost prices and in order to get the required return on investment. The prefabrication of linear elements still enables some degree of differentiation in length of section. As mentioned in Paragraph 3.4, the influence of CAD-CAM techniques in production will essentially be that while taking advantage of the production in series, yet quite a number of different properties of the individual elements can be provided for at wish, leading to characteristically different space structure applications.

  For example:
- Material of bar elements and node elements
- Length of bar elements
- Cross section of bar elements
- Diameter/wall thickness of bar elements
- Angles at the connection end of bar elements
- Diameter and strength of connection elements
- Diameter nodal elements
- Connection angles of node elements
- Design ('type') of node elements.

Although full automation has not been introduced yet in the author's factory, the future seems to promise that the usual ruthless mechanisation step can be avoided. The current half-mechanised, half-manually operated production gives ample possibilities for non-standard work. The next phase towards automation will not be the mass production of identical elements, but rather more to introduce CAM techniques, to produce elements in considerable diversity for the same costs as standard nowadays. In contradiction with the philosophy of Konrad Wachsmann written in his 'Wendepunkt Im Bauen' in 1959,[1] of a closed industrial system, directed more optimally towards the production and the producer, this means the realisation of open building systems, directed more optimally towards the consumer.

'Cock-Eyed' Aspects of Space Frames The shifting of labour from the warm/dry insides of the factory to the outside conditions with the eternal doom of the weather elements is a remarkable feature against the general trend in industrialisation and complete control of process. An intellectually even more negative aspect about working with space frames from the production point of view, is the cutting of strong and straight circular tube sections into smaller pieces, (often to lengths of only 1.2 or 1.0 m) only to invest an enormous material and personal energy with the result that a multitude of the original commercial tube length of 6 m is obtained. Obviously there are easier ways for a 6 m long tube to reach a span of say 12 or 18 m. The final goal is to get a more intellectual system, enabling one to divert stresses caused by external loadings into many directions so that each member has only a modest normal force to resist. This more or less intellectual goal is reached by the input of quite large labour investments. No wonder that space frames, especially in the smaller spans, are known to be more expensive than the conventional metal structures. As Stephan Polónyi suggested in 1986 in a lecture[29], the obvious solution is to make other types of space frames with prefabricated units using the full length of the chord elements. This thought leads toward prefabricated linear elements that either remain planar in a grid system of plane trusses or are fabricated as single triangular truss elements, but always with a less purely designed node, and therefore less attractive for client-architects. After the experiences of 7 years of enquiries about Octatube space frames by architects, one has to admit that

35, 36 Customs border station in Nieuweschans, designed by architects Benthem and Crouwel. Erection over an existing and still functioning expressway took place during the night, after assembly on an adjacent parking ground, transport in two parts on a 64-wheeled trailer and hoisted by mobile cranes. Size 24 x 51 m, module 3 x 3 m, depth 2.1 m.

37 Trial assembly of a 24 m diameter and 16 m high 'flame type' dome structure in Delft to check the geometry of all components, the hoisting method (ground level assembly, hoisted by a winched 18 m mast), and the overall geometry.

38 The final location of the gold-bronze colored single layered 'flame'-shaped dome structure with 562 light bulbs on its final position in Singapore, adjacent to the (gold-domed) Sultan Mosque. The dome covers a swimming pool.

the majority of enquiries stems from the design properties of space frames: the architecture of space frames is (even) more appealing than the structural advantages.

Site Assembly and Erection The different types of space structures all use different methods of site assembly and erection. The different systems matter, the site conditions matter (open building site, in-town situation, high rise situation, inaccessible situations of courtyards and mountain tops, etc), but also the economic situation matters (Western country or developing country etc). Most space frames are assembled on ground level, the bolts are pretensioned and then the frames are hoisted into the final position upon columns or other supports. In case of columns an off-set position is chosen for the assembly: the vertical columns can be positioned in the midst of a triangle in the frame, for example with an off-set of half a module in X and Y direction. Hoisting by mobile or building crane is a sequence of vertical hoistings, moving in X and Y direction over the missing half modules and then positioning onto the supports. This operation needs only to take a short time, from half an hour to several hours depending of the number of columns to be connected, the height and accessibility of the supports etc. Sometimes the internal size of the covered space is smaller than the outer size of the space frame; in which case after hoisting the missing row of elements will have to be connected, before finally letting the complete space frame down on the anchors. This requires either a longer suspension time, or temporary supports. Another solution might be for inaccessible situations like courtyard and atrium coverings non-accessible for mobile cranes, to prefabricate the space frame on the flat roof level in parts that are continuously enlarged into one direction, while being shifted over the atrium on specially constructed wheels and rails like the deck-hatches of a ship: sliding erection. On other occasions the limited size of the available assembly site might mean assembly in two halves or even smaller parts, hoisting them into position and connecting them air-borne. Air-assembly always is a more laboursome process because the position of nodes and bars cannot be adjusted at will like at ground level. The Octatube customs-canopy at the Dutch-German border near Groningen over an existing highway was too large to be built on site without interruption of the functioning of the highway. We therefore decided to build the complete canopy 24 x 51 m on a parking lot 200 m away at ground level. After assembly and pretensioning the space frame was split into two halves. The first one was hoisted by a mobile crane on a 64-wheeled lorry with extra extensions to carry the 24 x 30 m space frame. By means of its very steerable and also in height adjustable wheels, the first part was driven to the actual building site and hoisted on an overheight; the columns were hung underneath and the complete table was sunk on its foundations. The second half was moved shortly after the first operation, and was connected in the air. The mobile crane was needed during as long a period as 6 hours to enable the assembly crew to make proper connections. Needless to say, the whole operation took an evening and a long night to be performed.(figs 35,36)

Air-borne connections are the last methods to take refuge to. Also the safety of ground-level assembly labour is optimal compared with aerobatics.

Another form of assembly is usually asked for dome structures. Because dome structures cover interior areas, they tend to be inaccessible too. Sometimes the solution for a proper erection lies in providing a central mast from which the dome, suspended from its most superior or crown ring, will be assembled starting with the top ring, going downward until the lowest layer is reached and the dome is completed. Example is the 24 m diameter dome on the Far East Hotel in Singapore (figs 36, 37). On other occasions it might be possible to prefabricate the dome structure and to shift it horizontally on two sliding rails over the void to the completed situation. Or to assemble and to have it craned over the building onto the very anchors.

These situations are the only very short moments in a lifespan of a space frame when it can literally be called a 'space' frame, with reference to aeronautics. Needles to say, all the above described experiences, gained in the last 7 years, have their influence on the design of every new space frame application.

7 Application of Products in Projects

The implantation of the developed space structure products in building projects often confronts the author as a product-designer with a project-architect (who actually can be an architect, a structural engineer or an artist) plus an ever-changing set of conditions around the design. In these circumstances the space structure will have to be applied and fitted in. The process aspects are remarkable because of their variety. Large differences will occur from project to project, and from architect to architect because of the following personal attitudes and technical circumstances:

39 Opening music performance in the Haarlem music pavilion in 1985: steel substructure supports an aluminium Tuball-Plus space frame, covered by 3.3.1.laminated clear and non-hardened glass panels. Diameter 9 m, height 7 m.

- Different attitudes of the project-architect towards the role of technology in his overall design scheme: for example surpressed or visualised technology.
- The appearance of the space structure in a mechanical (material-confirmed) or an abstract (material-denied) mode of design.
- Style of architectural design of the overall scheme ranging for example from Traditional, via Functional Modernist, Late-Modernist, High-Tech, Structuralism and Post-Modernism, to mention only a few different attitudes the author has been confronted with in projects.
- The openness of a project-architect to be influenced by the product-designer: his flexibility to allow for a co-designership by the product-designer.
- The personal relationship from project-architect to product-architect as a possible positive stimulus for mutual interaction and improvement of each other's ideas, based on complete openness, mutual trust and challenge of each other's extreme capacities and ideas. Leaving complete freedom for each other's creativity and allowing for the respective benefit of having contributed to the design, or having made the design.
- Functional position of the product-designer only as a sub-contractor, as a producer or even as a co-designer in a growing rate of intensity and anticipation, caught between the extremities of complete dictation by the contractor on the one hand and complete input of know-how appreciated by the project-architect on the other hand.
- The financial relationship between main contractor and sub-contractor also is a major influence in the way that creative ideas can easily be cut off or surpressed, when no direct dialogue is allowed between the product-architect and the project-architect. This is sometimes the case when an enquiry comes directly from a main contractor, aiming only at a financial profit and not any technical or esthetical profit for the project, and forbidding any direct contact between the two architects.

To illustrate these differences in approach, a number of co-operations between project-architects and the author in his role as a product-architect in the last 7 years are illustrated in an arbitrary order.

1 *Music Pavilion* The former town-architect of Haarlem Wiek Röling is a convinced Functional Modernist architect with a strong affinity towards Structuralism. For the 400th anniversary of the most famous park in Haarlem, the Haarlemmerhout, he designed in 1984 a park pavilion in the form of a transparent geodesic dome on columns, inspired by the work of Richard Buckminster Fuller, and presented it in the form of a 1 to

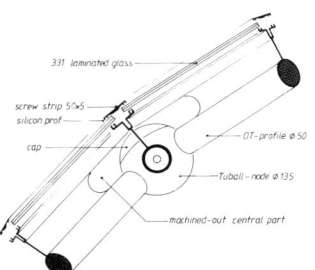

40 Detail of initial Tuball-Plus node as used in the Haarlem dome. Aluminium cast nodes with a diameter of 135 mm, and bars with a diameter of 50 mm with T-sections on top 50x50 mm, in one extrusion. The end of the body part has been machined out to show the form of the spherical node and to enable the erector to place the cap after pretensioning of the internal bolts. The installation of these types of nodes strongly resembles a dental operation: too many elements in too small a space, especially when electric cables for armatures have to be fed through, too.

41 Initial design model made by Wiek Röling, consisting of hexagonal and pentagonal faces as a good starting point for further development of the preliminary design.

42 Partial detail of the realised dome, showing the diamond-like outside and the continuous inside.

50 model. (fig 41) The dimensions of the dome were 9 m diameter, with a total height of 7 m. Wiek Röling asked the author how the dome could be realised. There were three alternatives, all departing from glass as a cladding material, plus an additional sub-division of the pentagons and hexagons into triangles so that the laminated glass panels had a realistic size and the dome structure was stable. The truncated dodecahedral geometry of Wiek's proposal was changed into a 3-frequency icosahedral geometry. (figs 39, 42)

The surroundings of the dome were a serene and ancient park, bordered by classical buildings; the design of the dome itself was, in all its modern premises, also quite severe and classical. So the structural design had also to be classical in its own right. Out of the three different schemes of structures and cladding systems, the one proposal in which the structure and the cladding system were integrated into one visually simple and purified system, was chosen to be the optimal solution in the situation, although the most expensive. It was the first time that this still experimental structural system was to be worked out in reality. The structure had to be a Tuball system, and was called from that time on: Tuball-Plus, details see figs 40 and 167. At the very time of the detailing of the Haarlem dome another project (canopy of the Raffles City Complex in Singapore) was in preparation in the factory. Drawing of the very details by the author, and the simultaneous solution of getting the node-cap on top of the node-shell after the pre-tensioning of all the bars, all of a sudden culminated in a spontaneous brainwave to machine a central part of the bar away in a semi-circular form. The characteristic Tuball-Plus detail was conceived. Only 2 hours after this Eureka-idea a full sample 1:1 scale was ready, and confirmed the imagined spatial appearance of the node detailing. Wiek Röling accepted the design with gratitude and so the decision was made to manufacture the first Tuball-Plus dome. In fact Wiek Röling encouraged also the detailing of the connections between dome and surrounding edge tube in a similar way. Also other details were worked out in close co-operation between architect and structural designer cum producer.

2 *Entrance Raffles City* The actual invention and development of the Tuball system was unknowingly enforced by Fritz Sulzer as the skylight and curtain wall specialist of the architect's office of I. M. Pei, New York. I.M.Pei was the architect of the Raffles City Complex in Singapore and had designed a flat double-layered space frame above the main entrance of 7.6 x 41 m long. As the author was also awarded the engineering of the glass

43, 44 Entrance canopy for the Westinn-Plaza Hotel in the Raffles City Complex in Singapore. An aluminium Tuball-Plus space frame with integrated electrical cabling and covered with silicon sealed laminated clear glass panels 5.5.1. The slope of the horizontal panels is 1 degree only: remaining water drips on the upper surface are visible. Because of the frequent rain in Singapore the guess of I.M.Pei's architect Fritz Sulzer that the roof surface will be kept clean regularly, was right. The adhesion of the structural sealed silicon was determined by the downward and upward windforces from the two adjacent 250m high hotel towers above the 30 m high basement.

45, 46, 47 and 48 4 pictures of the Raffles City Complex atrium skylight, consisting of 4 large elements 30x30 m in plan: 1 full square and 3 half-diagonal squares with additional wall surfaces. The structural element in each square is a Nodus space frame, covered with a skylight ,designed and developed by the author as a glazing system separate but interactive with the space frame system on which it rests. It consists of 20 different custom-made aluminium extrusion profiles that together form an internal drainage system for eventual leakage water. The system drains internally down from the top elements, via the sloped (4 degrees) elements in the flat roof, the sloped elements under 60 degrees in the walls, the vertical walls and finally through the lower inclined parts outside in the gutters on the roof. A quite complicated but safe route to take. The glass panels are double glass panels, heat strengthened and laminated, but clear glass. The sun screening function is performed by a specially developed architectural sun screen, composed of aluminium tubes dia 28 mm, spaced 45 mm, clear anodised, that graphically give a 'Moiree'-like effect. During the night the atrium skylights are lightened outside by short lantern posts placed in the gutters between the horizontal skylight elements.

skylights of this complex (figs 45 to 48), an initial proposal was made for the canopy in the Octatube system. In a discussion in Singapore Fritz rejected the proposal and asked for a more abstract system of purely circular tubes and spherical nodes being more in line with the overall abstract scheme of the building compared with the mechanical Octatube system. After one week of thinking and designing a new system was conceived not only purely consisting of circular tubes and spherical nodes (there were similar systems already available on the world market), but the extruded aluminium bar elements were also provided with an additional T-profile on top on which the laminated clear glass panels could be sealed directly with structural sealant. So the first contract in Tuball-Plus was the result of a positive rejection of an initial design proposal. As the Haarlem dome and the Raffles canopy were designed and developed in the same time, the respective requirements on these projects mutually influenced each other. (figs 43, 44)

49 Interior picture of the Serangoon Atrium.

3 *Serangoon Gardens* One of the most complex designs realised after the development of the Tuball-Plus system, was the atrium of the Serangoon Gardens Country Club in Singapore. The architect, Eugene Seow of Akitek Tenggara in Singapore, had designed a building consisting of two symmetrical terraced concrete structures, with an intermediate atrium. (fig 49 to 52) The covering of the atrium was thought initially as a cylinder in acrylic material, but the architect wanted a column-free space (35 x 21 m), and was not very charmed by the acrylic vocabulary. The author's alternative proposal was to make 4 intermediate linear gutters built between a double I-beam and to build a system of triangular space trusses in the Tuball-Plus system. The space frame module size was a full glass panel size (1.7 x 1.7 m). The design of this system of 5 adjacent cylindrical vaults was adapted to the respective heights of the adjacent concrete structure. After receipt of the contract, however, the structural project-engineer discovered that there was no possibility for the ends of the structural gutters to be connected to the concrete frame, as there were lightly reinforced balcony slabs cantilevering from the same structure in the same place. So at that moment the decision was made to change the structural system into 5 independent full space frame shells, only supported at the 4 corners, with suspended gutters in-between. A professional error. The responsibility in this contract included not only the space structure, but also the glass panels, the gutters, an electronically operated internal sun screen system and exhaust fans. Octatube was a nominated sub-contractor with co-design duties, but without influence on the rest of the building. The overall design of the building has strong visual influences from Structuralism in the composition of the independent concrete floor areas each supported by 4 corner columns, ending with 4 columns at each column position, even in the corners of the building. The space frame design anticipated that scheme. On the other hand, the interest of the architect in the structural behaviour and the details of the space frame design, especially in its spatial character

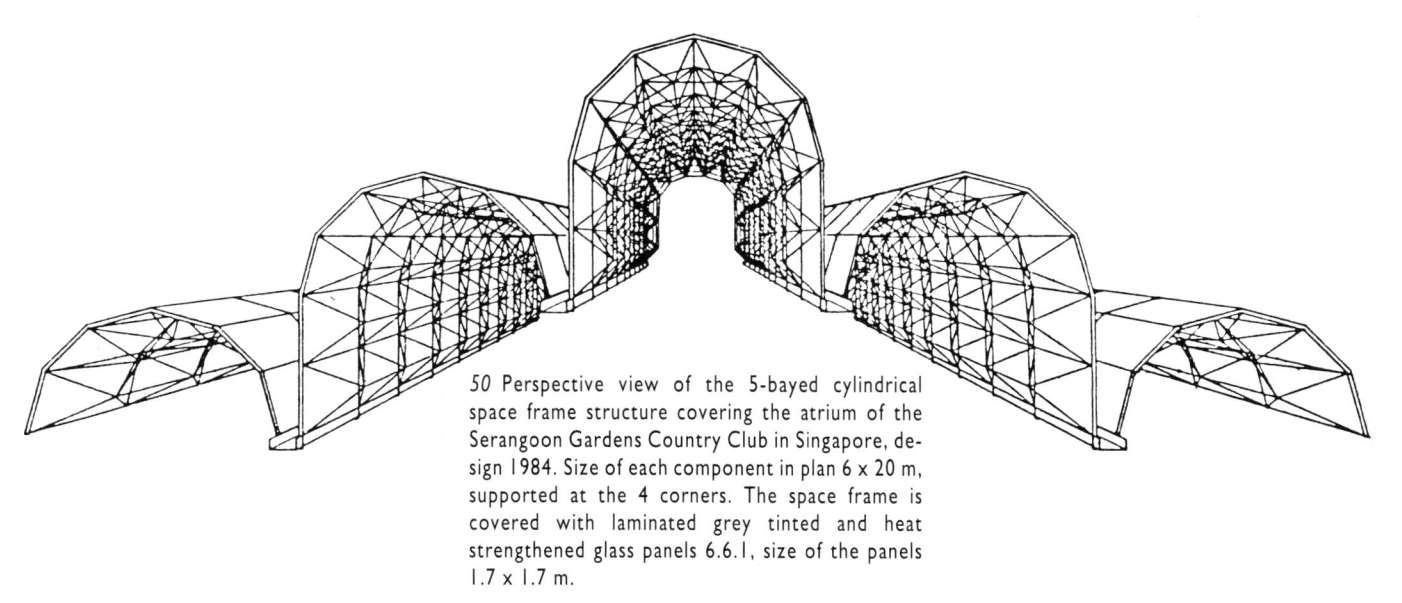

50 Perspective view of the 5-bayed cylindrical space frame structure covering the atrium of the Serangoon Gardens Country Club in Singapore, design 1984. Size of each component in plan 6 x 20 m, supported at the 4 corners. The space frame is covered with laminated grey tinted and heat strengthened glass panels 6.6.1, size of the panels 1.7 x 1.7 m.

51, 52 Exterior and interior view of the Serangoon Gardens Country Club in Singapore.

and the complex 3-D details stimulated the product-architect to optimise the frame details and elements. The end result is a glass waterfall on the outside and a complex spatial structure which cannot be viewed in one glance, on the inside.

4 *Entrance Zwolsche Algemeene* The first Tuball application in the Netherlands was built as an entrance canopy for the 'Zwolsche Algemeene' Insurance Company in Nieuwegein. Architect Peter Gerssen is a designer with a severe style of Late-Modernism in which ultra-functional plans are combined with avant-garde building techniques. His building was the first in the Netherlands to be built with a structurally sealed glass facade in black mirror-finished glass panels. His commitment to new technologies led to an interior of the entrance hall with a light grey tinted abstract space frame, covered with a two-directional gutter system and triple acrylic domes, suspended between two adjacent black mirror walls. Because of the sharp plan angles of 45 degrees, the mirror walls imitate the existence of a space frame 8 times as large as was actually built. (fig 53) The first design of the space frame as an alternative for a flat concrete slab was in Octatube, and cheaper, and used to convince the client of the spatial character of the entrance. Having done that, the details of the Octatube joint were further refined with flush bolts, rounded corners, untill a far more abstract appearance resulted. After this it was only one step further to change the system from the mechanical Octatube into the more abstract Tuball system which suited both the project-architect and the product-architect more.

The leaning of Peter Gerssen and his partner Cas Oosterhuis to abstraction and avant-garde technology in

Application of Products in Projects

53 Interior of the entrance hall of the insurance company 'Zwolsche Algemeene' in Nieuwegein NL. In plan a diagonally cut square 18 x 18 m surrounded by 2 mirror-glass walls, suggesting visually a space frame 8 times as large as the one really built. Covered with a two-way grid of (intersecting) steel insulated gutters and triple acrylic skydomes on top. As the colours of the gutters are the same as the space frame, visually the beam frame supports the space frame.

54 Interior perspective of the new 'Lichthof' in Mönchengladbach (D) : 5.1 m wide and about 70 m long. Height 5 to 9 m as the street level is sloping down and the space frame runs horizontally. The structure can be regarded as a grid of intersecting triangular space trusses to minimize the amount of bars and nodes optically. Supports in the longitudinal direction every 9 to 10 m. Module 2.2 x 1.3 m. Covered with insulated glass panels with clear laminated lower glass plates 4.4.1. The narrow and high proportions remind one of gothic vaults.

their architecture, started a discussion to describe the requirements for a dome structure on top of a hotel at Schiphol Airport completely without metal elements in 1987. This was one of the motivations for the author to start a long term Design, Research and Development program in-house for load bearing glass structures as mentioned in par 6.3. The dome itself remained an idea.

5 Shopping Arcades One of the projects that followed after the Serangoon project was a shopping arcade in Amsterdam South-East, designed by architect Ben Loerakker and the author, and consisting of a cylindrical barrel vault spanning 11 m wide and 33 m length. This space frame was composed of triangular space trusses and not a complete space frame: the same scheme as the original one of the Serangoon design. The barrel vault in the 'Amsterdamse Poort' was designed in 1986 on invitation of the architect, actually as a more simple duplicate of the Serangoon vaults, but with a more spacious monovolume. The arcade was realised in 1987. (fig 113-115)

One of the objections architects have against space frames is that there are usually a confusing number of bars and nodes. This was also the case at the design of a similar cylindrical space frame for the renovation of a shopping arcade in Mönchengladbach (Western Germany), 6 m wide, 7 to 10 m high and 70 m long. Architect Haasen did not prefer the full space frame, but the triangular truss space frame system. The span was 6 m in cross section and 16 m in longitudinal section. Only by reducing the span in longitudinal direction from 16 m to 8 m was a triangular truss system feasible, with actually a minimal amount of bars and hence minimal visual disturbance looking from the basement outward into the sky. The space frame structure with its inherent rigidity enabled the architect to renovate the adjacent buildings in a time long after the arcade has been built, while keeping the glass arcade in the designed condition. During a visit at the architect's office in Dusseldorf an unmistakable tendency towards Post-Modernism was felt by the author, after which a proposal was presented for the front facade that in a structural way still was purely Modern, but in its architectural outlook had a Post-Modern influence. Because of the German pre-occupation with concrete and brickwork as structural materials, structural space frame designs in Germany are expected to have another effect compared with applications in the Netherlands. Germany is in for 'Creative Structural Design', mixed with traditional design while both in the Netherlands and in Great Britain the occasional 'High-Tech' architects tend to make more complete 'High-Tech' architecture.

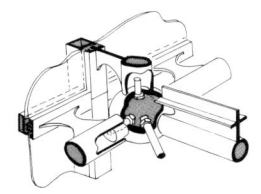

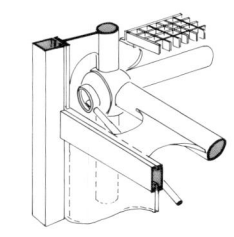

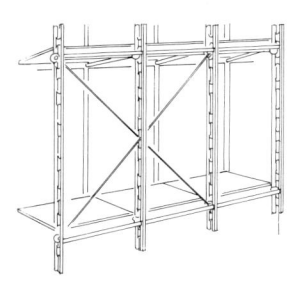

55 Design proposal drawings of Tanfield showing the perspective view, and an exterior and interior built-up drawing: a combination of Tuball-Plus flat skeleton with additional wind bracings and walkway maintenance grid elements.

6 *Curtain Wall Tanfield House* During one of the continuous in-house developments on stayed skylight structures in 1987, an enquiry from Edinburgh for a suspended curtain wall structure came in, and was proposed as a vertical Tuball structure with horizontal elements towards the building. After a few telephone conversations with architect John Perreur Lloyd of Michael Laird & Partners, the initial design proposal sketches (See fig 55) were sent over by fax. The author was phoned immediately after sending the sketches and invited to fly over to Edinburgh, where a discussion was to be held with the project-architect and the project-engineer. The designed system functions as a structural system for suspended glass 'curtain walls' around the 3-storey building, as a second skin, protecting the inner glass skin. In this distance between the two glass planes walkway grids are installed to facilitate window-cleaning, maintenance and fire escaping. The Tuball-Plus profiles provided standard connections, used in a non-standard way for all elements in this curtain wall system. During the building stage the frame system functions as a scaffold.

7 *Entrance Nieuw Welgelegen* In order to design a solitary intermediate building between two high rise office blocks of the project called 'Nieuw Welgelegen' in Utrecht, architect Bas Pickers of architects office Overhagen discussed with the author several schemes of an independent space frame structure resting on 6 columns and expressing an independence towards the two adjacent buildings. The discussions concentrated on the power of expression of the space frame structure, slimly covered by a complete glass wall cladding. For that purpose also a spatial soldered model of one of the alternative designs was made. In order to express the independence of the structure, the author proposed a sub-structure of a tree-like kind: four separate vertical tubes, bundled and diverging from a height of 2.5 m open towards the space frame. These trees actually were built and proved to be a strong structural element, not in the least place because the project-architect also combined the tree-bars with light armatures parallel to these bars. The architectural differences between the discussed schemes show strong independent and semi-independent buildings. So the space frame had to play its role as an expression in the overall architecture. (fig 96) The space frame with the 40-50 mm tubes is covered by a very reliable but visually dominating and heavy vertical window profiles 60 x 120 mm. Presumably some progress can be made in the field of refining curtain walling systems.

8 *Shopping Centre Schollevaar* In 1984 the author built the Octatube frame designed by architect Quinten de Wijn of AGS architects over the shopping centre 'Schollevaar' in Capelle aan den Ijssel. The space frame consisted of a complex of four different layers of space frames in 2 different modules 1.350 m and 2.700 m, connecting the car/streetlevel with the first floor or shop/pedestrian level. For that purpose the entrance frames had to follow the difference in height in a sculptural way. However, the covering elements (glass or metal panels) were not foreseen according to the tender documents. As Octatube was sub-sub-contractor under a metal claddings sub-contractor, there was not much opportunity to change the design to a more functional one. The end result was complying with the specifications of the architect, but was protested against immediately after the opening of the shopping centre by the shopkeepers, who expected a completely covered shopping centre, and found this a only half covered one. (see fig 56 for the original scheme, and fig 57,58 plus 103 for the current covering and glass cladding.) The sub-sub relation was cancelled and the author was able to make an improvement proposal on the roof over the shopping centre to reduce the influences of wind, draught and rain, this time in close co-operation with the architect. Because of the spatial complexity of the structure, 1:50 scale soldered models were used to have an accurate idea of the spatial appearance of the space frame. These models were soldered by the two designers jointly and in two weekends, giving them the idea of really building the frames or deciding where and why to leave out elements, and where to extend the frame. The proposal was accepted, and the models were even used during reconstruction to help the erection crew to position the new

Application of Products in Projects

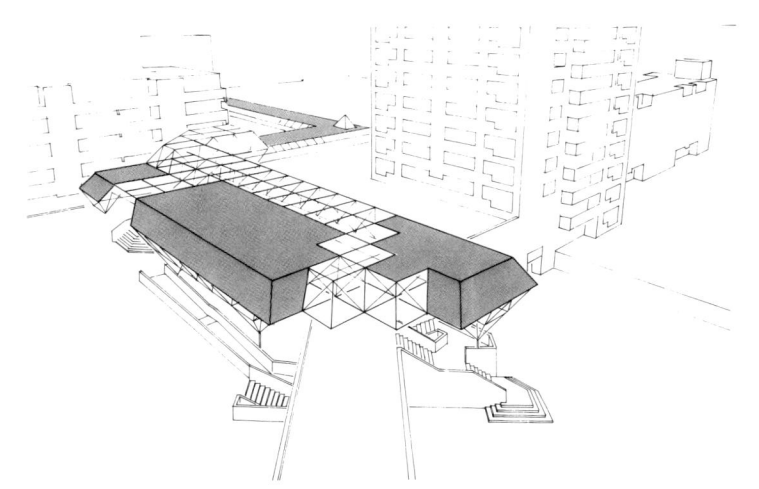

56 Bird's eye view of the original space frame covering for the Schollevaar shopping mall in Capelle a/d IJssel showing the sculptural open space frame elements. In a second design and building phase, started after inauguration of the shopping centre, a complete covering was realised. See fig 103 after realisation.

57, 58 The Schollevaar shopping mall with entrance canopies now open to all sides. The glass covering is tightly tailored around the space frame to produce a crystallised form of the multilevel space frame inside. Module of entrance canopies 2,700 m and 1,350 m in the arcades.

elements and to dismantle the redundant elements. The second co-operation was of course more intensive, responsive but also more effective than the first one where two layers of contractors complicated an open discussion between product- and project-architect.

9 *Council Room Townhall* Often enquiries start by a simple telephone question from an architect like in this case: 'How much does it cost to build a space frame in a quarter circular form?' Architect Berton de Bont of ZZOP architects struggled with a quarter circular form of a council room that before was designed in diverging laminated trusses and in concrete, but not to complete satisfaction. After receipt of the plans and sections of the proposed building, and the architectural ambience, the author made a proposal of a flat diverging double layered space frame in both Octatube and Tuball including cladding, glazing and roofing elements. For a correct presentation even a 1:50 model was soldered, displaying the graphical lay-out of this frame that appeared to be very delicate in the overall design and especially was to play an important role in the interior design of the council room. The design fulfilled the requirements of the architect: diverging straight lines (radiating from the position of the mayor to the council and circular lines perpendicular to these straight lines. Even the Aalto-like rooflight sheds as proposed by the architect could be realised in the proposal. The figure 59 shows the elegance of the space frame in the Octatube system with 40 mm diameter tubes and lengths ranging from 300 to 3000 mm. The space frame is hanging in the air during hoisting. The design resembled a multi-hull ship body. Although the relationship with the architect was quite open, the influence of the product-architect was not strong enough to discourage the use of high profiled steel cladding panels that by the heavy shadow lining overpowered the space frame in a particular daylighting. This relationship was also not strong enough to prevent the use of large airconditioning boxes, suspended in the space frame by the mechanical engineer, ruining the delicacy of the thin space frame lining. This project was a clear example that even a satisfactory involvement of the structural product designer can not be a complete guarantee to obtain a good overall result.

10 *Space Frame for Nederland 2050* In 1987 an exhibition was organised about a vision on the future of the Netherlands in 2050, in four different scenarios: the Careful, Dynamic, Critical and Relaxed Scenarios. On each of these scenarios several teams of Dutch designers (with different backgrounds) gave their vision of the fu-

60 The large hall in the famous Exchange of Berlage in Amsterdam during the exposition 'Nederland 2050'. A mezzanine space frame covered with black coated steel panels to accommodate the visual shows on the ground level, with a diagonally crossing space truss bridge at 10 m plus, supported by two tensegrity towers.

59 Erection of a space frame in the plan form of a quarter circle for the town hall of Huizen (NL) in 1985. Only during hoisting this structure was really a 'Space Structure' in all meanings of the word.

ture. The exhibition took place in the previous Exchange in Amsterdam, built in 1907 by Hendrik Berlage.

Architect Ben Loerakker was commissioned to design the exhibition lay-out and furniture. One of these furniture elements was a large Octatube space frame temporarily built up as a mezzanine roof to cover the exhibition space on ground level against daylight through the roof, and offering a roof area of 21 x 42 m on which a gigantic map of the Netherlands in 2050 was to be displayed. In open discussions with the architect all the design and erection problems were solved. Even the erection of the galvanised steel space frame, weighing approximately 12 tonnes, was satisfactorily foreseen by lifting from the stone supports under Berlage's roof trusses. Starting from the fact that the overweight was less than the winter snow load on the old roof. It was only after erection that the manager of the building suggested that his instructions were to remove snow from the roof every winter. But the building did not suffer.

The second set of problems to be solved was to design the bridge. The architect had designed a suspension bridge diagonally spanning the void above the space frame. Due to the inaccessibility of craning gear and the absence of tensile-stable reaction points the suspension bridge was left for a space frame proposal of half the price that by virtue of the diagonal position and its cross section of a triangular truss with metal parapets on top, had a tremendous spatial impact as figs 60 and 132 show. It was an example of how even a standard space frame, used in a non-standard way could produce a surprise.

The triangular bridge truss was supported by two tensegrity-towers that connected four upper chord nodes of the mezzanine space frame with four (twisted) support nodes of the bridge. It was the first time in the experience of the author that a tensegrity structure was used as a logical and very functional solution of a design problem. The persisting and challenging attitude of the architect to realise the diagonal bridge in whatever form, was rewarded with a strong spatial gesture.

11 *Tensegrity Maritime Museum* An equally compelling experience was the design of a tensegrity structure for the Maritime Museum in Amsterdam, designed in a very close co-operation between Krijn Giezen as the sculptor and the author as the structural designer. The design period included several years because of the unwillingness of the directors of the Museum to accept

Application of Products in Projects

61 Tensegrity structure in the courtyard of the Amsterdam Maritime Museum, composed of 4 mast poles, 12 guy cables and 2 vertical warped stretched membranes. The visual torsion in this sculpture is so overwhelming that visitors to the museum encircle the sculpture rather than dare to walk underneath to enter the building. Presumably not out of admiration for the sculpture: a really dramatic gesture.

62 Detail of the footing of the tensegrity masts. All tensile elements can be adjusted in a rough manner (chains) and a fine manner (turnbuckles), even regularly every year. Masts galvanised steel dia 160 mm, 16 m long; guy cables dia 10/12 mm. The foot plate could turn like a record-player on a lower plate with central pin to enable the movement during construction in horizontal direction, while the stainless steel pins ensured the vertical movement during the erection phase that had to be performed without a crane.

the sculpture in the internal courtyard of the 17th century building. Krijn Giezen is an artist very much involved in deteriorated naval materials like corroded anchors and chains and torn cottonfrayed ropes, while structural materials for a structure of this size can only be in the best position, and must be held in optimal condition. The first design was based on a macro space frame in which 4 membranes were prestressed, to have a closed system of forces, as the old foundations could not produce tensile forces of a considerable strength. The proposal was disapproved of by the management as being too far away from the past maritime vocabulary: the structure seemed too modern in their eyes. This same rejected scheme of 1981 would later be used for the Veronica tent structure. (fig 63) The fourth design proposal that also was the product of continuous discussions and insights between artist and engineer was a simple twisted tensegrity structure consisting of 4 tall masts in 16 m length, 12 guy cables and 2 stretched vertical membranes to dramatize the distortion of the structure, all in modern versions of old shipbuilding materials: masts, ropes and sails. (figs 61, 62) It took the personal intervention of the Dutch State Architect Tjeerd Dijkstra in 1984 to convince the directors of the museum to allow the erection of this tensegrity membrane structure. The structure itself is a purified example of a long search by two designers for a structure of simple elements with large sculptural qualities, or put otherwise: for a sculpture built from clear structural elements with a strong dramatic effect. The result was an integration of sculptural and structural design, effectuated in numerous discussions between two designers with a completely different background but with mutual respect for each other's opinion, and with a willingness to be influenced by the other. The preference of Dijkstra to build the structure on a 3:2 scale (with poles of 24 m, sticking out above the roof of the museum) was not adopted after comparison on model scale 1:20. At the moment of writing this book, the directors of the museum have tried again to remove this (in their eyes) 'too contemporary' designed structure from their courtyard!

12 *Tensegrity Hemweg* This design was the result of the winning of a select competition by the artist Loes van der Horst and the author as the structural designer cum manufacturer. They co-designed several cablenet structures and membranes before, mostly designs of the artiste, but in this case the structure had a more technical character. The influence of Loes was however large in establishing by means of a number of small models the

63 The Veronica Music Tent, in use every two weeks during the season at changing locations since 1982. Composed of a macro space frame in galvanised tubes dia 160 mm with lengths of 9 to 11 m, with a suspended prestressed membrane, calculated to resist windforces up to Beaufort scale 10.
For the different soil conditions there are 3 different types of foundations available:
- screw anchors for sandy soils;
- solid concrete blocks 1 m3 for quick sand;
- prefab concrete plates for in-city use.

64 The Hemweg Tensegrity Structure. (model in fig 23) Tubular elements not directly connected, only indirectly by cables. Masts dia 160 mm, cables dia 10 to 16 mm galvanised steel. During the winter 3 membranes are stored to remain only a graphical play of white tubes suspended or 'floating' in the air. When during springtime the membranes are installed again an extra outdoor area for the adjacent canteen is available.

definitive position of the masts, yards, cables and membranes to give a maximum quality in expression. (figs 23, 64, 129) The dialogue was very intensive. After 4 years the author realises that mainly due to the non-existence of time restrictions and ample personal time investments this very complicated structure could be developed into its final appearance. The contribution this piece of art made in the state-of-the-art of the space structures by the author is considerable as one realises that sometimes not too functional structures can free one's mind of too fixed patterns. And designing tensegrity structures is more characterised by the term 'Juggling With Structures'.

13 *Travelling Veronica Tent* During the manufacturing of the first tent structure in spring of 1982, one of the producers of the Veronica TV Broadcasting company, Geert Popma, asked the author to design a tent structure to be used for a travelling pop music show. The tent structure should be erected in one morning, and had to be visible from 3 sides. The project-designer, initially made a design that more or less looked like a gigantic blue drapery. In a few discussions with the clients, a macro space frame was decided upon under which a stretched membrane could be installed. At the time the producted was started of a very beautiful but also complex-to-erect tent structure designed for the Floriade 82 in Amsterdam that costed 3 full days to be erected. So the erection method had to be different and the structural system had to be improved as a result of that experience. This Floriade design was made by Paul Verheij, in co-design with structural engineer Joop de Graaf and the author as a co-designer cum producer. As the Veronica program was only meant for one year, and a lot of damage was to be expected, the steel structure was treated in hot dip galvanisation. The proposal to work with a white membrane initially was looked at rather sceptically, but the Veronica light crew advised that a tent in the evening could be given all kind of colours by projection of coloured light on it anyone could ever want; even laser light shows could work. (fig 63) The repeated request of the producer to speed up the installation time finally resulted in a tent structure that could be put up within 4 hours with a small crane, including the anchorage. The tent structure was designed, manufactured and erected in 4 weeks time. The tent has made such a visual impact as an eye-catcher on television that even after 7 years of monthly duty it is still regularly in use for showing pop-music programs on Dutch TV.

Application of Products in Projects

65 The 1 to 5 scale model for the tentdome in Jeddah to cover a private swimming pool for sheik Saoud Kaaki. Joint system with compressed tube ends sliding over the flanges of the star-like joint in powdercoated aluminium. Outer membrane in PTFE coated glassfiber, transparent PVC insulation of triple blister foil, internal membrane PVC coated polyester. Total translucency of 15% is enough in the Jeddah climate for a clear daylight covering without the need for an additional sunscreen.

14 *Swimming Pool Dome* In Oct 1982 the author attended a building exhibition in Jeddah SA, by sheer luck, together with Van Leeuwen Buizen, proudly presenting space frames and tent structures. The 1/20 scale model of the Veronica tent attracted much interest, especially from a client who wanted a pool covering. In the first place attracted by the design of the Veronica tent, the architect, M. Althaf from Madras (India) decided however that for a functional use the tent had to be closed. When a single layer structure is closed, the internal temperature rises because of the greenhouse effect. So during the technical discussion a second tent membrane was decided with even a transparent intermediate insulation material. So in one discussion the design changed from an open music tent to an aluminium dome skeleton with a double membrane. The ease of communication with pencil and fountain pen was in this case able to bridge habits and cultures and the architect regarded the structure as the crown on his work. He was interested in the field of lightweight structures, gave lectures on this topic on the university of his home town and informed the author that Richard Buckminster Fuller, well over 80 years of age, still gave seminars in India the year before. And although the tent dome did not have any resemblance to one of the designs of Fuller, such a common interest between project-architect and product-designer caused a special bond, with invitations to lecture. (figs 65, 157 to 159)

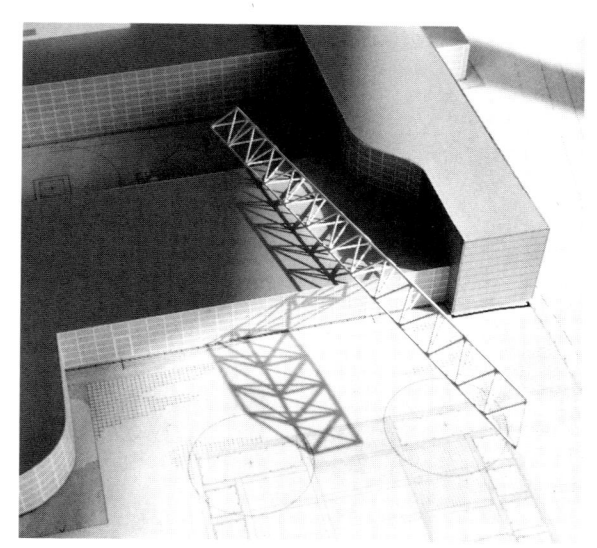

66 Model scale 1 to 100 of the printing factory Van Elburg in Sassenheim (NL) with the 40 m long diagonally running yellow space truss cantilevering 18 m, to indicate the abstract designed entrance of the building. In plan the space frame modules were designed as parallelograms, not as squares, to stress the relation with the building at the same time as the independence from the building.

67 Final realisation of 4 lily-like tent elements, consisting of poles dia 300 mm (7 m high), bracings dia 100 mm and tensile bars dia 10 mm, as a result of the respective material efficiency in bending, compression and tension.

Architecture in Space Structures

15 *Flower Tents Van Elburg* Architect Fons Verheyen invited the author to design a solution for marking the entrance to a new printing factory in Sassenheim. The designed building itself was quite massive in size and closed off from the outside by green-reflective glass panels and metal sandwich panels. Yet in this factory the most luxurious colour photographs were printed of flowers. Sassenheim is a village in the middle of the famous Dutch bulb fields. The main problem of the architect was to indicate the two entrances in the building for the public. The first idea of the architect was a tent structure, which according to the opinion of the author, did not cope very well with the technical outlook of the building and would be too flowerish and romantic for this type of building. After a discussion of one hour the idea came to hang a triangular space truss in daffodil-yellow over the main entrance, cantilevering 18 m. The truss made on a similar scale the same dramatic gesture as the building itself and the design would be in harmony again. There happened to be a ruler on the table with a length of 420 mm, so the proposal was to make a space truss with a length of 42 m exactly, running obliquely from the parking space to the main entrance of the building. The bars of the lower chord element were designed to run parallel with the building: so instead of square modules there were parallelogram-shaped lower chord modules. A second function of the space truss was combined with an emergency staircase in the inner courtyard, to enable an extra escape route in case of fire, from the upper floor. One day after this new idea a 1:100 truss model was soldered that in every respect underlined the spatial assumptions. The graphic designer of the printing house, however, urged the client and the architect that he preferred something more 'flowerish' so a new discussion was held; this time longer to change attitudes. So the second best solution of a system of lily-like tent elements was designed, composed of 4 equal units so that each had the form of an irregular pentagon. The irregularity enabled the position the connection between the five arms at odd corners, so that the tentmast elements are not in one line but are positioned on a curved line.

Identical entrance tent elements have been built in 2 other projects of the same architect in different colors in front of mirror-reflective office walls in Hoofddorp (fig 140).

Products

4 Space Frame Structures

Space frames are the most universally applicable space structures from the complete list of the membrane-like, truss-like and shell-like space structures. (par 2.2) Mainly because of the straightness of the composing bar-elements. They are more adaptable to different designs of buildings than the spatially curved structures. The author likes to stress the emphasis in his work on the design aspects of space structures, even more than the structural challenges, like maximum spans. But also more than the industrial aspects like production, or economical challenges like the maximisation of profit. The total complexity around every application is more interesting than the optimalisation of one single aspect. In this respect it is clear that both structural and industrial vocabularies had to be developed, but always keeping in mind that the space structure is a relatively small part of the overall architecture. This means that the space structure is influenced by the complexity of the total surrounding architecture, but also can have an important radiation in return on the architecture. When these applications are seen important, the art to design an application of a system of space structures in whatever circumstances and to optimise this application in all respects, is more important than inventing a new nodal system or minimising the weight of the structure. It is a designer's contra a specialist's opinion. All paragraphs of chapter 4 are written with this starting-point of being centered around the designed application in mind. However, the concerned projects will only be analysed in aspects directly related to the space structures. A full architectural project analysis will not be given, as this book is about the design aspects of space structures itself.

1 General Principles

Space frames can be used in buildings for two main reasons: structurally and architectonically. Structurally, they are optimally used when spans are large, when the roof areas have more or less square plans, or when cantilevers are to be made. Sometimes also the assembly of small prefab components appears an advantage when the building site cannot be reached by cranes, or when the shipping volume is small and compact. In other cases the required rigidity for local loads on a space frame (especially on flat roof structures), can be an advantage. Architectonically, space frames are interesting when the architect wants to obtain a spatial effect in his design, making use of the form and geometry of space frames, the colour and colour contrast of bars, nodes and cladding: the graphical lay out of the space frame, and the daylight penetration, through this lightweight structure. Space frames can be used in many different forms that can be visually slender. This slenderness is optimised when using a glass covering on cylindrical barrel vaults, domes or saddle-shaped spaceframes or even on a flat space frame. As a means of expression of visual lightness, space frames are used to balance heavy or let us say 'abstract' concrete buildings, or abstract parts of buildings. Usually, in the practice of the author the purely architectural applications outnumber by far the structural applications.

Obstacles   The number of annual applications of space frames in The Netherlands is growing rapidly yet in building volume it is not very significant. The most important reason for their relative limited applications is that architects think space frames are very expensive and too specialised; their designs often lack an accurate know-how on the optimal design possibilities of space frames, to minimize the costs, and hence these structures might appear to be expensive. A number of competitive systems is manufactured abroad and imported by commercial companies. In these cases a direct dialogue between product designer and project architect hardly exists, and no optimalisation takes place so that a real integration or implementation is only achieved after frequent discussions. This is valid for space frames imported into the Netherlands, but also for export frames from the Netherlands. Distance and the lack of personal ideas can be a handicap.

This book is partly meant to break through this vicious circle by informing architects on the design and application of spatial structures. Other reasons for the relatively high costprice of space frames, to be regarded as

68 Picture of the first Octatube space frame as a grandstand covering, cantilevering 18 m, on a total length of 70 m, over a stadium in Kuala Lumpur. Engineering was done in Delft, manufacturing and installation done locally by Octatube Malaysia, 1988.

obstacles to overcome, are:

1 Many systems are composed of ingenious nodal components, applicable in very different situations. Often the built-in capacities are much larger that actually used. And the costs of manufacturing these ingenious elements is included in each application, used or not. Sometimes the price of ingenuity is too high. This is one indication to follow a pragmatic rather than a theoretical route in future.

2 Sometimes the composition of separate nodes and joints works out very expensive when compared with conventional steel structures. For, essentially, in the space frame industry tubes of 6 m or 12 m length are cut into smaller lengths often as small as 1.2 m only to be connected in a later stage to a multitude of 6 m, of course with a lot of energy and financial input. So, a method to overcome this obstacle is to look for possibilities of prefabricating larger units like pyramids or trusses, to be easily connected on site.

3 Completely in contradiction with the general tendency in the building industry of reducing manhours on the site, a considerable number of manhours are now used outside the factory, where conditions are not as ideal as inside. A further goal in developing new space frames would be easy-and-fast connections on site.

4 Compared with conventional steel structures, most of the space frame systems can receive an excellent anti-corrosion treatment: most of the space frame systems can be hot dip galvanized internally and externally, and subsequently be treated with an efficient protection system like polyester powdercoating, which is very resistant against mechanical damage during transport, shipping, assembly and erection. It has a durable high-gloss

surface. Remarkable is that, because of the relative high costs of these coatings, as a result the price of a space frame can be composed up to 25-30% by the total costs of galvanising and coating. As normal steel structures have more simple paint systems, their price level will be lower accordingly.

5 Often architects design structures keeping in mind the possibilities of lineair steel trusses, leading to rectangular plans. In a later phase of further development of the project, space frames are considered as a possible substitute, and of course rectangular surfaces are not ideal for space frames because of the uneven routing of bending moments in the short and the long direction. So linear halls are not very well suited for space frames, unless the space frame geometry is deliberately adapted for these applications.

6 By choosing a very small module or a module not particularly suited for the different space frame systems, the square meter costs can be high because of the unfavourable bar length in relation to sawing waste of standard tubes, or the added cost of making more joints with annexes per m2. This consideration concerns only optimalisation of the space frame system itself, not the application in the architectural scheme.

7 Space frames usually are very rigid structures. Normally they are only used for roof structures, with modest live loads, and with a lightweight cladding and roofing. The system-rigidity is not wel used in these cases, which is an invitation for reducing the rigidity by reducing the number of bars and nodes: minimising the geometry. In other cases building physical requirements demand heavy reinforced concrete prefab roof-slabs on top of a space frame, for example in music theatres: heavy weight for acoustic reasons. In these cases loadings are so heavy that space frames can only be welded on site or bolted with additional welding. Most of the advantages of lightweight completely prefabricated structures are then lost. If possible, one should optimise the space frames with lightweight loadings and heavy loadings both in a different way. Actually, a reasonable budget price can only be obtained when the architect optimalises his space frame in the design stage, in dialogue with a possible producer, who then becomes co-designer in the preliminary design stage. A keen and clear sighted architect can design a medium-budgeted space frame.

Design Rules   Apart from applications where space frames are used as a substitute for an originally linear design of plane trusses, space frames will only fit in the overall design, when the architect has composed it in his conceptual scheme or in the visual idea of the architecture. This idea can be visualised by drawing the different cross sections where the space frame is used in the vertical wall, sloped wall, curved roof or horizontal roof areas. (fig 68) For architects one of the most exciting aspects of the use of space frames is the relative freedom for the positioning of columns and the many options to be filled in by the architect that lead to a distinctly personal spatial design. These options include: geometry, module, position of the frame, supports, colour, colour contrast, details, cladding, etc. For simplicity's sake first an explanation of the basics of flat space frames will be given, followed by more complex forms like stacked up frames in later paragraphs. A flat space frame could be seen as a horizontal flat plate, covered with a closed, transparent or translucent roof covering. Normally, the forces in the separate bars will be quite different, so logically the outer dimensions and wall thicknesses of the bars used, will differ. When using different tube sizes the project-architect can distinguish the size differences of tubes in the frame by means of the thicker and thinner shafts. Consequently, the routes of moments in which the loads are carried through the space frame to the foundation can be read. The opposite principle is to use the space frame purely as a spatial ornament, ignoring the moment-routing idea: and conceiving the space frame as composed of perfectly equal elements. In these cases all external diameters of tubes will be chosen to be the same (maybe some non-visual differentiation in the wall thickness); the result will be an overdimensioning of nearly all the bars. The debt to be paid to abstraction is a higher costprice, especially when the space frame is used in larger spans or heavier loads and when the space frame topology asks for differentiation: for example flat frames, supported by 4 single columns without beam-like or sprout-like intermediate elements (a space frame with heavily differentiated components).

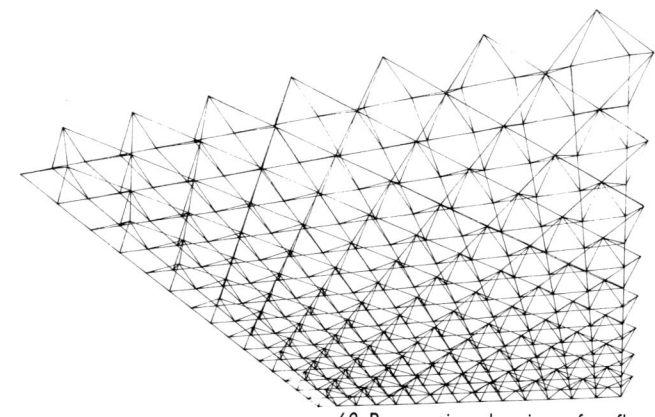

69 Perspective drawing of a flat space frame with geometry 'diagonal-on-square' module 2 m, spanning 32 x 32 m. Realised for showroom of machines and equipment Mahez in Amsterdam, 1988.

70 Entrance Canopy, Fascia trusses and atrium space frame for the Esso head office Benelux in Breda NL, designed by arch Kraaijvanger. Tuball space frames with welded fascia trusses for torsional rigidity and straightness.

Topology   In the graphical lay out of space frames 6 different types of topology (geometrical order of bars and nodes in relation with each other) can be distincted. (fig 71)
A Square-on-square set orthogonally
B Square-on-diagonal set orthogonally
C Square-on-double-square set orthogonally
D Square-on-square set diagonally
E Square-on-diagonal set diagonally (fig 69)
F Square-on-double-square set diagonally

For triangular instead of quadrangular space frame structures, the same subdivision can be followed; they form triangles and hexagons. The different topologies all behave differently according to the applied loadings, the position of the supports and the size of the frames. For example, for square frames supported by 4 corner columns the diagonally set topologies might be better because the routing of moments runs directly from the centre of the frame to the columns. In case of using orthogonally set frames the moments are drawn from the centre of the frame to the center of the edges. This is comparable with a reinforced concrete plate with 4 edge beams and 4 corner columns. The difference between square-on-square and square-on-diagonal or square-on-double-square often is a greater rigidity for the first topology, to be used only in larger spans or large loading cases. When using lightweight steel decking and live loads, square-on- square with perimeter supports gives much more rigidity than is asked for, especially when a tight cost comparison with conventional steel structures is performed. But space frames with a reduced number of bars and a reduced rigidity are not very easy to erect and have no capacity for large cantilevers. One illustration of the importance of the diagonally set frames are the Rai exhibition halls in Amsterdam, (fig 72) designed by architect Bodon and structural engineer Enserink, and built by Bailey. The largest hall 100 x 100 m has a diagonally placed square frame on top 70 x 70 m; so that this double edge truss acts as a reinforcement in the frame and as a support at the same time.

Torsional Stability   Roofs supported on all sides, are ideally for two-way double layered space frames when plans are square. Two-way means that upper and lower chord members run in 2 perpendicular directions (orthogonally or diagonally). When the design calls for a cantilevering structure, the torsional stability of the edges becomes a major point of concern. Under different types of loading the squares in upper and lower chord will be slightly deformed to rhombs and initiate a small sag of the structure. In these cases (of course depending on scale, loading and sensibility of the cladding material for deformations) a bracing is necessary: each diagonal divides a square into two triangles, avoiding deformation of its plane that way. This triangulation-function is performed by the bracing elements, but is applicable also for chord stiffening. This was for example the case for the large canopy of the Treasure Building in Singapore (fig 75) designed by DBS Architects, New York: a large equilateral triangle with plan size 100 x 60 x60 m, only supported on 3 columns, with maximum cantilevers of 27 m, and covered with a continuous glass skylight on top, very sensible for deformation. The architect proposed a two-way square-on-square grid, but during the international tendering stage the competing space frame manufacturers all advised a three-way grid. Had the architect been informed in a stage before bidding, he might have chosen a more optimal 3-way grid where the forces would be distributed more evenly over the tubes. In general we might state that space frames are very suitable for cantilevering roofs, and can even be stiffened for a larger cantilever, to prevent torsion for very sensible

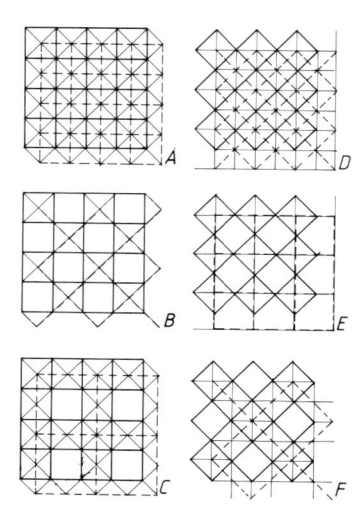

71 6 basic geometrical schemes for flat space frames; characterised by the geometry of the upper and lower chord members in comparison with the regular edges of the frame.

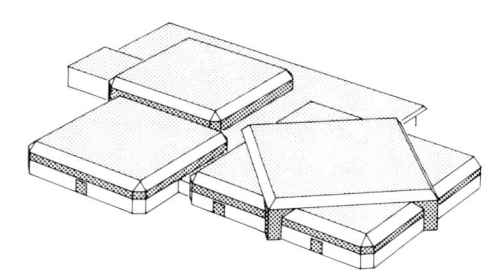

72 Isometrical scheme of the Rai Halls in Amsterdam: 100 x 100 m / 70 x 70 m in plan. The form of the roofs display the form and the structural action of the space frame plates.

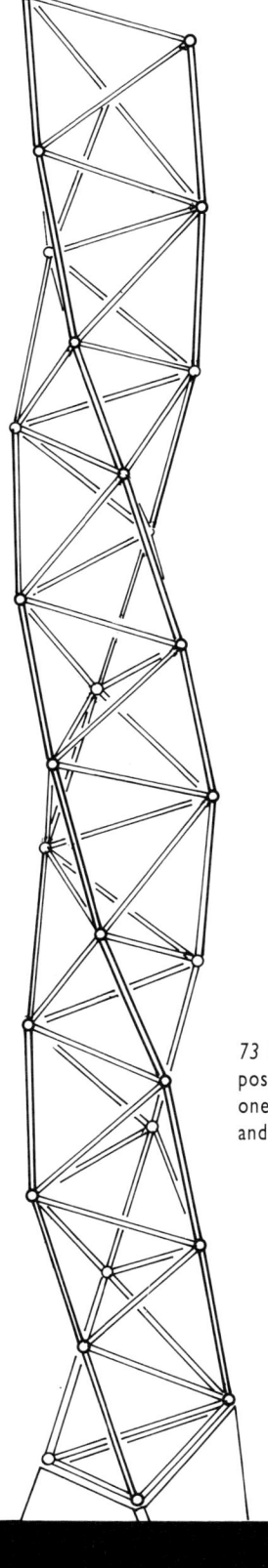

74 Post sevice train station in The Hague (Holland Spoor), size 35 x 105 m, slightly curved in plan.

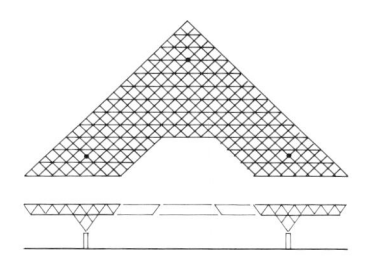

75 Plan of a 3-way space frame as a canopy with dimensional 100 x 67 x 67 m, supported by three internal columns, requiring large cantilevers of 27 m, for the Treasury Bank Building in Singapore. Specified maximum deflections of 7 mm at the tips appeared to be min 15 mm at tender stage.

73 Elevation of a standard space frame tower composed of regular tetrahedrons: one type of node, one bar length. Bars are located in a slow, a medium and a turbulent spiral.

76 The Van Rijswijk free petrol station canopy in Schiedam NL. Architect John Grootveld. The front edge is at 45 degrees in plan. The columns are rigidly connected to the foundations, the top of the columns is hinged. The cladding in translucent polycarbonate panels is suspended on gutters from the space frame.

roof coverings. In generally the effect of free cantilevering space frames is one of an almost effortless horizontal gesture almost independent of gravity. (fig 76, 81)

Cambered Space Frames   Because of the deflection of structures under downward loading, usually flat frames will be cambered into one or two directions depending on the spans and the loadings. This camber fulfils two purposes: firstly even in case of heavy deadweight a horizontal structure can be seen as a perfectly flat space frame or slightly positively cambered at the wish of the architect: a visual purpose. Secondly the outer shape of the cladding on top has to get a shape for positive rainwater drain. This can be obtained by using an extra layer of purlins in the required camber (or saddle shape) or by giving the space frame itself an extra camber. When the exterior top cladding used is profiled metal sheet, the minimal camber must be 3-5 degrees for spans of more than one sheet length. In case of a bituminious or neoprene/pvc roofing membrane over insulation on top of a metal corrugated sheet, the remaining camber must be at least 2 degrees.

The actual choice between an extra camber in the space frame or cambered purlins on top depends largely on the space frame system. Mero always is built with extra purlins; Nodus for simple roofs can be cambered itself: top chord members are square hollow sections and purlins can be omitted. Octatube uses different profiles depending on the complexity of the structure: multiple layered space frames must be provided with extra mullions. When using the Octatube Space Truss system cold rolled profiles are used as purlins in the secondary direction integrated in the system (which is limited to double layered frames.) Tuball usually has separate purlins and in some cases special aluminium extrusions used as a combined bar and purlin, called the Tuball Plus system. The above mentioned systems are explained in par 4.2.

Other systems consist of prefab pyramidal units, with open profiles or RHS-sections in the top layer and solid or circular bars in the bottom. As these systems have a rather industrial-mechanical image, architects favour more the use the four above mentioned less industrial systems of Mero, Nodus, Octatube or Tuball. When using pyramids it is only logical to form a cambered roof by shortening the lower chord members. In the Space Decks system all lower chord bars are manufactured as turn buckles so that its camber can be obtained on site and does not influence the manufacturing and stocking process. However, one should be careful with shortening of the lower chord bars at wish when the proper precautions are not taken like the temporary support of all nodes etc. Post-tightening of the lower chord members (after visual deflection) is even dangerous, because the extra tensions cannot be checked that are introduced during post-tensioning. So the actual stress distribution can be completely distorted. But in fact a post-lengthening system like the Space Deck System gives a good solution for camber possibilities and simultaneous manufacturing uniformity, enabling continuous prefabrication and stocking, independent from actual orders.

In reality only multiple layered designs, space frames in multi spans or very rigid space frames are never cambered. By choosing the built-in camber one of the basic ideas of space frames 'uniformity of standard elements' disappears because of the different bar lengths necessary to obtain this camber.

It is only natural that a completely flat frame shows a negative sag when loaded, after erection. Visually it can be annoying when this effect is to be seen close by, at eye level: from a pedestrian bridge, balcony of mezzanine floor looking directly into a multiple layered frame. Dust on the tubes can be seen in this case equally well!

One of the obvious disadvantages of giving positive camber is the resulting horizontal and vertical curvature at the gable edges which can visually disturb a panelled gable wall or curtain wall with straight horizontal lines. This point requires some attention during the initial sketch design phase, because it is very expensive to manufacture for example a flat square frame positively cambered with nodes and bars on the support line in a straight horizontal and vertical line: in that case almost all the bars will have different lengths. So then the system with separate purlins is easier.

The architectural choice of form, dimensions and material of the parapet or attica will be very important here. When only a simple and pure glass wall is placed against the space frame, there will be no technical intermediate element left: the solution is an equally simple (and yet complex) straight edge solution. The reader is reminded of the kind of details used by the Dutch architect Gerrit Rietveld or by Ludwig Mies van der Rohe that are so abstract that technical composition is almost denied. The designer's creativity is then ultimately challenged to accomplish this idea.

Structural Depth / Module Size   One of the axioms of space frames is that their nodes are equal and their composing bars have equal lengths. In this case in a regular frame composed of half octahedrons and tetrahedrons, the structural depth of the frame is 0.5 root 2 x module length or 0,707 M. The angle between bracings and diagonal chord bars is 45 degrees. So in most buildings the sloped orthagonal walls will have an elevation angle of about 54 degrees. Whenever the project-architect wishes to reduce the structural depth (for example because of details with wall cladding or additional glass systems) the diagonal angle of 45 degrees can be reduced to about 30 degrees. Or with the same ease enlarged from 45 to 60 degrees. Which means that the orthogonal angle will slide from 70 to 40 degrees. (But of course there will be structural consequences) This could for example be necessary when aluminium is used as a structural material: the loss of rigidity by the material must be balanced by a higher structural depth.

The choice of module depends in the first place on the design grid of the building. Columns are usually at the centres of the two grid lines in X and Y direction. The space frame will rest on steel or reinforced concrete columns at these centres. In plan the regular space frames are composed of square modules.

The standard commercial tube length from stock is 6 or 6.4 m. So from the point of view of minimal material waste the 3 m (or 3.2 m) module is optimal. The 3 m module has a structural depth of 2.1 m; (3.2 m module: 2.25 m height). For the larger spans the structural depths must be larger than 1/15 or 1/20 times the span. For lightweight optimal space frames structural depths must be between 1/15 and 1/18 of the span. So a horizontal module 3m with a depth of 2.1m is ideal for spans between 30 to 42 m. Below 30 m the depth can be reduced without major problems; above 42 m there will be a larger noticeable deadweight. For a span of 60 m and a depth ratio of 1/20, the depth will be 3 m, module 4.5 m etc. Tube lengths especially ordered at length from the steel mill, with a longer ordering time. A module size of less than 3 m means material waste during production and an increase in the price of the nodes per m2. Suppose the average node costs per m2 are 100% at a module of 3 m. When the module is reduced to 2.4 m (and the same nodes are used) the share of node costs is increased to 160%. The total lengths of tubes used is larger, but quite often of smaller diameter, except for practical tubes that already have the minimal cross section. The exact differences are very hard to calculate because of the large number of influences. Most probably one would have to compose a multi-dimensional graph to show relations. So, although it is hard to describe these differences in detail, it is clear that the consequences of optimalisation in view of pricing are quite large.

Span and Costs   The module size, span, mode of support and the total load will fix the bar diameter and size/strength of the node. Normally spans up to 45 m are

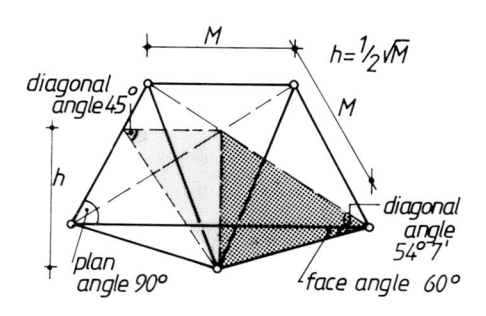

77 The standard relationship between the horizontal module of a space frame 'M' and the vertical height using bars of equal length.

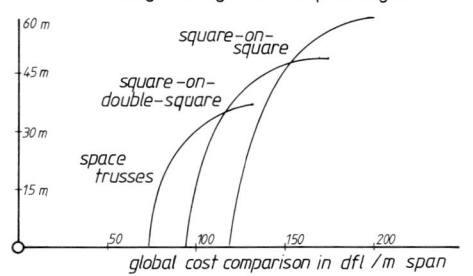

78 Global costing graph giving indications between span, different types of geometry and square meter costs for 3 m module, and 2.1 m depth. Live loads 0.5 kN/m2, in Octatube.

no problem for flat roof areas. For most space frame systems these spans are within the standard range. For larger spans the nodal strengths are higher than usual. For spans from 6 to 20 m in all space frame systems the smallest nodes are used. Normally larger spans are always possible, but at the expense of higher costs: a 30 m span flat frame is cheaper than a 60 m flat frame. When it comes to large spans (60 m and more) the only way to make space frames with relatively low costs is to make barrelvaulted or arched space frames. For example the author proposed in 1985 an ice scating rink barrelvault in Heerenveen NL 90 x 200 m, 20 m height, that was calculated to have the same price as a flat space frame spanning 50 m.

When one uses the individual nodal systems the lower spans tend to have minimal bars. So in that way a 15 m, 18 m or 21 m span could have the same m2 price. Because of the many practically sized or minimal bars a further reduction in span does not lead to a reduction in bar size or weight (comparison at same module). On the contrary: relatively the number of columns will increase, and hence the costs. Also in smaller sized jobs prices tend to increase because of overhead-intensivity. One also could state then that in using space frames, for the same costs larger spans can be obtained. Price graphs would be very handy, but no system manufacturer uses them because of the many variables. Indications are given from experience. In order to give the project-architect some

General Principles

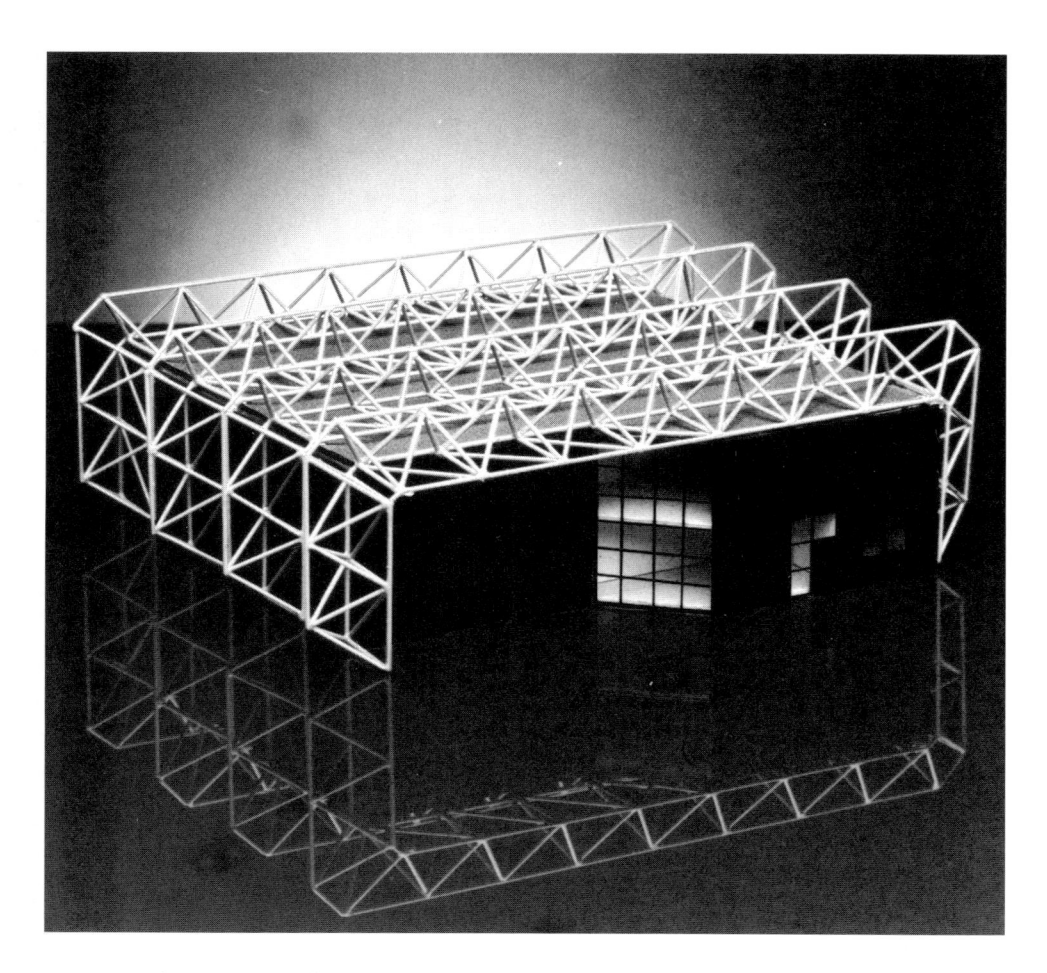

79 Design for a photographer's studio in Rotterdam with an external delta truss structure in plan 21 x 21 m, 6 m internal height with an indoor double office floor. Originally a white space frame and a black cladding as a negative picture. The internal volume free of supports or structures for an optimal work space.

indications a few budget prices can be given, that work out roughly:
- space trusses spanning up to 33m: Dfl 75.= to Dfl 125.=/m2;
- square-on-double-square space frames up to 42 m: Dfl 125.= to Dfl 160.=/m2;
- square plans with square on square grids 30 to 100m: Dfl 200.= to Dfl 500.=/m2.

All these influences are given in a graph fig 78. Price level mid 1988. It is always advisable to contact the manufacturers for budget prices in an early design stage; they are able to give more accurate prices depending on span, loading, module size, galvanising/coating, supports etc. In general one could state that space frames are easy for reaching larger spans, better than traditional structures, certainly for square plans; in general by using a minimal number of interior columns. For example a warehouse of 120 x 120 m with internal columns spaced at 24 x 24 m or 30 x 30 m can easily be realised with a very modest deadweight of only 0.18 kN/m2. When a space frame in square plan is supported along all edges with standard nodes, spans can be realised up to 40 x 40 m or 45 x 45 m, and up to 60 x 60 m with larger nodes. (Experiences in Octatube). Spans in flat frames between 60 to 100 m require special attention. In order to obtain a larger structural depth, two space frames square-on-double-square could be placed on top of each other (mirror wise): keeping the 3 m. module, the structural depth will then be 4.2m. (fig 19) Another solution would be to let the overall form of the space frame introduce a reduction of the bar forces: a cylindrical form, a dome, or by generating a hanging form or a suspended flat roof (that is, a flat space frame with outdoor columns guyed with cables in the same way as a suspended bridge). A longitudinal plan is not very suitable for space frames, as tubes in only one direction are stressed. The space frame is used optimally when the possible capacities in two directions are equally used. Another solution for longitudinal halls is to introduce truss-like elements producing more or less square frames in-between. These trusses can be made in the same space frame language: triangular in form, on top of the space frame acting as a skylight at the same time or hexagonal and stronger in cross section, or double XX. Experiences gained with these solutions show that these primary trusses tend to be very heavy. The concept of the linear hall is developed with linear trusses and a space frame can only adapt itself against (slightly) higher costs. Only in the Octatube system triangular or delta (space) trusses for linear spans have been developed. These trusses are popularly referred to as the Delta Octatube system.

Supports   One could distinguish basically (point- or) column-like and (line- or) beam-like supports. Columns are used when the reaction forces can be taken by the space frame and are relatively modest or when the space frame is supported by a truss-like element that in itself is supported by a single column. When the reaction forces in the frame become too large, the column would punch through the frame: large shear forces near the support. In that case an intermediate element will have to be introduced that distributes forces over a larger surface: its function will be to spread the forces concentrated in the column to a larger area just like a mushroom head in a flat concrete floorslab. An additional advantage of this plate support is that a considerable improvement in stability is obtained.

As to the position of hinged columns and the form of the edge of the space frame the following distinctions can be made:
- Mansard Edge (or sloped wall and flat roof)
- Vertical Edge (or vertical gable)
- Corniche Edge (or outward cantilevering gable)

Supports can be made on the outer edge of the space frame, or in one of the inner grid lines, so that a cantilever results. Space frames have a remarkable flexibility when it comes to the positioning of the columns. It is easy to place and relatively easy to replace columns at several positions under upper and lower grid nodes. They don't need to be in one straight line. In some cases it is even possible to change position after completion of the building. Enlarging the space frame is only possible when flexibility and a quite considerable number of over-dimensioned bars are available. The supposition that all columns can be replaced freely is pure myth: there is never more flexibility than one provides.

A truss-like support can be formed in two ways. As a separate flat truss in-between several separate space frames or as an incorporated spatial truss in the space frame system itself. The choice will quite often be made according to the magnitude of forces that will have to be carried. A space frame truss has its limitations in carrying the main compression and tension forces because of the maximum forces to be taken by the nodes to be used. For highly loaded trusses only completely welded trusses might work out efficiently, as for example in aeroplane hangars.

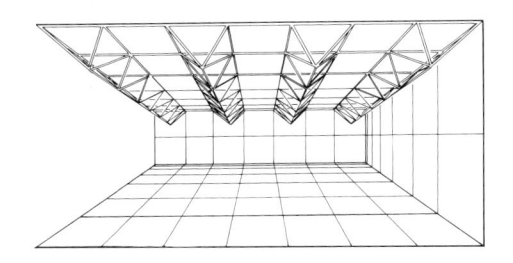

80 Perspective schemes of triangular or delta trusses spanning in one direction only. Because of the loss of transverse rigidity the single trusses will have to be stabilised against torsion by diagonal bracings in the upper chord planes or horizontal wind bracings. For amateurs these hybrid space frame types look fairly complicated already, but more understandable than a regular frame.

Roofing of Space Frames   Form and structure of the covering roofing material greatly influences the space frame by its deadweight and possible purlin distance. The possible choice can be made with profiled steel or aluminium cladding, (lightweight) concrete, stressed skins or a transparent or translucent skylight system. The choice of this roofing is also important for the visual texture of the material, color, acoustical properties etc. The most commonly used covering material is profiled or corrugated steel cladding. These panels can span up to 6 m single spans, but with the popular 'thin-gage' material 70 mm thick panels available in the Netherlands, spans are usually 4 to 4.5 m. Asbestos profiled panels are not very often used because of the small purlin distance (1.2 to 1.5 m) and because of the required roof angle, that does not coincide with the non-traditional and more abstract structural form of space frames. Aluminium profiled sheets are only used in case of a maintenance-free roof. The maximum purlin distance 1.5 to 2.0m is often a disadvantage for large moduled space frames: they require intermediate purlins. Also too often aluminium cladding appears to be sensitive to cracks during installation or walking on top during maintenance (or vandalism). Cracks that are easily visible from the inside, if they are not dangerous structurally. Lightweight concrete roofing is only used when fire proofing is a consideration of importance, or because of acoustic insulation. For normal projects this solution carries too much unnecessary deadweight. Sandwich panels made of foam glued between 2 metal sheets, or stressed skin panels made of plywood could offer a good solution when the architect wants a non-directional abstract cladding, and when the roofing elements can be supported on its 4 corners: the nodes. Having a flat ceiling surface is the most important consideration because usually these panels are rather expensive compared with metal profiled cladding, even when finished with a suspended ceiling material between cladding and frame. In the case of plywood sandwich panels sizes are to be obtained of 1.2 x 2.4 m or 1.5 x 3.0 m for regular plywood sizes or maximum 2.5 x 12 m for sandwich panels manufactured by the truck-industry.

Zygmunt Makowski advised in 1972 during a series of lectures he gave at the TU Delft around the design of a covering over the Feyenoord stadium in Rotterdam: 'First always choose the optimal roofing material and then design the space frame accordingly'. This also applies to skylights, for example for simple 'industrial' skylights. In that case the glass will have to be provided with a wire mesh or will have to be laminated because of fire and safety regulations. Glass itself, although almost maintenance-free, is rather heavy, has its limitations in span and suffers from thermal breakage problems. To solve these one could either use heat-strengthened or tempered glass instead of floatglass, or decide on plastic (acrylic, polycarbonate, or PVC). These thermoformed plastic sheets usually get a dome-like shape or barrel-vaulted shape. A span of 3 m is very suitable for this barrelvault type of covering. But one has to be very careful with the effects of thermal expansion and contraction in terms of watertightness as the thermal expansion of polycarbonate is 7 x that of glass! In the Netherlands it is a good custom to use double panels because of thermal insulation in winter with a reflective or absorbing outer skin for minimizing solar heat gain in summer. The most sophisticated glass systems in the USA even use a reflective coating on the inside panels to prevent warmth leaving the building, or combine a high percentage of day-light penetration and a high reflection of solar energy.

81 An overall view of the Veenman exhibition stand in Amsterdam 1986. (see also fig 154). A structure composed of 3 m module standard Octa-tube space frame with suspended tent elements 3 x 3 m. The structure rests on a central braced skeleton core 6 x 6 m. Total size of frame 25 x 20 m. Initially 6 edge poles were placed, but because of the inaccuracy of the floor of the old Rai Halls and the rigidity and straightness of the space frame, 4 out of 6 poles appeared to be hanging rather than supporting the space frame, so they were removed, with a freely cantilevering space frame as a result. The structure is built up every year in another adapted modular design (architect Frank Pluym).

For a certain range of applications such as covering a grandstand in a football stadium, street markets etc, transparent and maybe reflective coated skylights function remarkably well, but in fulfilling all requests they are quite expensive at the same time. Transparency or invisibility costs a lot of money. When using the skylights in a large span structure or large canopy one might expect large deflections due to upward and downward external loadings. An example is grandstand canopies. (fig 68) They should be covered with an elastic covering material rather than rigid glass materials. An all-glass skylight system would require a very high rigidity even for a space frame; so at the end resulting in high prices.

The last alternative roofing is the prestressed PVC coated polyester or PTFE-coated glassfiber weave membrane. In combination with a metal space frame the anticlastically curved membrane could be seen as a translucent covering for canopies, carports, shade structures for Middle East and Far East, or market coverings in West-

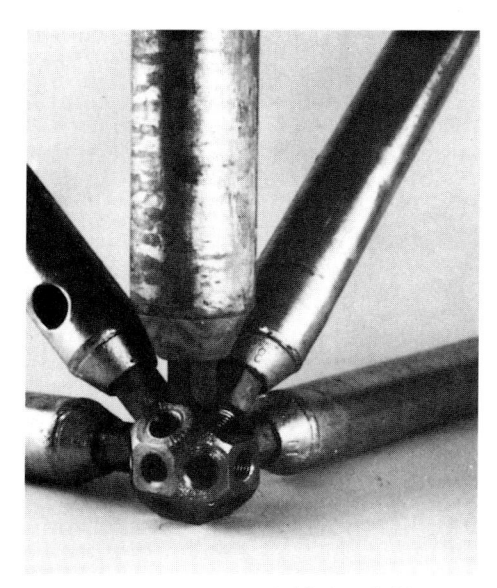

82 Standard Mero node with 18 threaded holes on the 18 facets of the solid sphere. The bars are always tapered at the ends. The diameter of the node is 1.5 to 2.0 times the average bar diameter. Bars hot dip galvanised, nodes electro-galvanised; powdercoated in factory. Manufactured by Mero, Würzburg.

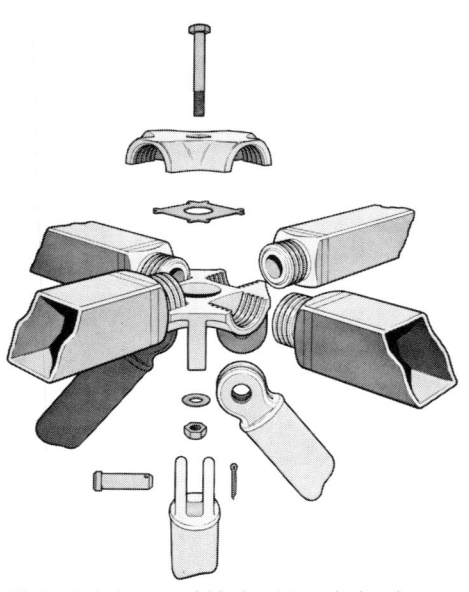

83 Exploded view of Nodus joint. 4 chord members are connected by one central bolt, connecting the upper and lower cast steel shells. Bracings are provided with cast steel fork connectors welded to the tubes by a stainless steel pin. A system with easy assembly. Mostly zinc coated and wet painted afterwards. Manufactured by Space Decks, Chard UK.

84 A standard Octatube joint with welded steel plates with M10 to M30 bolted connections characterised by the maximum axial forces in the CHS members. Hot dip galvanised and powdercoated, nylon covering caps over bolts and nuts. The flat-plate nodes can also carry open profiles for purlins, crane rails, columns etc. Manufactured by Octatube, Delft

ern European countries. (fig 154) Because of the special and tightly tailored form of the membrane, a contradiction in form between skeleton (space frame) and flying kite (membrane) can be very exciting, as experiences in several projects in the Netherlands show. (See par 6.1)

Roofloads and Deadweight Normally for larger roofs in the Netherlands a liveload is calculated of 0.5 kN/m2. The magnitude of this liveload is of course decisive for the choice of optimal grid geometry. As the deadweight of the space frame with spans up to 40 m often is less than 0.15 kN/m2, and the deadweight of the total cladding and skin also 0.15 kN/m2, one could conclude that the further optimalisation of the deadweight of the structure has only a marginal effect in the total loading. This decreasing optimising effect when going deeper into the matter from a certain point is equal to the economic law of 'decreasing marginal effect'. In general space frames are saving 30-50% in deadweight compared with flat traditional trusses, as studies in Octatube in 1978 for a number of projects have shown. A roof of 36 x 36 m supported along the edges does not have to be heavier than 0.13 kN/m2 supported along the edges while linear truss systems require 0.25 or 0.30 kN/m2. The deadweight however increases with the span.

2 Nodal Systems

In the Netherlands mainly five different systems of space frames, all using separate nodes-and-bars as the main category, are used regularly:

1 *Mero* This is the oldest commercial system available on the world market. Invented in 1942 by Max Mengeringhausen, with his mechanical engineering brilliance: the result is a very ingenious system that looks beautiful by the separate spherical nodes and circular tubes with conical ends. On a standard joint a maximum of 18 bars can be connected by means of one bolt - axially loaded - penetrating into the node from the outside. (fig 82)

2 *Nodus* A system developed by Hugh Walker of British Steel Corporation in 1972 to promote the use of their tubes and pipes. The bars are provided with welded ends; the joint is composed of 2 cast iron shells that fit exactly on the 4 ends of the horizontal bars. The chord members are rigidly connected in the node. The system looks very solid and is rather heavily dimensioned. On the regular nodes a maximum of 8 bars can be connected: the system is very practical for flat roofs. Per node only

85, 86 Non-standard Octatube nodes and assembly in case of an atrium covering with non-parallel walls, producing a diverging space frame module: from 2.2 m to 3.6 m over 24 m length. The lower chord edge members have been replaced by cold rolled U-profiles bolted directly under the nodes. (project: Logica, Rotterdam; architect Chiel Verhoeff)

87 Standard Tuball node in aluminium or steel with cast nodes and CHS profiled bars. Connections by pretension bolts from the inside of the sphere outward into the bar ends. Standard node size 2.7 x bar size, can be reduced to 2.0 x bar size. (Galvanised and) powdercoated. Manufactured by Octatube.

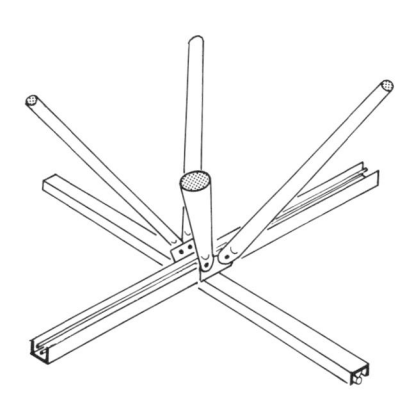

88 Custom made joint for Philips, as a very rigid and overhead laboratory frame for the testing of röntgen apparatus: Chord members are U profiles back-to-back with bent node plates in-between to connect the tubular members. The chord members are continuous up to a length of 6 m (ev 12 m), are punched and when connected do not suffer from mechanical deformation after erection.
Manufactured by Octatube.

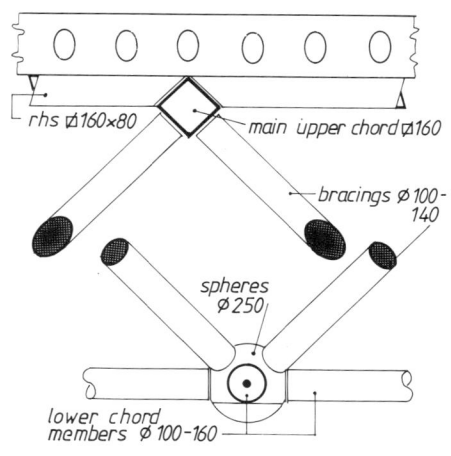

89 Non-awarded proposal for a welded space frame joint for a music theatre in The Hague. The space frame spanning 30 x 60 m, loaded by a 200 mm thick reinforced concrete roof, and extra suspended acoustic walls: high loads. The main span was chosen in the short direction as SHS elements, set diagonally to accommodate easy connections with the welded bracings, while the non-structural purlins in the longitudinal direction are RHS-profiles. (1986, Octatube)

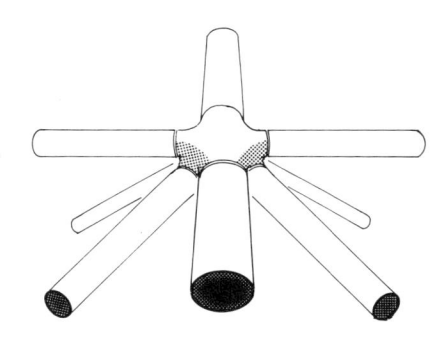

90 The new streamline joint consisting of cast steel nodes with hidden bolt connections for equal diameter chord members and smaller diameter equal bracings. Manufactured by Octatube.

Architecture in Space Structures

one single bolt is used, so the assembly speed is high. (fig 83)

3 *Octatube*   Designed and developed by the author as an architectural study on the TU Delft in 1973. The system consists of separate nodes and bars. The nodes are made of octagonal plates welded together; the bars usually are circular tubes, but also square tubes and C-profiles are used in steel, stainless steel, or aluminium. Even timber space frames are possible with solid square or rectangular laminated sections. Connection is by means of usually two bolts per bar end. Requirement for the bar is the flat strip at the end with a double bolt hole, corresponding with the bolt holes in the node. When using circular tubes as chord members, the flattened ends give the system a fairly fragile look, while the node itself almost becomes invisible, hidden between the connecting bars.
Maximum 18 bars per node. For flat roofs half nodes are used with maximum 13 bar connections. (fig 84)

4 *Tuball*   Developed by the author in 1984 as a more abstract and aesthetic antithesis of the more mechanical Octatube system, consisting of circular hollow
sections directly bolted axially to a spherical node. This node is hollow and divided in a 3/4 shell and 1/4 cap. The bolts are inserted from the inside of the sphere into the tube ends. After the pre-tensioning of the bolts, the cap is closed on the shell with only one single stainless steel bolt. The bars do not have conical ends so the spheres are generally larger than in the solid sphere systems. Because of the hollowness of tubes and nodes quite often electrical cables are fed through the members of the space frame to integrate lighting armatures, without cables ever coming into sight. The system is also in a geometrical sense quite universal in that flat space frame, cylinders and domes can be made with the same system: similar nodes with different positions of the drilled connection holes and connecting bars of different lengths. (fig 87)

5 *Streamline*   This fifth space frame system has been designed and developed by the author in 1989 as a consequence of the progressive (marketing) demand from project-architects for almost material-denying and ultimately abstract space frame systems in their increasingly abstract architecture and the growing use of slender skylights-bearing 'see-through' space frames. From these demands a search for ultimate elegance followed, that resulted in a battle between the structural efficiency and the aesthetic elegance. The system is composed of cast nodes and circular tubes and is connected by axial bolts. The junction between bars and nodes is hardly visible, and all corners between adjacent bars in different directions are rounded-off in a streamline effect. (fig 90)

Beside these regular systems occasionally other space frames are used. Firstly space frames in locally welded form, either completely welded at site, or partly in the factory, transported and connected/welded on site. This was the case with the first space frame systems in the 1960s, for example the Oktaplatte system, composed of half-spherical caps and circular straight tubes welded on site, and the welded square tube space frame for the Amstel-halls of the Rai in Amsterdam. Nowadays welded systems sometimes are used in the case of very heavily loaded space frames (See proposal for the Music Theatre in The Hague by the author in figure 89), in the case of linear space frame elements (See 'delta' fascia trusses in the Esso Europe head office in Breda, fig 70) or in case of small space frames made by local construction companies as a cheaper substitute for a prefabricated space frame at the required quality, especially in regard to corrosion protection. These welded space frames actually are not regarded as 'systems', but as custom-made space frames. Secondly the systems that can be regarded as copies of the systems already described like the Montan or the Zublin system are almost copies of the Mero system with only minor but patentable alterations. A third category that needs to be listed is the group of prefab pyramid systems consisting of elements larger than nodes-and-bars: pyramidal units composed of 8 bars welded together, to be connected on site with the 4 interlinking lower chord bars. Generally speaking these systems tend to be more low-cost than the described systems, though aesthetically they belong to mechanically connected steel structures, and are regarded by architects as not in line with modern architectural developments. Their application is not very frequent in The Netherlands. Examples are the Pyramodul system, the Space Deck system, and a derivation of the Mero system: the Mero-Deck, combining cost-efficiency with the aesthetics of the spherical and conical connections in the lower chord. A fourth category of space frames are prefabricated larger elements in linear form, forming space truss grids. These systems do not follow the seemingly 'cock-eyed' manufacturing routine in most space frame systems. Although these systems may profit from prefabrication advantages, their application is mostly limited to structures without torsion; the overall rigidity is not within the normal range of space frames. Quite unlike most other space frame systems a crane will always be needed during the assembly of the elements. An example of one of these systems is the Octa Truss Grid. The maximum length of these elements is fixed by the length of commercially available steel tubes, by hot dip galvanisation baths, by powdercoating facilities, by the container shipping and lorry transport dimensions, and by the limitations of the steel corrugated covering sheets. The practical maximum length will be 6 m, but as this truss grid system is very vulnerable for torsion there will also be a great influence of the position of the supporting columns of the surrounding building. The total ground plan of a space truss grid has to be square or nearly square in order to make an optimal use of the used materials in the prefabricated elements. The first application of this structure was the covering of the Dukenburg shopping centre in Nijmegen NL in 1988, designed by architect Peter Sigmond.

3 Flat Space Frames

Space frames in the most common, popular and simple form are flat frames. Flat frames can be applied as roof structures, but also as floor structures because of their flatness. They can also be used as vertical or sloped walls. In the form of linear elements space frames can also be used as bridges and towers. There is a large variety of geometry, topology, support systems etc to make a simple and straightforward design for given loadings and location in the total building. For this purpose most of the general principles treated in paragraph 4.1 are valid. The basic underlying principle that supports flat space frames is that these space frames can be composed of identical nodes and bar elements. This is a requirement from the production side, and is appreciated in architecture that in the contemporary form uses mostly flat space frame roofs. This axiom of mass produced similar elements is rapidly vanishing due to practical influences of all kinds.Most of these influences are treated in this book. And not in the last place because of the influences the author wants to introduce from, and to, the surrounding architectural scheme.

So a remarkable effect of self-fulfilling prophecy (stressing the possibility of non-standard space frames means that at the end a large number of non-standard space frames will have to be produced), is that a major part of the author's projects are space structures complex in geometry and detailing, (independent of their scale). One gets what one asks for. So in a number of the realised flat space frames in the last years even the relatively simple basic geometry was made complex. May be the subconcious knowledge that standard space frames can be boring in the long run, plays a role here. Also that all implantations of space frames require apart from the very structural design also an architectural effect, a surprise or a gesture that makes every space frame (standard or not) a special one for the project-architect. Thus producing a continuation of intellectual incentives for the product-architect to stay alert. The author realises that he displays an unconscious inclination to complicate even simple elements for the sake of visual pleasure , less out of statical function, and more an intellectual game to make simple schemes complex. And indeed: 'Why should one design a simple solution when also a complex solution is possible?' This point of view is a personal one of the author, and not at all representative for the state-of-the-art in the space frame industry. The difference is also one of emphasis: mass-produced space frames are producer-centered and architecture-adapted space frames are consumer-centered. One of the most clear examples of the adaptations of space frames to the requirements of the surrounding architecture is the geometric adaptation. This deviation from standard space frames with standard nodes and bars to very irregular space frame geometries, resulting in individually shaped nodes and bars, can be explained via a number of gradual steps. (fig 100) The zero situation is a standard frame with equal node and bar elements, for example in a square module. Although a similar deduction can be given treating triangular modules, it is however not interesting enough to be explained in full. The five steps towards geometric sophistication will visualise how to solve a general design design problem of global dimensions within the space frame itself.

1 Height Deformation   Quite often the direct relationship between the horizontal module and the vertical structural depth is disconnected, as often requested by the architect out of reasons of span,heights of the vertical cross-section of the adjacent building etc. Another spatial angle than standard (45 degr. diagonally or approx 54 degr. orthagonally) means other lengths of bracings and chord members. Most of the available standard systems of space frames will accommodate this deformation as it frequently is requested.

2 Length Deformation   In order to adapt the originally square module grids to the overall size of the space frame in the total architectural scheme a rectangular module can be chosen as the optimal solution, when the project architect wants to have the same size of edge distance all around the space frame. In which case the two

91 Steel flat Tuball space frame 17 x 25 m module 1.7 m, depth 1.2 m, covered by a lightweight concrete roof, with integrated lighting in all upper and lower chord nodes, supported by 4 octahedronal support bars on each of the 4 columns. Cultural Centre in Drachten NL by architect Abe Bonnema.

92 Flat space frame cantilevering over existing buildings of Holiday Inn in Leiden NL, to change an existing outdoor garden into a sub-tropical hotel garden: Holidome. Design by the author as project-architect in 1978. Even the glass curtain walls are suspended from the roof structure, so that existing roofs are not loaded. The chosen geometry square on double square appeared to have an insufficient torsional stability at the corners, and had to be stiffened at those points. The American owner took the suggestion by the author about the tree-like supports too literally: the supports were clad with palm leaves and coconuts after completion of the building.

93 Customs office building in Hazeldonk (NL-B) in Octatube with a single aluminium roof decking on top, and insulated roof panels suspended to form a free office space. Total plan size 17 x 68 m, module 1.8 m, depth 1.2 m. Geometry delta trusses with a double fascia delta truss. Architects Benthem and Crouwel.

94 Tuball space frame for Auping, Deventer NL. Module 1.2 m, combined with hardly visible halogen lamps in all lower chord nodes. Architect Roeterdink of Postma Partners, with industrial designer Frans de la Haye.

Flat Space Frames

95 Tuball space frames for shopping centre De Klanderij in Enschede (NL) in metallic grey. Architect Spruyt, De Jong, Heringa.

97 Tuball space frames around the main Octatube office in Delft. Size 12 x 30 m in plan. The frame carries the roof level of the first floor plus the sun shading tent structure on top. Architect author. (1985)

96 Entrance hall for Cap Gemini office, Utrecht supported by 6 tree-like supports. Architect Overhagen.

98 Customs complex in Hazeldonk (NL-B). (fig 93) The free-standing canopy 24 x 42 m in module 2.4 x 2.4 m and depth 1.7 m in Octatube square-on-square, has been provided with a suspended roof of double metal cladding. The detailing of this roof-type has been developed especially for this project by Octatube and has been used in a number of buildings afterwards. Architects Benthem and Crouwel.

directions of chord members will have a different length, and the space frame node is non-standard in plan angles, and of course, also in bracing angles as a consequence of this deformation from square into rectangle. But the frame itself 'fits in' excellently.

3 *Regular Angle Deformation* In case the plan boundary lines are not rectangular but rhombic, the total space frame lay-out will have to be deformed to fit into this scheme. Then the angles in plan between the chord members are not 90 degrees. An example of this geometry is the proposal for a petrol station canopy for Elf in Berlin where the chord directions were deduced parallel to the 'random' adjacent building site boundary lines. In fact in this proposal there is a third even more complicated direction and group of chord members to give the space frame an excellent torsional rigidity as the supports are internal and large torsional moments are expected thereof. The modules are hence designed as irregular triangles, but fitting perfectly in the boundary lines.

4 *Radial Angle Deformation* When the projected ground plan of the space frame is a part of a circle, the chord members can be adapted to the radial and meridional directions of the circle, while the bracings follow these directions automatically as they connect the upper chord and lower chord nodes. This results in a large variety of individually different node and bar elements which in the circle form are repeated in small series. A shining example in this case is the design of the roof over a

99 Petrol station in Schiedam with suspended translucent covering. (fig 76) Module 3 x 3 m, total size 21 x 45 m, on 5 columns in irregular places of upper and lower chord nodes. Architect John Grootveld.

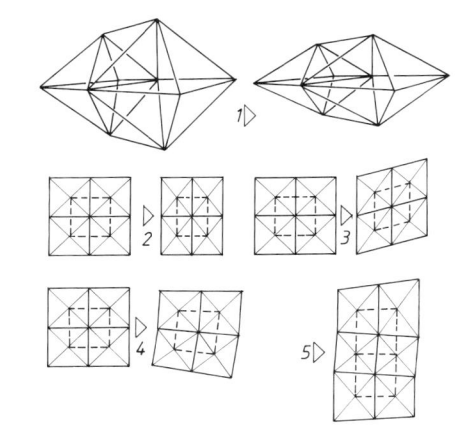

100 The degrees of freedom to design flat frames:
- Standard space frame
- Shallow frame
- In square plan
- In parallel plan
- In trapezoidal plan
- In random plan.

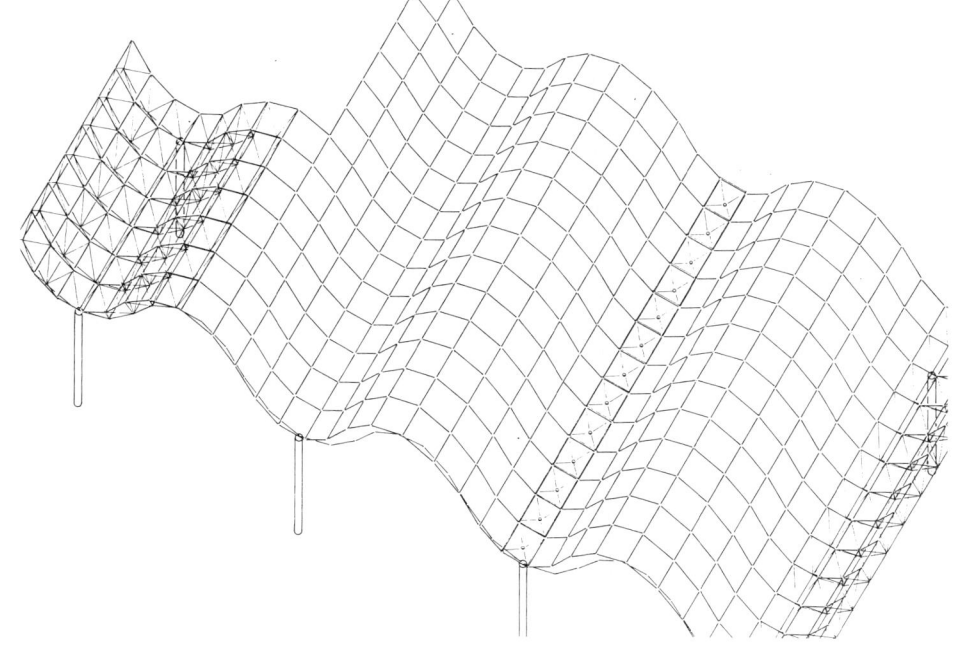

101 A double layered waving space frame as a result of the ultimate degree of design freedom. Design for a Shell petrol canopy in Pforzheim D., by the author 1988.

Flat Space Frames

council room in the town hall in Huizen NL, as described in paragraph 3.7.9. Another example is the design of a quarter circular show room for Volvo-trucks in Waddinxveen NL where the modules range in width from 2.1 m to 0.8 m, while the length bars are always 1.8 m.

5 *Irregular Angle Deformation* By filling arbitrary quadrangular plans with flat space frames, the resulting space frame will be composed purely of individually different node and bar elements, leading to increased energy input in the engineering phase, the production and the building phase. Some of the extra energy will in future hopefully be reduced to almost zero because of the effects of CAD/CAM programs, but the selecting and identification of the individual elements in the factory, after each surface treatment and on the building site will still cause a memorable extra amount of labour energy and money. An example of this ultimate deformation is the proposal for the Prinsenhof Museum music pavilion as illustrated in fig 116 in a slightly curved form.

Another example is the waving double layered space frame illustrated for a canopy in fig 101, that could be covered with structurally scaled glass panels in a flushly detailed manner. But by and large the illustration of geometric deformations and adaptations of space frames show that if the project-architect insists on this space frames can be fitted into almost any flat roof area of an overall architectural schemes. The other illustrations of this paragraph are typical examples of work done by the author, and are believed to be self-explanatory.

4 *Stacked Space Frames*

These applications of space frames are essentially a vertical addition of flat space frames on top of each other. But there are remarkable influences by this type of application on the architectural, the structural and the industrial design aspects. The resulting structure has a much more complex internal structural action that in most cases cannot be simulated by hand calculations and requires a computer analysis already in the first design phase. The industrial system normally used in these cases can only be a bar-and-node system with the result that a complex structure is actually composed of standard elements of equal lengths. Welded structures, pyramidal- or grid-type space frame structures are not suited for these applications. The architectural aspects of these applications are also quite remarkable:

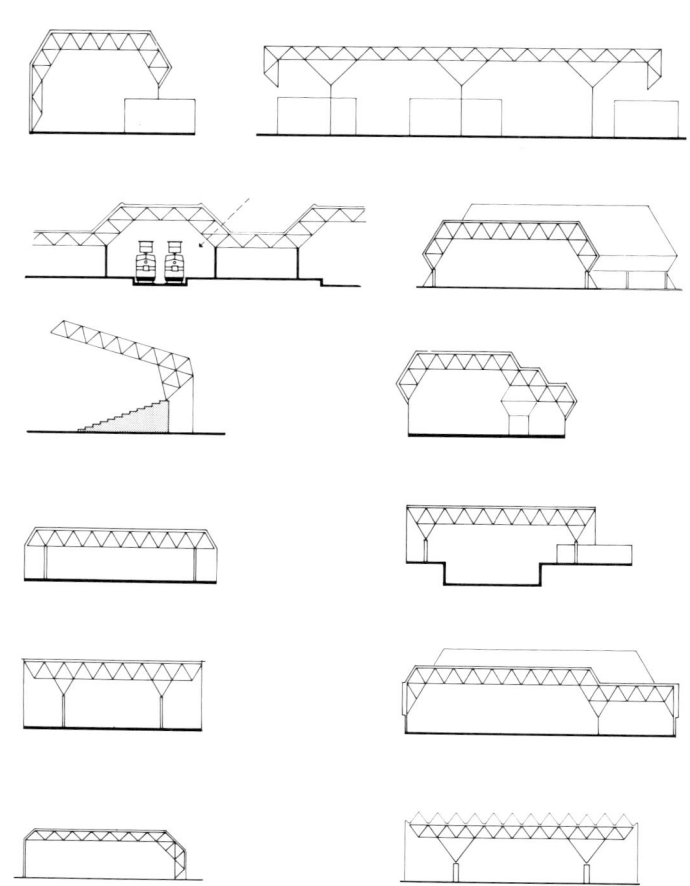

102 Different cross sections of space frames showing how these structures can influence the architectural space by form and position, and integration of wall and roof parts: Arcade, Railway Station, Subtropical Garden, Integrated Roof and Wall, Swimming Pool, Freestanding Space Frame, Sporting Complex, Exhibition Hall.

• In the first place stacked frames are deliberately chosen by the project-architect to solve a functional, spatial or a visual problem in the overall architectural scheme. Usually the height and frequency of the stacking will be a result of the spatial connection of adjacent spaces like one- with multi-story heights in (vertical) sections, or the transition in level height above stairs or ramp areas in public or semi-public buildings. It can be used to follow the lines of visibility in theaters or galleries above the chairs. But only in case the architect also desires to work with horizontal frames giving horizontal ceiling or fascia top lines in stead of sloped ones. Out of the same spatial reason space frame walls can have the same (horizontal) section: to connect smaller with larger floor areas, or to express openings or entrances.

• In the second place the result is interestingly enough rather complex, not to say sometimes confusing. This is caused by the large amount of bars and nodes in the

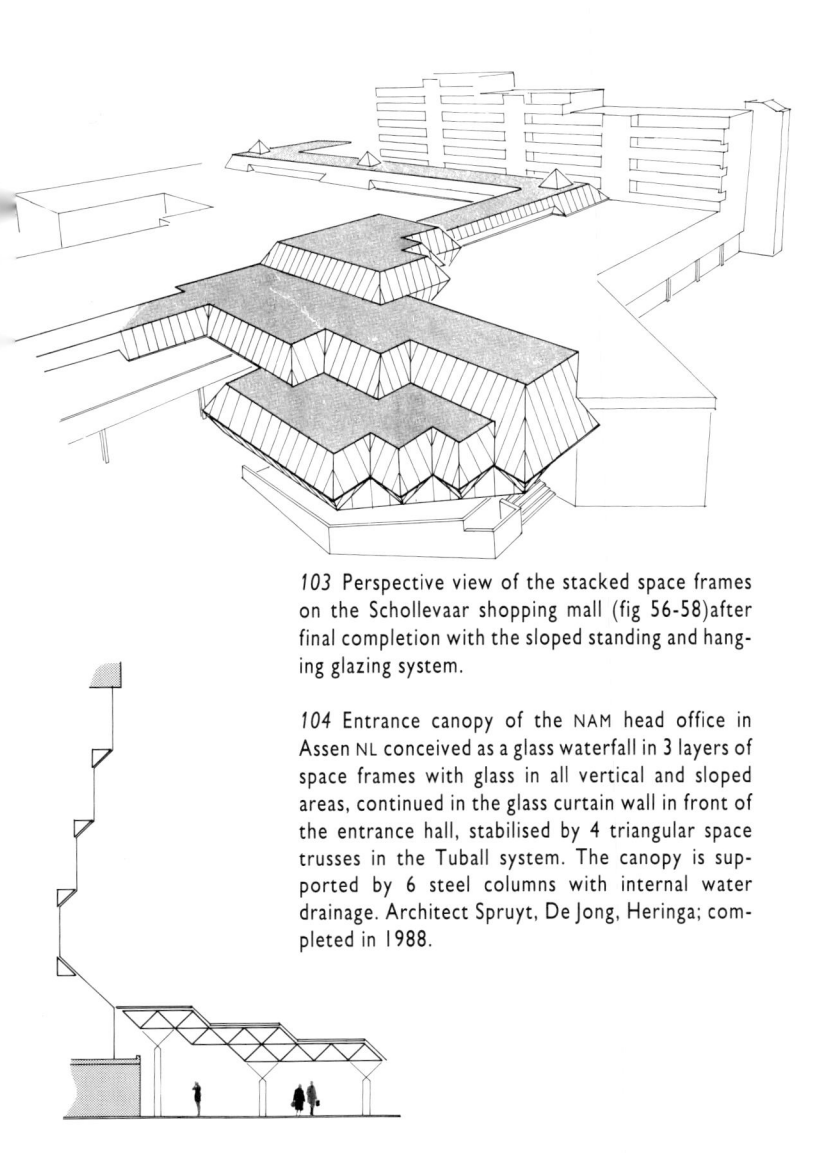

103 Perspective view of the stacked space frames on the Schollevaar shopping mall (fig 56-58) after final completion with the sloped standing and hanging glazing system.

104 Entrance canopy of the NAM head office in Assen NL conceived as a glass waterfall in 3 layers of space frames with glass in all vertical and sloped areas, continued in the glass curtain wall in front of the entrance hall, stabilised by 4 triangular space trusses in the Tuball system. The canopy is supported by 6 steel columns with internal water drainage. Architect Spruyt, De Jong, Heringa; completed in 1988.

space frame that is usually built in the square-on-square geometry. The photographs in this chapter illustrate the over-density of bars by the existence of which the average bystander cannot visually comprehend the statical action of the structure. Sometimes the ease of visual understanding of the structural action that is displayed in most of the flat frames, but also in the curved space frames, cannot even be followed here any more by professional eyes. And usually the resulting structure does not give a strong emphasizing character to the overall architecture, but on the contrary a complexity in shape that when large enough in size looks more like an 'anthill'. In the case of over-emphasizing this terraced character, the realised space frame will look like the result of deliberate struggles in the design stage to get more fluent spatial connections. The advice therefore is to use the stacking principle only in a moderate frequency, and preferably in harmony with straight lines or volumes for reasons of visual balance, or to use stacking only in a small, regular and controlled presence.

- In the third place, once the final decision on the stacking character of the design has been made, the resulting space frame has to be worked out in detail- and in shop drawings. The space frame itself, as already pointed out, is normally composed of equal nodes and bars of equal length, and does not form a particular problem. In contrast with the space frame, the preparing of shop drawings of the cladding elements is usually very complex because of the many different elements deriving from horizontal and vertical (different) corners, and corners that are both external and internal (i.e. the worst of all). A cladding consisting of prefabricated metal elements like purlins, gutters, panels, skylight frames and the connecting metal flashings, usually requires an increase in the amount of energy (and accuracy) compared with the original space frame elements. This is especially the case in the design of stacked space frames, as opposed to flat frames and curved space frames, where the spatial corners can be different but usually in a small degree. Yet, once the contract is signed for such a space frame, the art in engineering is to get a perfect result displayed in, for example, the fact that all skylight screws tightening the glass cladding around such a stacked space frame are exactly at one height, no matter what, and how many corners are covered around the frame.
- In the fourth place the resulting frame and cladding will be rather expensive as a whole because of the large amount of engineering hours involved in the preparation of these metal elements, and the more careful and longer lasting assembly and erection on site. Very often one of the problems will be how to assemble the space frame: as already described flat frames are assembled on the ground floor (or on a flat area) and lifted into position. Some of the stacked frames can only be assembled when air-borne which is more time-consuming and dangerous work.

Square Dome-like Halls   One of the remarkable forms of stacked space frames is realised when the elements of reinforcement of a flat space frame only contain space frame bars and nodes. In case of the Rai-complex in Amsterdam (fig 72) the horizontal roof frame was reinforced with a space truss in the form of a rhombic cross section, only composed of space frame elements. In the same way of thinking the design of the author's final studies at the TU Delft in 1973 was a Labour Union building in Utrecht. This design contained an exhibition wing in the form of a space frame with a peculiar cross section. The structural form was designed as a reinforce-

Stacked Space Frames

105 Interior of the Bakesteijn tennis halls in Zwijndrecht NL. Architect Piet Peutz.

106 Graphics of a part of the roof and wall frames of the Bakesteijn space frame during construction. The omitting of bars and nodes (square on double square) in the roof, is continued in the wall areas forming separate octahedrons and tetrahedrons, leaving openings in the structure, to be appreciated by the educated visitor.

107 Interior of the Quintus sporting hall in Kwintsheul NL, showing independent space trusses with separate wind bracing in the upper chord plane. The light armatures are chosen in a non-directional way, in order not to conflict with the squareness of the space frame modules. Architect author, 1978.

108 Exterior corner of the Quintus hall: carefully detailed and realised, underlining the special form of the space frame cross section. The initial design envisaged a completely translucent hanging glazing system in the inward sloping parts all around the building, which would have given the roof a floating character at night. The idea was abandoned after study of the functional aspects of badminton players being dazzled, by afternoon daylight at low angles.

Architecture in Space Structures

ment of a flat frame only supported on the 4 corners by an edge truss in sloped form, consisting of space frame elements in the appropriate geometry. (scheme fig 102) The hypothesis was that the surrounding rhombic edge trusses would reinforce the flat slab by the 2-hinged flattened arch form in cross section and by bringing the shear forces from the horizontal frame to the edges, via the trusses to the 4 corner columns. The expectation was that the middle parts of the trusses would deform horizontally outward but as they were built in a rigid geometric form, this deformation would be well within acceptable limits.

In 1978-1979 the author worked with architect Piet Peutz in a sporting hall complex in Zwijndrecht NL as a structural engineer and as a space frame contractor in the building of a similar shape designed by the architect. One year before, the author designed as an architect a sporting hall in Kwintsheul NL, took care of the structural calculations as the project-engineer, and tendered the space frame. The comparison between the two buildings brings a feedback on the hypothesis of 1973, and illustrates the virtues of the even more economical geometrical system of delta or space trusses. The Zwijndrecht complex was designed in the Nodus system, but during tendering the Octatube system appeared to be far cheaper. One of the reasons was that the proposed geometry in Octatube contained less tubes and nodes as a result of the analysis of the 1973 scheme. In this scheme the large amount of bars and nodes in square-on-square-offset geometry showed that even more elements were used in the sloped areas than in the flat roof area. The resulting rigidity would not be appreciated, so it made sense to reduce this rigidity. This was done in the Zwijndrecht scheme by choosing a square-on-double-square geometry in the flat areas and by omitting bars and nodes in the sloped areas. The total complex consisted of 2 halls 35.1 x 35.1 m (2 tennis courts) and a longitudinal hall 35.1 x 51.3 m (3 courts) based on a 2.7 x 2.7 m module. In the longitudinal hall the statical analysis showed that the major part of the forces was carried in the shorter direction. As a consequence of this, the longitudinal hall was covered by double triangulated trusses and 3 zero-trusses in the other direction only for the looks. As figures 105 and 106 show, the complex was composed of space frames in 3 different roof levels with the sloped wall frames around. As we decided to assemble the space frame on ground level, the assembly had to be done in 16 separate parts, each followed by hoisting the assembled layer for 2 m on temporary posts to enable the lower layer to be assembled underneath. For that reason special temporary adjustable frames were fabricated to support the flat roof elements in the middle. Assembly took place mainly on ground level.

It was during one of the 16 subsequent hoists that a special aspect of the experimenting with structures was proven: building new structures is still to some degree a question of trial-and-error. Not as frequent as in the middle ages when Gothic vaults collapsed before mastermasons got the right experience. Most of the risks can be analysed now beforehand. In this case a difficult building site with a complex building form and a number of different floors offered only limited space for positioning the mobile cranes. The problem arose during the hoisting of the large hall that in fact was composed of double delta trusses spanning the short direction and the 3 only cosmetic and minimal delta trusses in the other direction. The hoisting points taken by the crane and only fixed at the last moment gave large compression forces in two of the lower minimal tensile bars. These bars did not only buckle but also folded at the two ends, where the flattened ends evidently were too long. The space frame was put down again and after the changing of the two tubes to thicker tubes, the hoisting was completed. The thick tubes still are present as a proof of this trial-and-error incident. The flattening of the tubes was from that time on for Octatube bars not taken as maximum outside the nodes. We also learned to be extra careful when hoisting a space frame from an unfavorable hoisting position. So sometimes trial-and-error frightens. However, a negative result can be changed into a positive learning result and lead to an improvement in the entire system.

The Quintus sporting hall in Kwintsheul was designed to have a similar geometry. The cladding was conceived as a tightly fitting metal skin around the building. As the function of the hall was only a sporting hall in a small village whose handball teams already played in the National League, more expressive means of a 'High-Tech' nature were felt to be superfluous. One of the original ideas to have the upper part of the sloped walls in metal cladding and the lower inward sloping part completely in glazing so that the structure would be visible from the outside inwards and so that in the evening the roof structure would visually 'float', was sabotaged by the handball league. It requested that all sporting halls should be closed boxes because of the possible daylight blinding effect of the late afternoon sun. So the facade was to be completely covered with metal cladding. A special, curved cladding type, rather new at the time, was imported from the UK, to give the effect of accurate and neat detailing. The money to enable this rather expensive effect was gained from the space frame that simultaneously was altered by the requirement to divide the hall of 30 x 48 m into two parts 30 x 30 m and 30 x 18 m by means of a suspended partitioning wall. This wall could only be located within the volume of the space frame and did literally cut through all lower chord members in longitudinal direction, that already should attract less bending moments than the shorter direction. So the decision was taken to change the geometry into a hybrid geometry of triangular space trusses, in upper module of 3 x 3 m and on a distance of 6 m, supported directly on columns each 6 m. The larger part of the sloped area became redundant for the main structural function and was only used for wind bracing by the triangulated elements and for a balcony for video and television cameras.

Jaap Oosterhoff commented on visiting Quintus, that he appreciated the resulting triangular trusses in the Octatube system by the relative graphical simplicity and by the 'bamboo' effect of the Octatube bars that were flattened and slightly widened near the joints.

5 Macro Space Frames

A special view on designing space structures in architecture becomes apparent when the architecture in space structures is regarded more literally: instead of designing space structure volumes, these spatial volumes can be enlarged on such a scale that an inhabitable space results. In these cases the structure is used as a place to live in. This item was very popular in the 1970s and was worked out in the studies of several architects, but has not lead to large-scale application. The stepping stones of these design concepts were:
1 The proposals of Archigram in the early sixties which showed space frames used as platforms suggesting complete freedom in flexibility of use. (fig 109)
2 The proposals of Yona Friedman who designed in the sixties giant space frames hovering over Paris in a second spatial layer in which containerised living areas were conceived. His proposals never came further than a town planning stage in design, published in magazins.
3 Stephane du Chateau designed and built a Community Centre in Rennes (Fr), where a macro-formed space frame was used as the primary skeleton that dominated the interior spaces.
4 The Dome Books issued in the USA in the early seventies as a result of the expression of an alternative way of life, in which many dome structures were described in self-build packages.
For students at architectural schools, designing with

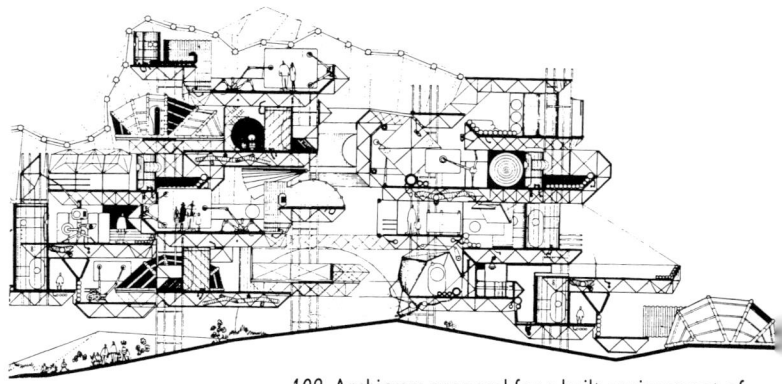

109 Archigram proposal for a built environment of a flexible society

polyhydronal volumes meant sharpening the 3-dimensional insight of students, and for non-conformative designers it was an alternative for designing in the Cartesian grid. In the Netherlands this way of thinking led to academic studies, stimulated largely by the late Joop de Graaf, teaching structural design at the Amsterdam Academy of Architecture. Greatly influenced by the spirits of the Dutch Structuralists like architect Pieter Blom, but even more stimulated by the then close-packing euphoria, a number of designs were made to show the potentials of polyhedrons as a close-packing system suitable for human use. Also these studies did not result in realisations. As a result of contacts laid at the 3rd International Conference on Space Structures held in Surrey, 1984, the author was stimulated to make a design proposal for a small housing estate in Wateringen NL in a close packing form. This stimulation was caused by the lecture of Francois Gabriel of Syracuse University, and was worked out in Delft by one of his former students, Neil Stempel. Although a more conventional design scheme was built, the author used this close-packing design as a simultaneous comparison with a realistic scheme. At that time a certain stimulus was the building of the tree-houses of architect Pieter Blom in Rotterdam, in which scheme a cubic volume was used, supported on one of its very corners, instead of normally on one of the faces. In the overall townscape of Rotterdam this complex of 'tree-houses' also inhabited by the Rotterdam Academy of Architecture and some little fashion shops manifests itself rather extravagantly, arousing excited discussions. A few years before, the author designed a house in a macro-form space frame , using the Octatube system as the basic skeleton: the horizontal floors were designed as frames of H-profiles, supported by nodes and bars in the space frame system under the well-known 45 degrees spatial angle. The module size is 3.6 m, the floor to floor height 2.8 m. This study was published in 'De Architect' of May 1981, and was a realistic proposal in a technical sense, but not very convincing as a design. These close-packing or macro-frame designs should be regarded as brain crackers in the sense of a study subject. In real life the building process usually is filled with enough errors, mistakes, and the consequences of miscommunications so that hardly anybody favours an even greater complexity of the current design geometry. Also the resulting architectural overall shapes are rather complex and amorphous (and in this respect typically 1970s), and not at all appealing in the current decade of cleanliness, abstraction and large architectural gestures. It represents more an inward looking attitude than an open-minded attitude, ready for the changing influences of time. The fact that a fully equipped building system was developed that can be built at any moment, does not reduce the significance that essentially it is an historical architectural idea.

One of the positive influences of macro frames, has led to the concepts of large space frame modules with for example 6 m tube lengths, and a storey height of 4.2 m in which tent structures are suspended. Several of these schemes are treated in paragraph 5.2 and 6.1 In this case the macro frames are the primary structures while the internally suspended stretched membranes form the covering. Another positive effect of the thinking in macro-frames are the proposals for more or less independent structures as building volumes in the form of large polyhedral forms: extended, flattened or deformed in another way. (see fig 108)

6 Single Curved Space Frames

Flat frames can be curved structurally or only technically. 'Technically' is a reference to a light camber in a flat frame to get a positive water drainage. 'Structurally': in case of large spans the arched form can help to minimize the bending moments by following the pressure-line, as a consequence of which the space frame will mainly be loaded by compression forces while the tensile forces are taken by the supports as horizontal reaction forces or by tensile tie-bars. This principle is valid both for small roofs and for large spans. In smaller spans usually the span-to-depth ratio is very small, the rigidity is very high and so no horizontal reaction forces are to be expected, apart from direct horizontal wind loading. This is the case with the barrel vaulted double layered space frames of 6 to 10 m span and a module of 1.5 to 2.0 m, with a structural depth of 1.0 to 1.5 m. In larger spans and more shallow depths horizontal spring forces will grow, but the structural designer is able to choose the re-

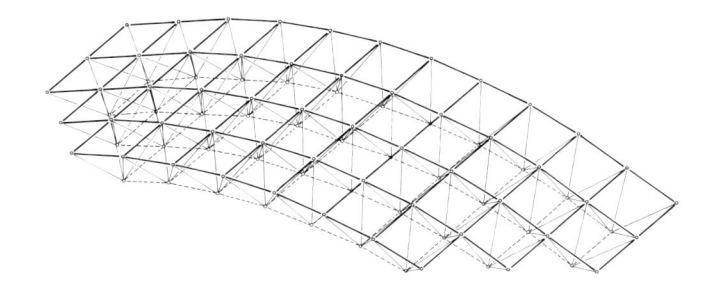

110 Slightly curved double layered space frame as an entrance canopy for the Mohammed Sultan office building in Kuala Lumpur MA. To be clad with structurally sealed glass panels. Octatube proposal 1987.

quired rigidity of the arched roof structure according to the capacity of the sub-structure to receive horizontal forces. Doing so, usually large dead-weight savings are reached compared with flat roofs.

An example is the proposal for an ice rink in Heereveen, NL, (1985) having a span of 90 m with an arch of 20 m height submitted as a space frame proposal in the overall form of a cylinder with two half domes at both ends. The proposal was done in hot dip galvanised steel Octatube, and resulted in a deadweight of only 0.25 kN/m2. The alternative in the same geometry and laminated timber as the structural material of the shafts of the Octatube bars, weighed even less: 0.20 kN/m2. In both cases the tendered costs of these 2 space frame proposals were found to be as high as a normal 50 m span in a flat frame. So by taking the same advantages as two or three hinged two-dimensional arches, used in conventional steel structures, also space frames can be reduced in weight and cost. When the architectural design asks a cylindrically formed space frame, to be clad with metal corrugated sheets, sandwich metal panels or glass panels, the structural scheme can make use of the reduced internal forces in the dimensioning of the composing elements. The result will be a slenderly dimensioned space frame.

A semi-cylindrical section gives the clear advantage of positive water drainage and strong form recognition. Structurally this form can be realised in two basic methods depending on the supports. In case of continuous supports on both sides of the span, the space frame is composed of arches, and can in reality be built from triangular curved space trusses: for example the shopping mall in Amsterdam Zuid-Oost NL. (figs 113 to 115) Here the structure rests upon an adjacent reinforced concrete structure. The design of this space frame was made by architect Ben Loerakker in co-operation with the author. The size of this arcade structure is 11 m wide, 5.5 m high and 34 m long, composed of a Tuball space

111 Interior detail of a cylindrical structure of one of the entrance canopies above the MRT underground stations on Orchard Boulevard in Singapore, formed by triangular trusses and clad with flat aluminium sandwich panels.

112 Interior views of one of the MRT entrance canopies in Singapore.

frame in module size 1.7 x 1.7 m on the outside chord members. In Photograph 114 the geometry can be seen as triangular trusses spaced 3.4 m apart, acting in fact as a 2.5-D structure: a composition of space trusses without interconnections of a structural nature in the longitudinal direction. The structure is clad with 6 mm laminated clear glass. As the arcade is ventilated at the bottom all around her perimeter (50 to 100mm) and the shopping street it covers is open on two opposite sides, solar accumulation or green house effects do not occur. The weight of these barrelvaulted structures might be as little as 0.05 to 0.1 kN/m2 in aluminium, while the same cylindrical forms in steel will weigh 0.15 kN/m2.

When the supports are not continuous but only located at the 4 ends of the cylinder, the space frame will be used in its full form: the shell theory will be applicable. In the cross section the space frame acts as a series of arches, and in the longitudinal direction as a shell and as a beam simultaneously. Depending on the largest span the loading of the separate elements can be quite considerable, and hence the deadweight of the barrelvaulted space frame will grow. Example is a 5-bayed semi-cylindrical space frame shell for the Serangoon Gardens Country Club in Singapore, realised in 1985 in Tuball. (fig 49 to 52) The size of each bay is 6 m wide and 20 m long, only supported at the four corners. Due to the building masses of the adjacent concrete structure that also functionally had to be followed, the 5 semi-cylinders were elongated by vertical space frame elements so that a total effect of a glass waterfall results. The structure consists of cast aluminium spheres, aluminium outside bar members and steel support nodes plus steel tubes in the bracings and lower chord members. All steel components are hot dip galvanised, the complete structure powdercoated. The structure is covered by laminated glass panels, with an outer panel of 6 mm grey tinted (solar energy absorbing) and heat strengthened glass, laminated by 3 PVB foils of 0.38 mm thickness, on 6 mm clear glass panels. The panels weigh approximately 1.5 kN per piece and had to be placed by hand. The resulting deadweight of the structure is 0.30 kN/m2.

The same space frame system of a semi-cylindrical form enheightened with vertical wall elements is conceived for the Arcade in Monchengladbach (D) of 70 m length and 5.5 m wide, composed of a space frame module 2 x 1.3 m supported every 10 m by free-standing but rigidly to space frame and foundation connected column supports. (fig 54) At a suggestion of project-architect Haasen, the tubular columns had to be placed as near to the shop fronts as possible, keeping the connections with

Architecture in Space Structures

113 Overall view of a shallow 12 m dome partly clad with panels, partly with insulated glass, and the main arcade on the Amsterdam Zuid-Oost shopping centre seen from the first parking floor above the shopping centre. Architect Ben Loerakker.

114, 115 Interior and exterior of the cylindrical arcade 11 m wide, 5.5 m high and 34 m long in a delta truss system supported by all lower edge nodes: more elegant and minimal than the Serangoon atrium.

several joints in the space frame, and so resulting in columns that stick like independent elements inside the volume of the space frame. In order to minimise the costs, and to minimise the dazzling graphical look of a full frame, a special bar-topology was developed for this arcade : although the space frame has a discontinuous support (every 10 m), a grid system of interconnected triangular trusses was chosen, clearly with less rigidity than a full space frame, and hence the main horizontal triangular truss had to be triangulated in the rectangular module faces additionally. This space frame is at the very edge of structural possibilities, because the composing triangular truss elements suffer from torsional moments. The resulting independence of the space frame on the steel columns is used in a future second building phase to completely replace the adjacent one-story buildings by a two-story complex around the space frame arcade. This space frame is completely closed-off and the covering glass panels are insulating glass panes 6 mm outside, air space 12 mm and 3 + 3 mm laminated inside panes. A special detail developed for securing the watertightness of this arcade, made the introduction of additional skylight frames neccesary, so that the space frame module of 1.3 x 2 m is covered by two separate glass panels each 1.3 x 1 m in size.

The author has made several proposals for tennis halls for projects in Italy, out of which one proposal can be described as follows: a system of large triangulated arches spaced 18 m and a length of 36 to 40 m, with a single layered triangulated network in between, combining the full functional height of the tennis courts with as shallow as possible a structural depth. This type of structural scheme is a mixture of a 2-dimensional triangular space truss and a single layered cylindrical vault that is hybrid in its combination, but attractive in its costs.

A small example of a cylindrically formed space frame was proposed (but not awarded) for the Sultan Mohammed Office Complex in Kuala Lumpur, where the architect built a mixture of a Late-Modern all-glass office tower with a Post-Modern neo Louis XIV marble porch in front. The void between office building and porch had to be filled in by a transparent skylight. The proposal of the author was to design a slightly curved Tuball space frame, covered with a continuous laminated glass panel, bent in situ. The perspective drawing in fig 110 gives an overview of the proposed space frame between the marble porch and the glass office with internal and external corners in plan. Structurally this frame was to act as a slightly curved flat frame.

A second example is the design by the author for the

Single Curved Space Frames

116 Model of a diverging and cylindrical / conical double layered space frame canopy as one of the original proposals for a contemporary music pavilion on the Prinsenhof courtyard in Delft. Design Author.

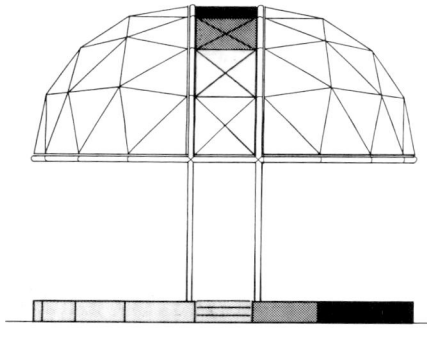

117 Final proposal for the Prinsenhof Music pavilion in Delft 1988. The two distinct faces are directed towards the street and towards the garden as the pavilion is situated on the borderline between a garden and the street. The grey tinted glass panels form the elongation of the separation between street and garden. Design Author.

covering of the reception atrium in the Exchange of Rotterdam. This complex was recently enlarged with a high rise office tower with two typically outward curved facades, filled with green glass. This new office tower acts as a city landmark in Rotterdam centre. At the time of the first discussions with the client, the author suggested to him that most probably the observer could see this green tower through the glass atrium roof when this was covered in transparent glass material. So one could see from the inside what the rest of town could see from the outside. Also it would be very logical to give the atrium (sized 10 x17 m) the same curved form as the green walls of the office tower, but then in cross section. The project is completed in April 89.

A third example is the atrium covering of the Museum of Education in Rotterdam, sized in plan 7 x 17 m, where the transparent glass covering had to enclose a volume in which also a 3.6 m high elevator tower is situated. The design was made in consultation with the artist Toni Burgering who acted as the project-architect.

A last example in the category of cylindrically curved space frames is one of the proposals by the author to build a music pavilion in the courtyard of the Prinsenhof-Museum in Delft NL, invited by the city council. A total of four alternative designs were made at 4 different locations inside the courtyard, each leading to another form. The site directly against one of the long walls of the museum complex led to the proposal of a slightly curved space frame that slightly diverged in plan, too. The roof frame was proposed as a lightgrey Tuball-Plus space frame, with laminated clear glass panels on top, sealed with structural sealant, and giving a flush surface easy to be cleaned. The position of the pavilion is under large chestnut trees. The supports are slender vertical steel columns, rigidly connected to the concrete podium structure. The total design concept was aimed to be abstractly detailed and coated in minimal visual dimensions with almost invisible glass, and with a form and geometry that indeed is 20th century. Abstract designs like these can be appreciated as separate items, like a modern car standing in front of an ancient building can be appreciated as an independent design in contrast. The pavilion was to stand parallel to the Museum at the back, but 1.5 m in front of it. The size of the total pavilion is 5 x 7 m, with a free height of 2.5 m above the podium. The definitive choice was however a special dome structure, shown in fig 117.

7 Dome Space Frames

During the last decades geodesic domes have again popularised the use of dome structures. The term 'geodesics' is a contemporary title ascribed to the arcs on a spherical surface which represent the shortest distance between any two points on that surface. When applied to the architectural structural systems it becomes "... a frame of generally spherical form in which the main structural elements are interconnected in a geodesic pattern of approximate great circle arcs intersecting to form a three-way grid,...". (From Richard Buckminster Fuller, US patent nr 2-682-235).

A geodesic subdivision is only one way to conceive a dome geometry. The geodesic domes as invented and developed by Richard Buckminster Fuller are the most well-known geometrical types of spherical domes of our era, but other types are at least as frequently built. Spherical dome structures are a geometrically simple

118, 119, 120 Overall view, interior and details of the main dome dia 15.5 m over the Orchard Boulevard MRT station in Singapore, clad with aluminium sandwich panels/insulated glass panels. The five lower panels are 4 double smoke exhausts hinged on both sides and one service door, hinged on the upper side. All elements have been detailed with an internally surrounding welded steel gutter with details; working like a car door type 'hatch back'.

and pure form of dome structure, but other types of dome structures that are non-spherical rotation surfaces also do exist, as do dome surfaces with the characteristic property of a double positive curvature but with an irregular geometry. A geometry with positive curvature. Basically different skeleton-like dome structures are characterised by the subdivision of the dome surfaces:
- triangles
- rectangles
- pentagons/hexagons

Of these categories only the triangulated dome is stable in its own plane when built with hinged connections. The square subdivision will need additional wind (or torsional) bracings, or will need rigid connections. Pentagons and hexagons will need additional bracings (compare fig 41) or need to be stabilised by tensile elements and perpendicular naves. (compare fig 133) These requirements influence the statical systems and, of course, the design of the space frame system. The span of the dome and the chosen module will influence the sensibility of the structure against local buckling. For spans larger than 30-40 m. usually a double layered grid is chosen, with outside or 'chord-'members of squares, rectangles and trapezoids. The dome designs realised by the author were up to 20 m high. Single layered and triangulated as visually minimal glass covered domes, (bar length max 2.5 m), and up to 40 m as domes covered by stretched membranes with bar lengths of 8 to 11 m. The

Dome Space Frames

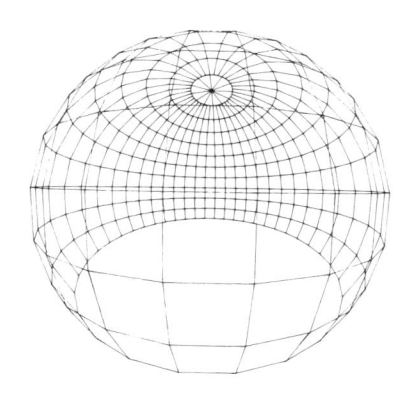

121 Computer perspective of the outer chord members of a double layered space frame dome structure, as one of the proposals for a Science Park in Rotterdam (1987). Architect Joost Paré (AGS).

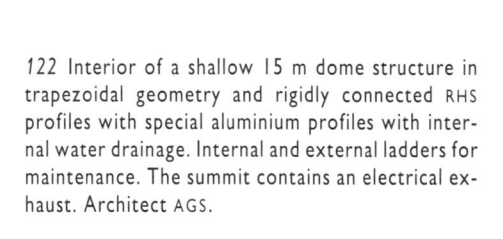

122 Interior of a shallow 15 m dome structure in trapezoidal geometry and rigidly connected RHS profiles with special aluminium profiles with internal water drainage. Internal and external ladders for maintenance. The summit contains an electrical exhaust. Architect AGS.

123 Third and final proposal for the Rotterdam Science Park dome: diameter 70 m, height 48 m, in a double layered three way grid: internal chord members in hexa/pentagonal geometry, with suspended prestressed double membranes in between. In the air space between the 2 layers is 80 mm rockwool insulation. Module size some 6 m. (model is simplified, only the outside layer is shown).

124 Model scale 1 to 100 of the Octatube proposal for the dome of the Basilique de la Paix in Yamasoukro (Ivory Coast). Dome 90 m diameter and 75 m height. As the concrete substructure already had a height of 100 m, and the marble works were executed at the same time as the roof structure was to be built: the logistical problem of erection overruled all other design aspects. The structural design was an alternative to the traditional flat truss scheme by the project architect.
The overall design of the basilica is a 2 to 1 scale copy of the St.Peter's basilica in Rome. The model was presented by the French contractor Sitraba to the President of the Ivory Coast republic, but the tender was not successful. A similar structure is currently under construction.

125 Soldering of the model took about four weeks with three to four designers (1987). Computer drafting of the presentation drawings two days and one engineer.

figures in this paragraph show different types of geometries. In the single layered triangulated dome structures the most practical geometry appeared to be not the geodesic geometry but the 'network' geometry. In this 'network' geometry the dome surface is formed by concentric horizontal rings of equal bar elements that in the areas between the rings are triangulated. See figs 118, 119 and 126, 127. The advantages of this geometry are the relative freedom to shape the cross section of the dome and the ease of connecting the dome to the horizontal perimeter structure. The shaping of the cross section becomes an evident freedom when one realises that dome structures are quite unique architectural phenomena and are in size always strictly regulated by the project dimensions. that is to say: all dome sizes are always different. There is no standard. That is valid in plan size or diameter, but also for the diameter-to-height ratio. Semi-spherical domes like the Singapore MRT of fig 118 are special types of dome. Most of the domes will be more shallow like the glass atrium domes for Tanfield House in Edinburgh (fig 126). Special items are the designs of church domes (figs 124, 125) and mosque domes (figs 14, 127). Mosque domes are more vertical in section and also non circular, like the flame-like dome in Singapore (figs 37, 38) and the pointed Malaysia dome proposals. Network geometries give the designer flexibility to decide separately on horizontal sections and vertical sections. Another possible distinction is that of the composing structural system:
• continuous structural material as is the case in shell structures with reinforced concrete, and glassfiber reinforced polyester. These structures have not been part of the author's work and will therefore not be dealt with in more detail;
• discontinuous structural material, ranging from a shell surface with openings, and prefab concrete (beam-and-slab) elements oo pure skeleton structures of metal, timber or plastics.

As the main interest of the author is in space frames in several forms, only his dome structures are illustrated that are composed from bar-like elements. Domes have a form that contributes enormously to their rigidity, so the actual thickness of the dome structure can be very thin. Just compare the thickness and size of an eggshell with its rigidity, or the 50 mm thick reinforced concrete domes sprayed over an inflatable flexible casting, designed by Dante Bini often spanning over 30 m. Spherical domes have the property of containing a maximum vol-

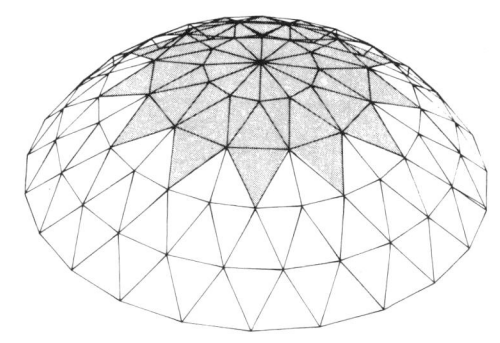

126 Perspective drawing of a shallow 15 m diameter skylight dome for three atrium coverings on the Tanfield House head office in Edinburgh. Architect Michael Laird & Partners (John Perreur Lloyd). Rastered top elements aluminium sandwich panels, lower elements are double glass consisting of laminated 4.4.1 lower plates and solar reflective upper plates (intermediate proposal). Realisation May-July 1989.

127 Perspective computer proposal for a standard 18/22 m diameter dome structure for the smaller state mosque domes in Malaysia, in anodised gold-bronze Tuball-Plus and dark blue enammelled steel sandwich panels. (1986) The geometry of the structure is a network geometry: horizontal rings with triangulated bracings around an imaginary central axis of rotational symmetry, like modelling work of a pottery / vase. (design author)

ume inside a minimal surface compared to other enveloping forms. This property is, however, not often used in architectural reality (apart from liquid gas storage tanks or pneumatic domes), as it is only a theoretical basic datum that functioned as an intellectual challenge during the early development of modern dome structures.

8 Saddle Space Frames

Anti-clastically formed (or 'saddle shaped') space frames continue a technological development of shell structures that began in this century with reinforced concrete, continued in laminated timber and in glassfiber reinforced polyester, but practically has been stopped in all those materials. The high costs of labour, scaffolding and of formwork have ended these developments, but of course also the changed architectural styles aiming more at a silent and modest than a jubilant impression.   From a structural point of view this geometry is also worth while looking at for space frames. The same advantages in material gain that were the goal in developing concrete shells, can be obtained in designing single layered and triangulated space frame shells for smaller spans and double layered saddle formed space frame shells for larger applications. In history one of the last works of Felix Candela was the Olympic stadium in Mexico, composed of a grid system of macro-trusses filled with individual smaller hypar shells in the form of an aluminium (triodetic) space frame. His Mexican successor Castaño also has built a number of these single layered saddle shaped space frames in the Triodetic system in aluminium. And at last in Japan a saddle shaped double layered space frame has been built over a theater by Nippon Steel. The computer is now increasingly used not only during the statical analysis but also during the subsequent phase of element engineering. This has enabled the semi-automated preparation of elements of different lengths and angles to be executed at only a modest extra price compared with equal elements. This fact could be regarded as one of the virtues of the use of computers in the field of space frames: computers make space frames composed of different elements possible at relatively low extra costs compared with standard frames. An absolutely indispensable datum for those renaissance of saddle shaped roofs is that the resulting architectural expression is appreciated by project-architects. This is more a question of personal taste and suitability in the overall architectural scheme and style than purely technical hindrance. The eventual renaissance of 'truss-like'

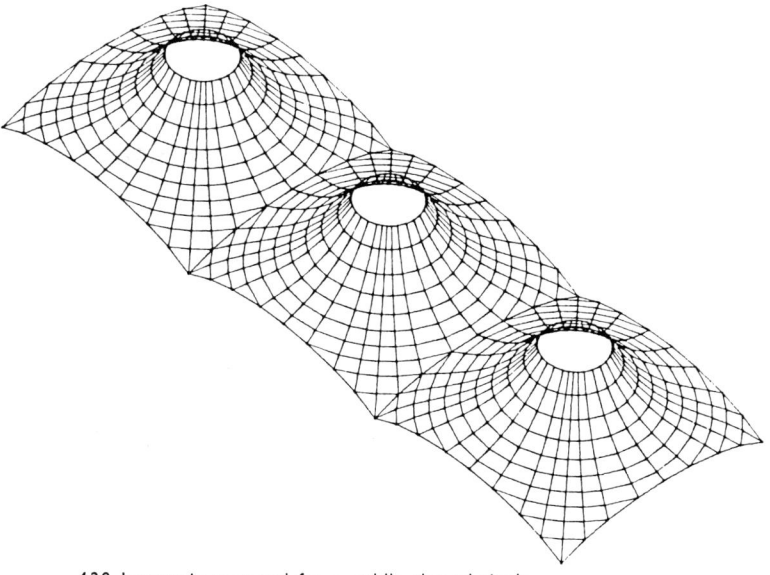

128 Isometric proposal for a saddle shaped single layered space frame to be stabilised by the plywood infill panels (instead of stabilising diagonal bracings), for the Circus Theater in Zandvoort (NL). Architect Sjoerd Soeters. In contradiction with dome structures the horizontal elements get compression forces, the vertical elements tension. The idea was to introduce a continuous prestress cable in the vertical elements producing a rather hybrid structural system: something between a cable net structure and a space frame structure: Or a prestressed space frame. Because of acoustical problems, the roof will be built in reinforced concrete.

saddle-shape structures will have to be prefaced by an exact analysis of the rise and fall of saddle shells in other materials. Saddle shaped space frames should also gain from the knowledge of membrane and cable net structures of the 1960s and 1970s in regard to the complete freedom of form and lack of regularity displayed in these forms, and the strict geometrical regularity of hypar shells.

5 Tensile Structures

Space frames are structures that essentially are only loaded by normal forces acting either in compression or in tension. In order to cope with loadings from changing directions that sometimes result in tension for one loading case and compression for another loading case, the average space frame elements are dimensioned to take both kind of forces. All bar elements are normally tubular elements. This could be called a pragmatic approach. A more theoretical approach is based upon the more extreme distinction between tensile and compressive elements, and dimensioning both groups of elements purely on these tasks. As compressive elements usually can take a certain amount of tensile force, but, reversedly, purely tensile elements cannot take any buckling, the mechanism of pre-tensioning is introduced, to turn passive tensile forces into an active tensile sub-system that also can resist compression forces. In this case in the neutral (= purely pre-tensioning) situation all tensile elements have a certain amount of tension, and the compressive elements have a certain amount of compression. External loadings may result in heightening of the tension in the tensile elements, for which purpose they are well equipped. It may also result in reduction of the pretension (tension and compression can be added). This is only possible to a certain degree, until the total pretension has been neutralised in fact by the introduced compression. The group of tensile structures consists of three main categories:

• Tensegrity Structures with a continuous and active tensile sub-system and a discontinuous compressive sub-system, integrated to closed structural entities.
• Stretched Membranes with spatially curved actively prestressed membranes or cablenets as main features with additional tensile elements and compressive elements for a final stabilisation of these open structural systems.
• Spatially Guyed Structures where the main character is the enforcement of other types of structures by individual tensile elements. This category of structures contains simple underspanning poles for reinforcement of beams, and larger underspanning or hanging masts under tensile roof surfaces (membranes and cable nets), compressive roof surfaces (tensegrity domes) or bended roof structures: flat plates, beam-and-plate structures, but also guy systems in flat trusses (e.g. Polonceau trusses) or spatial trusses (bicycle wheel roof systems) and suspension of all kinds of outward turned structures where horizontal elements are suspended from poles and masts via guy cables.

129 The Hemweg tensegrity structure in Amsterdam (See fig 64).

1 Tensegrity Structures

The culmination in the art of 'Juggling with Structures' is formed by the so-called tensegrity structures, invented as an artistic-academic feature by Kenneth Snelson, and brought to its worldwide popularity by his teacher Richard Buckminster Fuller. These structures are composed of linear elements that are loaded only by normal forces: either tension or compression. These elements acting under tension and compression are distinctly separated and as a further characteristic compressive elements are never connected directly. Therefor the connection cables have to be prestressed. The result is always an entity of forces, an equilibrium of tensile and compressive forces that allow these structures to be independent of any site or situation. As the starting point formulated here is rather theoretical, it is no wonder that the development of these structures was greatly stimulated by inputs from the mathematical and mechanical side. The sculptural and non-functional result of these structures betrays inputs from artistic designers that regarded tensegrity structures as the most 'l'art pour l'art' structures: structures of mainly academic and artistic interest. The author was lucky to cooperate in the case of two tensegrity structures with artists, profiting both from their spatial insights as from the sculpture budgets that allowed for a larger degree of experimentation than is usually possible in building industry contracts. A personal effect was gained by introducing stretched membranes inside these tensegrity structures to enlarge the dramatic effect of the structure as a sculpture, and to have a more practically usable roof. The first of these two sculptures was the structure at the Hemweg Electricity Plant in Amsterdam (fig 23, 64, 129), the second one was the sculpture at the Maritime Museum in Amsterdam. (figs 61, 62)

In addition to the above information on these projects, a distinction has to be made between relatively simple structures and more complex structures. From the intellectual point of view the more complex, the more attractive the object should be, the higher the reward after completion. A relatively simple four-poled twist tensegrity such as at the Maritime Museum has a direct, single-sided and overwhelming impact compared with the more fractured and complicated Hemweg structure. So even in complex structures the designer's opinion marks a route towards simpler and clearer design solutions, that combine simplicity with spatial effects and visual strength. The author sees a main impulse radiating from his experiences of designing with tensegrity structures as the liberation from conservative ideas on structural design which often lead to repetitive schemes. Thinking in academic terms about these absolute tensegrities enlightened the way of looking at structures in general, and of manipulating or juggling with structures.

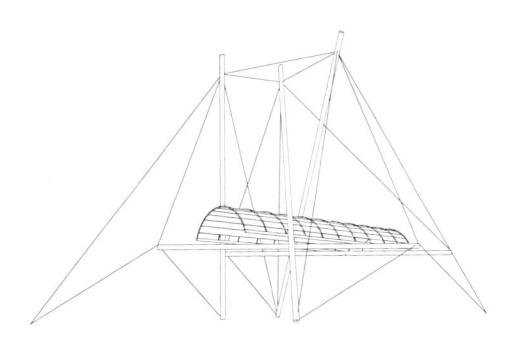

130 Perspective design drawing for an entrance canopy with a red acrylic barrel vault stabilised with stainless steel masts in a tensegrity structure, for Fashion Garden, Amsterdam. Architect Jan Dirk Peereboom-Voller. Completion June 1989.

131 Overall picture of the tensegrity canopy for the 'Nederlanden van 1870' office in Diemen (fig 134).

132 Construction picture of the tensegrity supports of the triangular truss bridge in the Exchange in Amsterdam for an exhibition in 1987. (fig 59)

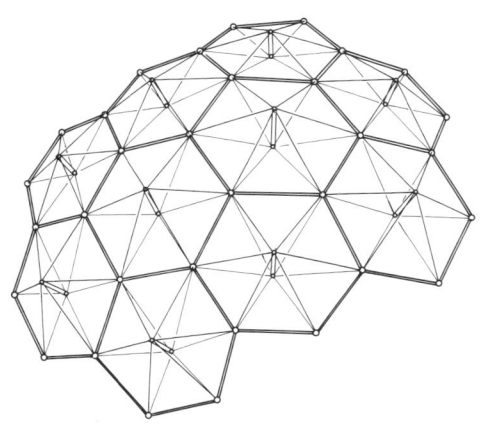

133 Design proposal for a 70 m tensegrity dome over an exhibition area in Sevilla. Because of the relative high deflection of this type of structure, the most suitable cladding system is a prestressed membrane: PTFE coated glassfiber (flexible and high temperature resistant). The overall structure is built up of hexagonal and pentagonal 'bicycle wheels': steel bars 6 m in length, stabilised with double guy cables over a central tensegrity mast.

134 Model for an entrance canopy in front of the office of De Nederlanden van 1870 in Diemen (NL): a floating space frame suspended and stabilised by a cable system fixed by 4 tensegrity poles, piercing independently through the space frame. (fig 131) Length of poles 14 m, space frame 5.4x12,6 m. The 4 pole footings rest upon a roundabout in front of the 9 story office building, so that the actual canopy reaches out towards the building. The height of the office tower is balanced by the height of the poles. Designed in 1987 by the author with architect Maarten Grasveld.

Two more examples of this enlightened design process are the tensegrity bridge supports in the 'Nederland 2050' exhibition in Amsterdam 1987 (par 3.7.10), and a design for an entrance canopy for 'De Nederlanden van 1870' insurance company in Diemen NL. (fig 131,134) In this latter design the architect of the office building, Maarten Grasveld, invited the author to co-design an entrance canopy that was in harmony with his high-rise building. The entrance lobby had no expression as yet, and at that place the facade was to be 9 stories high and the front piazza with a small roundabout for car traffic, rather compressed. The design was presented as a tensegrity structure as a self-supporting vertical structure consisting of 4 poles 14 m high, standing on the concrete edge of the roundabout / flower basin, in order to obtain a gesture in harmony with the 'overpoweringly high' building at the background. The actual roof was to be a Tuball standard space frame cantilevering from the tensegrity structure, and reaching towards the building tipping just above the main entrance's small turnstile. The space frame was to inhabit a flat suspended sandwich roof panel with integrated drainage and lighting.

Generally speaking there are some drawbacks for tensegrity structures to become popular structures.
- Firstly, they are very complicated structures, that only recently can be calculated by computer programs capable of coping with large deformations and the overstressing or overpressing of cables.
- Secondly, the geometrical complexity of most of the tensegrities make them only wanted by very persistent designers with a completely 3-dimensional insight. This claim is valid for the primary structure but even more so for the eventual cladding system, that automatically leads to hand-made 3-dimensional modelling.
- Thirdly, really building tensegrities and especially establishing the theoretically required pretensioning stage is a very labourious process by virtue of the high degree of interconnection between all the elements. Consequently there is high degree of freedom (of external loadings to be distributed in internal stress-distribution patterns). It makes the erection crew members want to have 14 arms at the same time, like the Indian Godess Shiva.
- Fourthly, the relative large deformations under external loadings make these structures only suitable to be combined with cladding elements of equal flexibility and deformability, for example stretched membranes, leading to a certain limitation of functional use.
- Lastly, the geometrical wildness of these structures makes them not very practical to design with as an application in an overall architectural scheme.

So most of the applications realised by the author are free standing sculptural elements. The tensegrity bridge towers from fig 132 were rented out to the exhibition at the time, and later have been used in The Hague for a music programme on one of the squares in The Hague NL. Four different space frame towers were used one of them was composed of the two tensegrity bridge supports, stacked on each other in a double-twisted spiral with a platform on top, where a Japanese drummer was performing.

2   Stretched Membranes

Amongst the different types of space structures, the category of the stretched membranes takes an outstanding place by virtue of the spatial curvatures in its design: more than other categories it is a combination of science and art, of scientific know-how and designers' emotion. Many steps in the process of design and realisation of these stretched membranes are taken emotionally or visually, more than on the basis of dry and real facts. And indeed: at first sight the visual examination of stretched membranes is already ruthless. Membranes show every wrinkle: a large risk both for the designer and for the producer. But when a membrane structure finally is completed, it can be a pure source of visual delight. Stretched membranes are spatial structural systems where the membranes under tensile stresses take a major part in the structural behaviour of entire structures. According to this definition there are two major different types of stretched membranes, characterised by the nature of the pretension: either from overpressure (pretension caused by air perpendicular to the surface of the membrane), or from pretension in the surface of the membrane:
- Pneumatic Membranes
- Prestressed Membranes

Both types of stretched membrane structures have been developed mainly after the second world war, that essentially gave her influence in two impulses. In the field of the pneumatic structures the American radomes built by Walter Bird in his Birdair Company were responsible for the first pneumatic structures to cover the newly developed radar installations at the end of the war. In that time pneumatic structures were the only type of non-metallic structures for completely covering the radar machinery. Prestressed membranes have been studied thoroughly and made popular by Frei Otto, who was motivated in post-war Germany by the lack of available material to build bridges and roofs: directly after the war

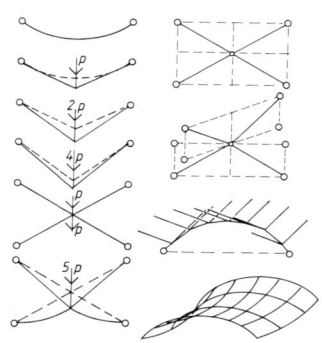

135 Diagram of development from a single suspended cable to a prestressed cable net or membrane weave.

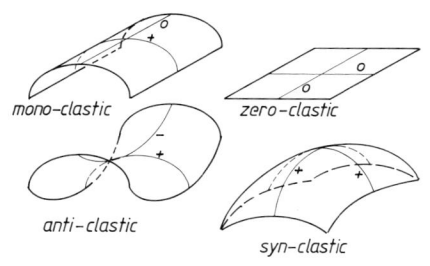

136 Diagram of anti-clastically, mono-clasically, zero-clastically and syn-clastically curved membranes.

137 Hot air balloon

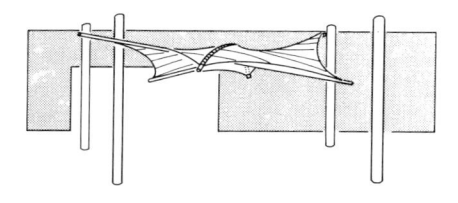

138 Open air-supported structures: the Genova and Balloon sails.

139 Diagram of the flying kite in the Hemweg canteen, Amsterdam. The form of the kite and the instreaming air above it would cause a lifting movement. Design Loes van der Horst.

he developed his minimal material theory in his dissertation 'Das hängende Dach' in 1952.[5]

Prestressed Membranes Prestressed membrane structures belong to the most basic structures in a structural sense in that they are composed of materials that can only resist tensile stresses for the membrane surface and mainly compression for the masts, arches and other bar-like elements. The nature of these differences has been followed very thoroughly by its developers: tensile surfaces that also could resist bending stresses were not appreciated as purely stretched membranes, for example the two olympic stadia designed by Kenzo Tange in Tokyo, 1964. The roof areas of the indoor gymnasium and the swimming pool were formed by pre-curved steel sections with steel cladding on top: mechanically these roofs behaved neither as a suspended roof, nor as a conventional beam structure: the beams gave reduction in bending moments comparable to a purely suspended roof, or the suspended form gave the beams a far larger span. The result had advantages of combining two techniques.

From Cable Crossing to Membrane The technique of prestressed membranes is based on the logic of stabilising a roof structure using only tensile material. When a cable is spanned between two points, it will sag because of its own dead weight in the form of a catenary. Depending on the sag, the form of the catenary almost resembles that of a parabola that is more easy to calculate, but that strictly only resents the deformation of a weightless element under loading uniform in projection. The height of the sag is an indication for the resulting horizontal forces; the vertical forces remain unchanged. (fig 135) The influence on the suspended cable by an external force can be imagined as a sharp V-formed line that is sharper when the magnitude of deadweight and load differs. The resulting form of the cable can exactly be calculated by its bending moment, numerically and graphically. A second and equal loading will cause an additional deformation of the cable that is in magnitude less than the first one. That is to say: each next loading has less influence. This process might be continued until the additional deformation of the last added loading is acceptably small. Presuming the cable is still strong enough to hold the tensile forces, the added loadings and the consequently declining deformations indicate that for practical reasons cables are only workable in structures when they are preloaded. In real practice this preloading can be done by adding a large dead-weight like reinforced concrete, (symbolizing suspended structures) or by introducing counterspanning cables that result in an equally large preloading force: a cable crossing, symbolizing prestressed structures. External vertical loads in downward direction will work out as an addition of the tensile forces in the upper cable and a reduction in the lower cable. The process of adding more deadweight can continue until the lower cable has no pretension left. On that very moment all additional stresses will go directly to the upper cable. Going to this ultimate stage only has the advantage of smaller deflections compared with the initial stage.

As structures with minimal deadweight suffer from external loading under different magnitudes and directions, this cablecrossing principle is able to resist both downward and upward forces. In addition to that, when the lower cable is twisted 90 degrees the cable crossing still acts, but is spatially stable. Adding more hanging cables in the cable crossing, combined with more (downward) spanning cables, has the principle of the anti-clastically curved cable net as an outcome. (Fig 6) As a result of the described principles in general the suspended structure has larger deformations under external loading than the prestressed structure. Loadings are likely to change in direction or magnitude: upward and downward wind, snow on one side of the structure, caused by wind direction and slope of the roof, etc. In this respect the prestressed principle applicable to all external loadings, is a more adequate answer in its structural requirements than the suspended principle.

For a fair overview of the entire solution for practical building purposes, the resulting reaction forces of the cable action schemes will have to be taken into account. For practical applications also the consequences for the entirety of the system are important to regard. As for elements necessary to make a balanced whole, like guy cables and reinforced concrete foundations it is extremely important to realise that it is no good to concentrate upon minimising the prestressed part of the structure when the rest of the total structure is not taken into account. In many studies only the virtue of the pretension principle was under study rather than entire structures. Only in the case of tensegrity structures the entirety of the structure is always regarded. Frei Otto used the above described principles in his books:[5, 6] 'das hängende Dach' and in 'Zugbeanspruchte Konstruktionen 1 und 2'.

Prestressed membranes are made of a woven membrane or (in a larger scale form) a cable net. Both materials have elements with similar properties in two perpendicular directions: warp and weft. In coated weaves properties between the warp and weft directions differ only in the magnitude of small percentages, while usually cable nets have cables of similar cross-section and strength in two directions. The consequence of this similarity is that this material is used optimally when in both directions stresses are equal. That is, the stresses from pretension and external loading should be divided over the two directions as equally as possible. The two cable directions should therefore be designed in the same curvature and span. The typical form-type resulting from this technique is anti-clastically curved (two cables in different directions). Compare this with the form of a linear suspended roof: zero-clastically curved or with the form of a hanging square roof: syn-clastically curved. (fig 136). Domes are also syn-clastically curved structures, but then upwardly directed. No wonder that 'bungalow' type tents can be blown from the camping site by severe winds, and no wonder that occasionally circus tents are reported to be damaged by windstorms. These types of tents do not have the right type of stabilising membrane. In fact the recognition of the pretension principle has been very important for the further development and manufacturing of tentstructures, as Peter Stromeyer has recognised (being one of Europe's master tent builders in the fifties and sixties) when he supported the investigations of Frei Otto in the 1960s.

Cutting Patterns An important indication for spatial stability is the development of separate strips of which a membrane is composed. Classical tents like the big circus tents are not or hardly tailored: they are made of straight-edged rolls of cotton weave. A real anti-clastically formed tentstructure needs to be composed of strips of material that have each been tailored, or slimfitted: the hollowness of the sides of the strips is decisive for the shape and potential smoothness of form and hence the capability to take any external loading. Hollow-cut strips are typical for anti-clastical tents, as bulging strips are typical for syn-clastical tents (like pneumatic structures). The underestimation of the importance of a good cutting pattern for a spatially curved membrane is responsible for the continuous manufacturing of ill-cut tents that fold and wrinkle. The central axiom in tent structures is that a tent only is optimal when both warp and weft are utilised in the same order of magnitude: wrinkles always mean an over-stressing in one direction and simultaneous understresssing in the other direction. That is why a good tent should first of all be visually without wrinkles.

Pneumatic Structures Although Walter Bird built the first pneumatic structure in 1946 as a radome of

18 m, gas heated warm-air balloons and zeppelins were quite well known even in the 19th century. (fig 137) But they were not regarded as possible inspirations for terrestrial structures. Everybody knows now that there are many tools in our daily life based upon the pneumatic principle that simply are non-existing without this very principle: the pneumatic tyres of a car mean so much for comfort of machine and man that without the over-pressurised air, cars would fall apart after the first test drive. And inflatable life jackets, life boats, emergency exits for large passenger planes or water mattresses for health and air inflated mattresses for therapeutical purposes at the benefit of autistic children. And we also know the same principle in the form of open pneumatic structures in yacht sails, parachutes and wind-gliders. (fig 138) The development of pneumatic structures has been very substantial in size in the fifties and sixties, but during the last 2 decades it took place mostly in the United States. In Europe pneumatic structures are hardly used any more after the first oil-crisis in 1973 that made electricity and heating more expensive. Apparently not so in the United States, where the applications that have been developed during the last 2 decades mainly are coverings of big indoor stadia, covering spans of 100m and more. For these applications the normally used a membrane fabric of the seventies, PVC-coated polyester weave, has been replaced by the more durable and incombustable PTFE-coated fiberglass. On spans of such a magnitude the membranes have been reinforced by a macro-scaled cable net to take up the main stresses. These reinforced pneumatic structures have only a deadweight of approximately 0.05 to 0.10 kN/m2 and can be regarded at first sight (apart from the foundations) as the real lightweight structures.

Tents Always Stir Going back to the reality of prestressed membranes and inflatables, the foretold comparison means that an open structure will receive more suction on its surface by the two-fold action of the wind than a closed volume. Open prestressed tent structures can hence be attacked by higher wind loads than closed off tent structures and inflatables. (This also applies in conventional structures for the loading of open canopies like petrol stations compared with closed halls). For prestressed membranes this also means that by the changing hollow and bulky forms of the anti-clastical surfaces by definition a very quick-changing pattern of upward and downward forces will be the result of external windloadings: Pretensioning is a must! Compared with sails, the aim of structural design of stretched membranes is to obtain a steadfast structure, and not a moving one. But the principle can be used to stabilise the membrane skin. The description of the air streams around a sail illustrates which air currents occur around our buildings and with what result. With soft structures like stretched membranes this can be very important because external wind loadings can cause a deformation. Other negative consequences of unexpected wind attack are the same as those at more conventional buildings (which deserve more attention). Wind means for a tent structure that there will be a deformation from the neutral, prestressed or inflated form. Wind, but also snow and rain means deformation of the tent structure. We have to remain in control of this deformation, but nevertheless deformations will continue to exist. For the tent structure of the Veronica Broadcasting Company in the Netherlands designed by the author, 1982, the statical analysis of wind loadings could be tested on site by several severe wind storms. (fig 63) Windstreams around a surface of a stretched membrane can easily be assessed by woollen threads on its surface. These threads indicate the direction and the local pressure or suction on the surface of the membrane.

During the design stadium of a double indoor flying kite project as a work of art in the canteen of the Hemweg Electricity Plant in Amsterdam, the aeroplane wing principle was also valid. By the instream of the airconditioning the designed flying kites would start to lift at a given speed of the air and deadweight of the kites! These kites would really lift off only by the action of the artificial airco. Talk about integration of art and aircondition technology! (fig 139)

Statical Analysis Statical analysis of tent membrane usually is a rather complicated matter when all consequences of external loadings are taken into account. Prestressed and inflated membranes each follow different procedures. Prestressed membranes can result in quite different statical results by the integration of the compressive elements. These elements can form an independent skeleton, that surrounds a tent, or can interplay harmoniously in the total system that composes tensile and compressed elements inseparably at the same level. The statical analysis of this last action is far more complicated than the first one. During the last years in a number of places in the world adequate computer programs have been developed to simulate the statical analysis of stretched membranes, but these programs are rather protected from regular use outside the originating engineering firms. The times of openness as displayed by Frei Otto are over. Hence a manual approach is indispensable.

140 Modular Tent structures in office projects in Hoofddorp (See par 3.7.14).

141 Model of movable tent roof for leisure park 'De Efteling' in Kaatsheuvel NL. Height arch. 25 m., span 60 m. ground plan E 60 m. diameter (not realised)

142 Temporarily entrance canopy for the palace of Her Majesty the Queen of the Netherlands in The Hague. This structure is only installed for reception of official guests.

143 Tent structure of a stage covering for AVRO's Sterrenslag in Kaatsheuvel NL 1987. Size 20 m wide, 8 m high and 8 m deep.

144 Sun shade tent structure on the south terrace for an old age home in Dongen (NL), 1975, designed and realised by Egbert Töns and the author.

Physical Behaviour   Apart from the material development of the correct membrane material being the first obstacle during the development of membrane structures during the last 3 decades, the second obstacle is formed by the physical behaviour of membrane structures. The lack of material mass, and the low insulation value of the thin skins lead to poor summer conditions, often referred to as a 'greenhouse' effect. This effect is slightly hindered by the white reflective skin, sometimes reinforced by aluminium foil, and by ventilation: the chimney effect in stretched membranes and electrical fans on inflatables. In winter, on the other hand, the insulation value is very low, a large energy loss is expected through the membrane. The comfort is low because of the large flow of cold air. In practice many of the inflatables for human use like tennis halls have been provided with an extra internal skin to double the insulation value. This second skin is mostly suspended without additional overpressure inside the structural inflatable, in the form of an oversized drapery, with wrinkles and folds, improving the acoustic climate at the same time because the 'drum' effect disappears. In order to improve this scheme, a second blower with outside air would prevent internal condensation between the two skins. And of course, it would be a great step foreward in the development of membrane structures if one of the manufacturers of fabrics would develop a skin with the same structural properties as usual, but coated with an additional insulation layer, preferably translucent, with a dampproof interior finish and still high-frequency weldable. An alternative solution would be to use separate skins at a distance of 0.3 to 1 m, where space in-between would be ventilated with outside air, as most of the first year schoolbooks on building physics show, while the outer part of the inner skin is provided with a 30 to 100 mm thick insulation layer of mineral wool. Alas this coincides with a loss of daylight penetration, as the usual insulation materials are neither transparent nor translucent, but the inner climate as a whole can be regulated. (fig 128 Circus Theater in Zandvoort NL)

Considerations of physical nature show how one-sided the initial development of membrane structures has been in the past: the aim was to use a minimal amount of material and a structural efficiency, neglecting at the same time most of the other complex factors that make structures more complete buildings. The development of stretched membranes was solely focused on one aspect, neglecting physical, functional and formal requirements, leading to an unbalanced design. As a consequence of which the early oil crise of 1973 with the raised energy costs came as a shock at first, and as a knock-out blow afterwards. It showed that developments like these, could better be performed within the overall complex pattern of the totality of the built environment, rather than taking only one element, ennobling it, while ignoring other design factors. That is why membrane structures now only are used for applications without severe acoustic or thermal insulation requirements: in the Dutch climate only coverings of outdoor spaces like market and street coverings, entrance canopies and , of course, temporary structures that can be dismantled within a short time and travel all around the country. (figs 145,146)

In other climates like Mediterranean and desert climates, membranes are mostly used as shade devices, and because of the surface temperatures have to be made of PTFE-coated fabric. For the public designs in the Western European countries in general one has to anticipate the danger of vandalism and graffiti-spraying on the skin. Most of the applications to frequently visited places like coverings of shopping centres, are hindered by the high requirements from fire-prevention officers. PVC usually is not allowed, in the United Kingdom even the use of PTFE material is hindered by the anticipated toxic fumes during fire.

Energy Costs   The high energy maintenance costs of membranes caused by heating a single skin, are obvious. At the same time inflatables and air-inflated structures (cushion-shaped with a higher overpressure in spaces without human access), require electricity to maintain the overpressure by a fan or compressor installation. The average costs of overpressure are usually one quarter of the costs of heating a non-insulated pneumatic structure, which can be considerable. A legal conclusion could be to replace the overpressure by another form of stabilisation: in stead of a continuous overpressured column of air, better take a more discontinuous outer or inner skeleton, from which the membrane is suspended or spanned over: this type of stabilisation does not require any additional overpressure for stabilisation.

The Italian structural designer Dante Bini has taken the intermediate solution by using the pneumatic way of blowing up structures to erect by inflation a temporarily supporting membrane that carries a metal outer skeleton. After the concrete casting and hardening the inflatable 'formwork' is removed.

Another trend in the United States is to replace the pneumatic principle of the large football domes by a system of hanging masts pushing the membrane on top upward, and stabilised by a complex system of underspan-

145 Sunshade cum entrance canopy in the form of a stretched membrane at the Octatube head office in Delft (NL).

146 Cable net structure composed of white double polyethylene cables dia 6 mm with alu clamps providing a graphical and sculptural play of lines against the dark background. (1976). Design Loes van der Horst and author.

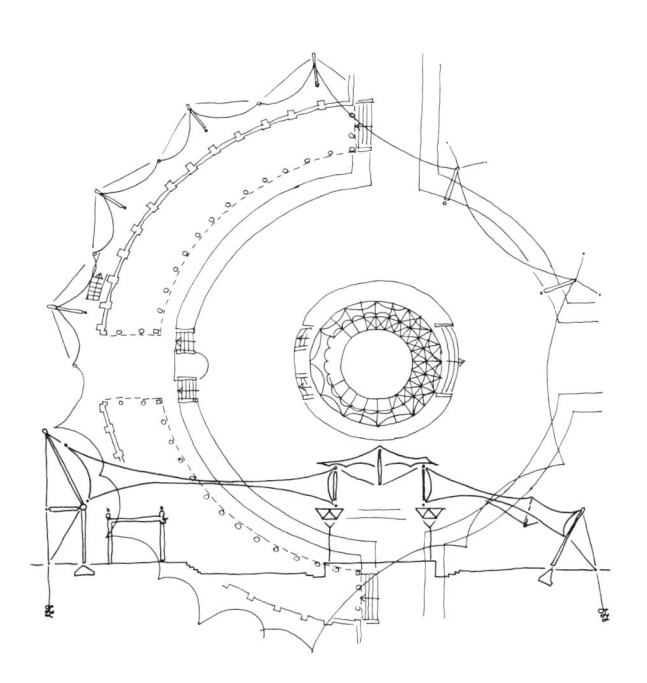

147 Proposal for a circular mobile tent structure to cover a part of the Baroque Royal Gardens of Het Loo palace in Apeldoorn (NL) during the Holland Festival 1988 by Anke Engelse and the author in 1987. Diameter 66 m.

ning cables: more a tensegrity principle.

Although the metal dome structure is a very material-efficient structure, of course the total amount of metal material is larger than the minimal amount required in an identical pneumatic structure. Pneumatic structures are the most material-efficient space structures. But when the design process consequently aims to fulfil more requirements, hybrid structures will be the result, that are not the most simple and straightforward structures, but fulfil a higher degree of total function of the building. Several examples of membrane domes have been designed and built by the author according to these principles which are described in more detail in the illustrative figures of par 6.1.

Anchor Solutions   A further obstacle is formed by the problems usually neglected in the first studies of membrane structures: the foundation. Often membrane structures are referred to as the most lightweight structures ever developed, but they are only that when foundations are not added as structural elements. There is more than only the visual light and translucent upper parts of these structures. Like in a sailing yacht not only the sails are important, but also the mast, the stays, and the body of the vessel, the same is valid for earthbound structures. Essentially there is a distinction between an open and a closed structural system. The open systems are composed of the stretched membranes, masts, arches or other compression elements and guy cables leading to anchors that in itself usually are not regarded as being

Stretched Membranes

part of a design job, but should be. Closed systems, on the other hand, regard the external pattern of forces of mainly compressive forces as being an integral part of the total structural stystem. There are advantages for both points of view. But we must not see stretched membranes as open systems at the edge of which the boundary forces are conjured from the ground level miraculously. We should rather regard systems of a closed entity of forces: tensile and compressive forces. The Dutch soil is very weak in producing tensile reaction forces. In most cases the solution is to design heavy deadweight foundations made of reinforced concrete, as tensile foundations in the form of grout anchors or screw anchors will not hold in the soft peaty soil. On the other hand government regulations might lead to the approval of heavy deadweight foundations as the only directly calculable types of foundations, which can lead to surprises: in case of the Munich Olympic Games cable net roofs, the deadweight of the underground reinforced concrete structures was responsible for approximately 80 % of the deadweight of the total structure. And when only 20 % of the total structure is visible, a lightweight appearance is easily obtained. All because the Munich municipal authorities did not allow for anchortype foundations. In order to evade heavy foundations, several alternative solutions can be strived for. Firstly there are a great many possible anchorage systems that all mobilise the deadweight of the soil to counterbalance the tensile forces from the structure. The simplest of these are screw anchors: large corkscrew-like anchors with a central axis and a saucer at the end that hold a conical form of soil. The practical end values of reaction forces obtained with screw anchors in different soil conditions (e.g. peat, sand and clay) can show large mutual differences in magnitude: sometimes up to 100 % so in these cases site tests will have to be performed. Other foundation systems like reinforcement nets with foils, filled with sand, also use the cheap deadweight of sand to form reaction forces. Harpoon-like anchors are not very often used apart from the grouted alternative:'grout-anchors', and herins simply are too weak.

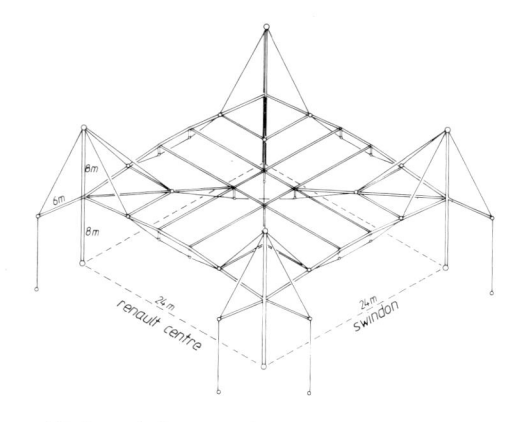

148 Renault Centre in Swindon by Norman Foster

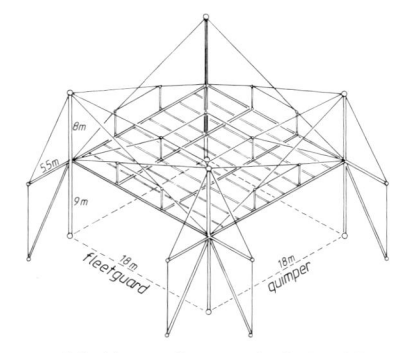

149 Fleetguard Building in Quimper by Richard Rogers.

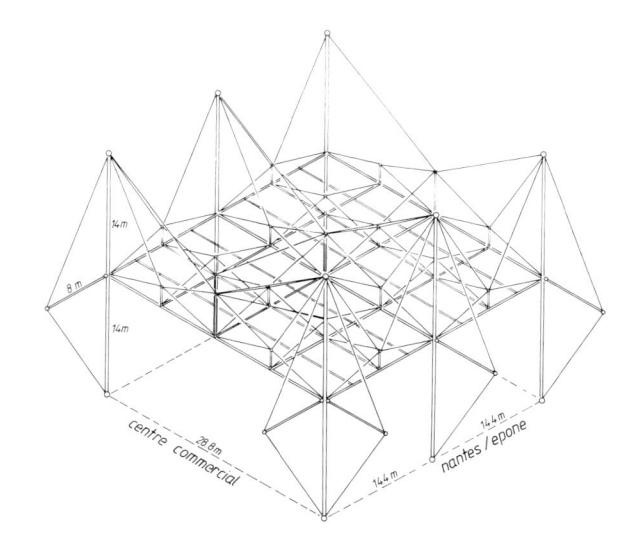

150 Centre Commercial in Nantes/Epone by Richard Rogers

3 Spatially Guyed Structures

Spatially guyed structures are 3-dimensional versions of the single guyed structures in the 2-dimensional plane. The guy principle is a means of strengthening weak structural elements. In roof structures the guy principle can be explained as an internal or as an external scheme. The internal guy principle can be explained as follows: A beam on two supports (fig 151) can be reinforced in the case of a longer span or heavier loading by an underspanning cable and stud, after which the structural scheme acts as a combination of a beam to take the local bending and a vector-active springwork in which the elements are stressed by normal forces; compression and tension. For reversable loadings the springwork has to be in the two directions of the loadings. These schemes still are 2-dimensional. Once this beam on 2 supports is seen as a beam crossing, an intersection of 2 beam elements perpendicular on each other, provided with two underspanning cables or in the case of reversable loadings 2 double springworks, the principle of the 3-dimensional stabilisation (with guyed cables) of beam elements is explained. Essentially it still is a means of strengthening a relatively weak structural element, loaded on bending. This principle is valid, for beam-like elements (still 2-D), beam-grid elements (3-D) and plate-like elements (3-D). These elements still have relatively weak cross-sections in comparison with the loadings, and can be strengthened and stiffened to adequately spatially stabilise wall or roof structures. These schemes are all comparable with a beam-on-two supports. When the same principle is worked out on the basis of a 2-dimensional beam on 2 supports with two cantilevers, its spatial consequences are seen in fig 151. The 3-dimensional structural schemes have a certain degree of statical indeterminancy, depending upon the degree of interconnections of the elements. This means a certain reserve capacity to reroute moments when one tensile element should break, or a compression element should buckle.

Externally stabilised cable stayed structures have been built and published in a small number in the last decade. There are quite a number of well-known buildings realised in the Eighties that have these guyed schemes, but most of them are linear schemes; only three of these buildings are known to be 3-dimensional:
- The Renault centre in Swindon by Norman Foster;
- The Fleetguard building at Quimper Fr by Richard Rogers and Ove Arup;
- Centre Commercial in Nantes and Epone Fr by Richard Rogers and Ove Arup.

One of the notable characteristics of these cable-stayed structures is their mutual differences; they seem to be invented for each application all over again. Therefore the author has initiated a study by civil students to analyse cable stayed roof structures and to extract a more generally applicable system for square module plan elements, 15 x 15 m to 30 x 30 m being a reasonable plan unit. The supposition is that the roof has a light deadweight, so that a double staying system has to be used. The designed system is illustrated in fig 152.

The second study with 3-dimensional guyed structures has resulted in cable stayed glass planes that either can be used as wall or as roof planes; this idea is presented in par 6.3 as it is a combination of glass and metal structures.

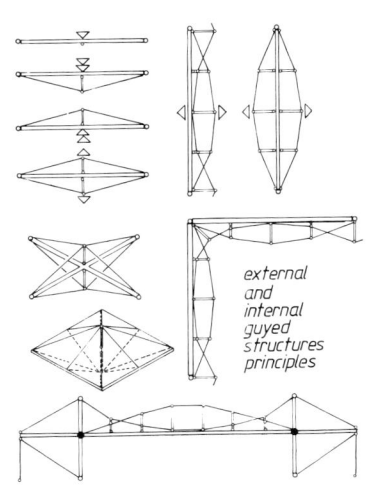

151 Deduction from beam to guyed structures.

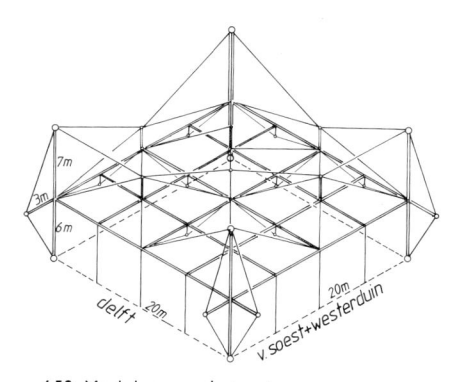

152 Modular guyed structure.

6 Integration of Structures and Cladding

This last chapter is filled with examples of combinations of load bearing space structures and enveloping cladding and glazing systems, as a personal speciality introduced by the author in the field of space structures. Due to his background as an educated architect, he feels that a building design problem is only partially solved when the structure is designed. Often in case of a complicated space structure the presentation of the design concept of a structure means only the start of a larger circle of problems. Who is capable to design and to realise a suitable envelope around the structure? In other words only then is the design problem beginning to be profiled as an attractive intellectual challenge. Preferably the design solution should go towards a specially fitted (or even better: integrated) solution. The choice and design of structure and cladding have a large mutual influence in that for example the spanning capacities of the cladding often determines the module of a space structure. But there are more active and reciprocal possible relations between structure and cladding. The three following paragraphs show a variety of different claddings, from sculptural stretched membranes, via more conventional metal cladding and sandwich panel systems to separate and integrated glazing systems, even to the ultimate design proposals of glass panels taking structural compression and acting as an essential structural part that also covers and keeps wet and draughty weather outside.

Apart from these integrations of structure and envelope, there are also other integrations possible: for example an integration of structure and electrical circuit, or structure and heating with water as a medium or air-conditioning. All of these combinations can be compared with the biological model of skeleton, skin, nerval and brain system, blood system, lungs etc that in a human body are not literally integrated, but work closely in one integral system: the human body.

1 Space Frames and Membranes

Space frame membranes are a light-footed variation on the macro-frame theme (See par 4.5). The essence of the design concepts of space frame mebranes is that on the one hand large scaled space frames are stable and autonomous structures. They are an adequate answer to the absence of strong soil conditions in the Netherlands from which tensile reaction forces can hardly be obtained in case of open membrane structures. In these macro frames stretched membranes are used as secondary covering items that do not contribute to the overall stability of the primary space frame structure. This category of structures is of course a mixture of space frames (in any of the paragraphs as mentioned in chapter 4) and stretched membranes. Until now the author was only able to design and realise a small number of space frame membranes that can be grouped into 3 types:
1 Normal sized flat space frames with suspended or covering stretched membranes;
2 Single layered triangulated dome frames with suspended stretched membranes;
3 Macro-scaled space frames with internally stretched membranes.

Apart from these three categories more variations are possible, however not yet realised by the author, like: barrel vaulted space frames with suspended membranes for temporary coverings of warehouses, factories, festivals, and tennis court coverings. (model sportshall Ring Pass, Delft); saddle shaped space frames with a suspended or covering membrane in the same form, or regarding the space frame as a macro-modular unit and the membrane as a smaller-scaled micro-modular unit. An example of which form could be like the Olympic Games Sports Palace Dome in Mexico City, structural design by Felix Candela,1968.

1 Flat Space Frames + Stretched Membranes
Stretched membranes in PVC-coated polyester or PTFE-coated glassfiber have a capacity to span 6 to 9 m in a continuous form of lower and upper support points. As the idea to combine a flat double layered space frame usually applies to an outdoor covering, the flatness of the overall design requires only modest curvatures in the membranes. For modest spans up to 30 to 40 m the space frame can easily be designed in a 3 m module so supporting points in the space frame are possible in a 3m grid or a 6 m grid. When the height of the membranes shall be as shallow as for example 1 or 1.5 m, metal gutters can be used fixed on or under the space frame, between which

153 Space frame and stretched membrane on top for an entrance canopy of a storage building in Oegstgeest. Architect Jan Brouwer 1983

the lower edges of the membranes can be fixed, while the upper points are either suspended from the upper chord members of the space frames (when the membrane is suspended) or supported by additional poles standing on top of the space frame upper chord nodes (when the membrane is covering the space frame). The gutters can be designed in a linear or a two-way grid fashion, but the membrane can of course also be designed to hover over the space frame with curved edges, without the use of straight lined gutters.

The earliest application shows a small membrane 8.1 x 9.6 m over an Octatube 1.8 m moduled space frame, supported in downward direction on the 4 edges by a steel gutter, and in upward direction by 4 poles standing on the lower chord nodes and a central pole on the upper chord node. (fig 153) The colour of the PVC membrane is grey, which is an assurance that cleaning out of visual purposes is not necessary, but which gives a rather dusky atmosphere underneath the canopy. A fact which is not relieved by the dark green coloured space frame. (After 5 years of use the dark green space frame members show a condensa-tion of calcium underneath the bars: tracks of dried condensation water). The building is designed by Jan Brouwer Associates for a small hospital warehouse Endegeest in Oegstgeest NL and is one of the early Dutch 'High-Tech'-image cable guyed buildings (1983).

A second example is the membrane covering over the factory entrance of the Octatube factory in Delft NL, designed by the author as an independent and free floating membrane, tied down at intervals of 3 m around the perimeter of 12 x 12 m, and supported in the central area by 5 adjustable poles with saucer heads, fixed on the Tuball upper chord nodes. (fig 145) The membrane can be ad-

154 Veenman exhibition stand on Efficiency 86 in Amsterdam, consisting of a regular space frame and membrane elements. (fig 81) Architect Frank Pluym.

justed afterwards at the bottom of the 5 poles by an axial thread, and chains with turnbuckles at every edge support. This membrane functions as a covered canopy for the factory, but at the same time as a sunscreen for the two story office building on the north side of the membrane. The radial cutting pattern also distinguishable in the photograph, gives the membrane a flowerlike character. The material is white-translucent PVC-coated reinforced polyester fabric that gives a Mediterranean outlook when the sun shines. The membrane serves also as an entrance gesture for visiting architect's tours.

A third and actually the first conceived example of a suspended stretched membrane under a standard Octatube space frame of 3 m module was designed in 1983 by the author in co-design with architect Cees van der Hoeven, as a permanent building site covering in The Hague NL. Underneath the covering a continuous retrainings program for building-trades workers was scheduled. The design was not realised due to lack of funds and functional necessity. (fig 155) Yet the design provided assumptions which in the course of time were applied in a number of other projects. The space frame was a double layered flat frame, in three parts stacked on each other. This was done out of the functional necessity of different free heights. The total designed space frame plus membranes was regarded as a permanent building site scaffolding structure, that, however, was professionally made. The horizontal membranes were to be conceived in one height, so partially suspended underneath and partially covering over the space frame. The membrane module size was 6 x 6 m, surrounded by a two-way grid of steel gutters, through which on several places the space frame components pierced. Solving these details is solving the whole design.

The fourth example and a less complicated successor of this scheme is the canopy of the Beyersdorf Cosmetic factory in Almere NL, designed with architects office Op ten Noord/Blijdensteijn in 1987. (fig 156) The space frame sized 17.5 x 35 m, was provided with an underspanned square grid of steel gutters 5 x 5 m, running along the module lines. As the space frame was also supported on these very axes, the intersection of the vertical column supports with the suspended horizontal gutters was an interesting detail to solve. The upper points in the membrane elements were suspended from the upper chord nodes of the space frame. Due to the square on double square geometry of the space frame, the volume of the space frame itself was simultaneously used for the necessary membrane volume. It gave a compact and yet graphical look as a result. The space frame is supported on 8 vertical steel columns rigidly connected to the foundations. The top connections (intersecting the gutters) are regarded as hinged connections. Structures of the above described type are very well suited for semi-permanent functions where a standard hot dip galvanised Octatube space frame is covered with a multitude of prestressed membrane elements on the roof, and may be on the upper parts of the walls, while the lower parts of the walls can be closed by a simple industrial glazing system. One of the proposals for a two-year exhibition structure near the Euromast in Rotterdam has been designed in this way with architect Jouke Post. The structure is purchased for a period of 2 years, to be dismantled and sold back to the manufacturer again, and re-used in

155 Model of the first proposal of Octatube space frames with integrated membranes in 1983.

156 First large scale application of a regular Octatube space frame 21 x42 m realised in 1988 for Beyersdorf in Almere (NL). Architect Op ten Noord/ Blijdensteyn.

157, 158 The 40 m diameter exhibition dome of the Autotron Car Museum, first built in Drunen (NL) and after 2 years moved to Rosmalen. If required the second membrane can be built on top of the existing one to get a better building physical behaviour.

Space Frames and Membranes

another project. Module of the space frame 3 m, structural depth 2.1 m. The possible spans are multitudes of 6 x6 m (element size): 18 x18 m or 24 x 24 m, supported on the edges at a distance of 6 m. The size of the tubes are diameter 63 to 76 mm, the nodes M16.

The use and re-use of these structures and also the membrane modules profit from the bolted connections of the separate elements that frequently can be used, a property that is normally very rarely exploited in permanent space structures.

A more permanent alternative to the space frame + membrane scheme was developed for use in covering sewage wastewater treatment plants in rectangular and circular ground plans. As the internal atmosphere is most aggressive, the concept was to use a suspended horizontal membrane in the form of a thin (=2-3 mm thick) polyester reinforced glassfiber shell in the same form as a prestressed flexible membrane. As the polyester shell is more rigid, it needs less pretensioning to be stabilised. As a structural system it is halfway between a stretched membrane and a rigid polyester shell. Moreover, the considerable costs of a thick polyester shell are avoided. In this case only a quarter of the price of an all-polyester shell structure will be spent, with the additional costs of a hot dip galvanised and additionally coated steel space frame. Several proposal designs have been made but until now not any of the designs have been realised.

2 *Triangulated Dome Frames + Membranes*
Continuing this design and development of coverings for sewage waste water tanks, an alternative was developed in 1981 by the author for oxidation beds that require a conically formed free height. As mentioned in paragraph 5.2, the material used is PVC-coated polyester fabric. The author has designed a series of possible dome frames to be completed by a suspended stretched membrane of a nature as described under the flat frames, be it that in the case of dome frames continuous membranes are possible without gutters. The upward curvature is caused by the regular suspension points, the downward curvature is caused by the dome form and the lower perimeter gutter. The erection of the membrane is easily performed by hoisting the individual points from the frame joints. In the final situation the suspension point details contain a small length of galvanised chain for rude adjustment and a turnbuckle for finer adjustment during erection and afterwards for regular maintenance. These membranes are completely high-frequency welded and fulfil the usual requirements of watertightness and air-tightness in these applications without problems.

Two examples of this dome frame + membrane scheme have been realised: a 15 m dome for a swimming pool in Jeddah (see par 3.7 and fig 160 - 162), and a 40 m dome for the Autotron Museum in Drunen NL. (fig 157, 158) The 15 m dome was a shallow single layer triangulated dome structure in the so-called parallel-lamella geometry that is divided in 6 triangular parts in plan, that are subdivided parallel to the 6 main lines and horizontal rings. The structure was in white powdercoated aluminium because of the short distance to the Red Sea. The nodal design was made special to suit the single layered state of the dome, the required local resistance against local buckling, the triangulated geometry and the connection of the suspension thread through the joint. The tubes are flattened at the end like the Octatube space frame system. This frame system is called the Hexadome system. The covering is a double tent: outside a PFTE-coated glassfiber weave with enough resistance against the high local surface temperatures in a white color. The lower membrane with a similar form was suspended approx. 300 mm lower with 3 layers of transparent insulation material (30 mm) to get a good temperature insulation value. The structural tubes are provided with electrical cables to feed in total 19 light armatures. The inside of the dome gives an exuberant impression because of the micro-curvatures in the membrane surface, while on the outside the clear-white color of the perfectly smooth membrane surface gives more the impression of a melting ice-mountain. The structure and the membranes were trial-assembled in the factory in Delft, before shipping to Jeddah. (see fig 65) Due to this preparation time, the total erection time took only 5 days. The poor state of the concrete foundation anchors and the curves in the supposedly straight edges on the base of the dome were responsible for making good activities during two days of that time.

The second Hexadome was built as a geometrical enlargement of the first structure to a total free span of 40 m. The structure has element lengths of 6 to 8 m and a diameter of 160 mm in hot dip galvanised and coated steel tubes. Although the element weights are too high for manual assembly and erection, the total erection time of the structure, the lower ring, the metal cladding, and the single stretched membrane took about 3 weeks. The principal details are similar as the Jeddah dome. The foundation in this case, was formed by a double set of prefabricated concrete blocks of 0.5 m3 each, with additional central tensile screw anchors to activate a conical volume of ground under the foundations in case of vertical uplift reaction forces. The concrete beams between the support points were chopped-off concrete piles, laid

159, 160, 161 The 15 m diameter Hexadome with double and insulated translucent membranes, built in Jeddah. (fig 65)

on galvanised steel brackets. Two years ago the dome structure was dismantled in Drunen NL and moved with the Autotron Museum to Rosmalen NL, including the foundations. The concept of the partly concrete and partly tensile foundations was developed for the design of the retrainings project in The Hague.

The two Hexadomes with the different spans and the same geometry leads to the conclusion regarding the distance between the suspension points that the optimal distance of 6 to 9 m over the total envelope can be reached. Hence for smaller spans not all nodes/suspension points need to be used.

3 Macro-scaled Space Frames + Membranes

Starting from the polyhedronal units of tetrahedrons and octahedrons, being the basic elements of a regular space frame, structures of a large scale can be made with enough space inside for human use. When the elements have a length of 6 m and more, the average height is 4.2 m and more. So in this volume a stretched membrane can be connected inside the macro-frame units. The membrane does not add to the overall stability of the structure: the space frame structures form a closed entity with a secondary membrane stretched inside. The advantage of these schemes is especially for temporary structures: there is practically no restriction on the building site as the space frames form a stable entity. Inside these frames membranes with an inviting and jubilant form can be stretched, resulting in sculptural structures. When situated on the streets and market squares of old Dutch towns they look more like 'space age' structures in strong contrast. One of the first of these macro-framed membrane structures was designed by the author for Veronica Broadcasting Company in 1982 (fig 63) and is still in monthly use after 7 years. The structure is composed of 4 tetrahedrons with bar lengths of 9 to 10 m (in fact there are 3 different lengths), made of hot dip galvanised steel tubes of 160 mm diameter. The nodes are designed and developed with the aid of 1:5 scaled cardboard models, to check easy hinging during manual- and-crane erection of these heavy elements. They are a refinement in this case of the Octatube principles, be it that all nodes are more rounded-off to prevent damages during erection and dismantling that often occurs after broadcasting in the middle of the night after the set has moved out. One of the surprising effects of this structure apart from the regular appearance on television, is that occasionally the designer sees his structure built on places he never expected, like in 1985 on a pair of pontoons in the harbour of Amsterdam during the Sail '85 happening. This experience shows that such a particular

Space Frames and Membranes

162 Standard 6 m module aluminium macro-space frame with internally prestressed membrane, complete with a triangular space frame stage platform with plywood boarding, for the shopping centre Amsterdam Zuid-Oost, (1987). Design author.

163 Macro space frame in standard 6 m Octatube with 4 separate prestressed membranes for an exhibition stand for Modulex, Hoofddorp (NL), designed and realised 1986 by industrial designer Rogier de la Rive Box and the author.

situation between the oldtimer sailing ships is quite an appropriate one in ambience: masts cables and sails speak the same language, only with a different structural form.

The Modulex Exposition structure is designed with industrial designer Rogier de la Rive Box, and is composed of standard Octatube space frame M16 nodes and 6 m long tubes of 120 mm diameter in hot dip galvanised and powdercoated steel, as a large scale (2:1) space frame, in which volume 4 separate hypar formed membranes are streched. The structure has 4 support nodes 6 x 6 m that can be raised at will on 4 pyramids 1.2 m high. (fig 163)

2 Space Frames and Metal Cladding

Concerning the cladding of non-transparent materials, reference is given to Par 4.1 'Roofing of space frames'. In this paragraph 6.2 only examples are given where the cladding elements are more integrated with the space structures than in the usual independent systems. In these examples mutual relationships are either semi-independent or interdependent. This close relationship can be the result of purely structural reasons, or architectural detail or product-design, and sometimes of purely economical reasons.

Benthem House   The experimental house of architect Jan Benthem in Almere was designed in accordance with the regulations of the first designers competition 'De Fantasie' to have only a lifetime of 5 years, which in the meantime has been extended officially. This design of Jan Benthem and Mels Crouwel is a simple glass box 6 x 8 m, with a row of 4 different adjacent rooms (kitchen, bathroom, 2 sleeping rooms) each sized 2 x2 m, so in total 2 x 8 m, with opposite to the 4 boxes a 2 m deep balcony. The totality of these simple volumes are placed upon an Octatube space frame sized 8 x 10 m with modules of 2 x 2 m and a structural depth of 1.4 m. The temporary situation in the polders around the newtown Almere could cause problems by the setting of the new soil. For that reason the four supports on prefab concrete slabs were provided with post-adjustable footings. The relative short life cycle had its conclusions in limited budgets and materials and building techniques that enabled dismantling and re-assembly. For a number of prize-winners of this competition winning (and being allowed to build the designed house) seemed the surest

164 Picture of the Jan Benthem House in Almere.

165 Proposal drawing by the architects of the Jan Benthem House in Almere.

route to bankruptcy, when no grants could be obtained from sponsors, or smart technical systems could be used. One of the smart systems in this house was the omitting of the upper chord members of the space frame, and routing the acting compressive and tensile stresses in the covering sandwich panel floor. This floor was made by rigidly connecting three large sandwich panels from the coach-work industry sized 2.8 x 12 m, consisting of two layers of 10 mm plywood with 50 mm intermediate polyurethane foam. The sandwich plate was connected by woodscrews with the flat Octatube upper nodes, and formed the first integrated example of primary and secondary structural elements. (fig 164)

Orchard Boulevard Station The integration in the roofs over the MRT central underground station of Singapore at Orchard Boulevard, has another nature, and is actually only a variation on the Tuball-Plus system normally filled in with glass panels. The three roofs are: (figs 111, 112 and 118 to 120)
- a central semi-spherical dome 15.5 x 7.75 m;
- a semi-cylindrical entrance barrel vault 6 x 28 m;
- a semi-cylindrical entrance barrel vault 8 x 22 m.

The dome is a single layered triangulated network dome with panels sized maximum 2.4 x 2.4 x 2.4 m, being the largest commercially available aluminium sheet and heat-strengthened glass sizes, that also could still be transported in a standard container. The details are exactly conforming to the standard Tuball-Plus system. The panels on the roof parts of the two canopies and on the upper rings of the dome are manufactured as alu-

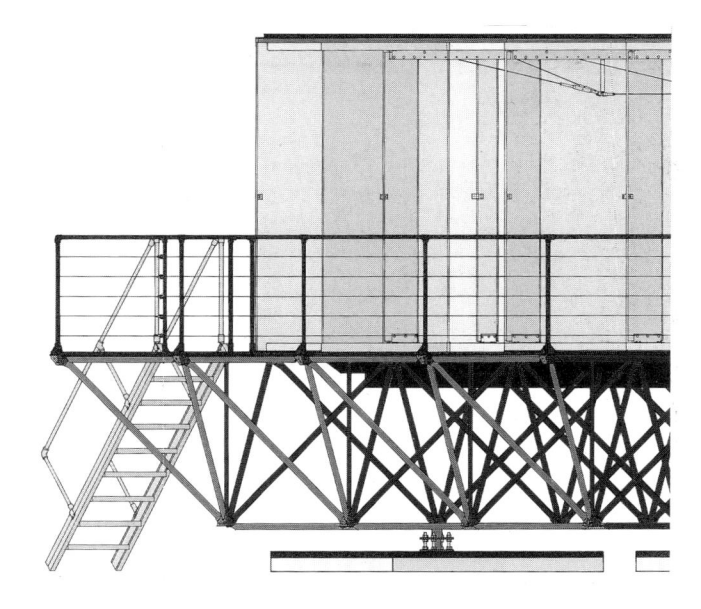

Space Frames and Metal Cladding

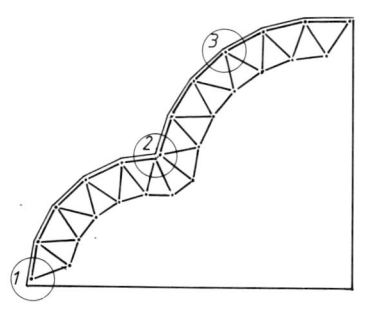

166 Section of Somerset underground station, Singapore.

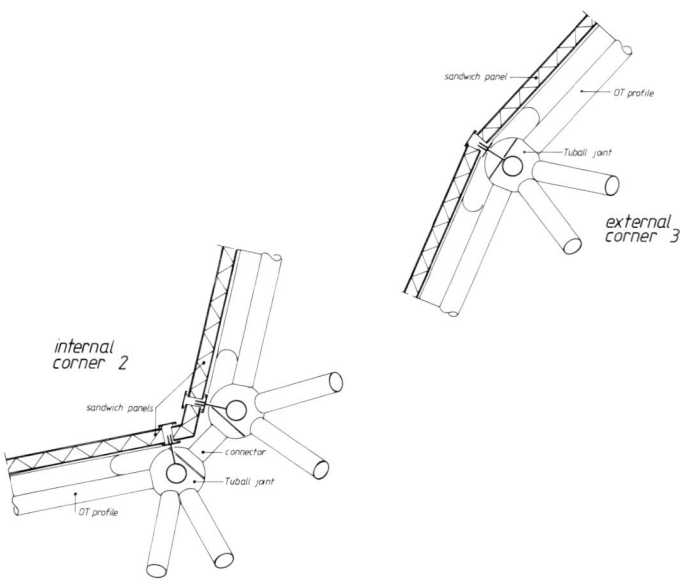

167 Typical details of the Tuball-Plus proposal for the Somerset MRT underground station in Singapore, as proposed by the author in 1985.

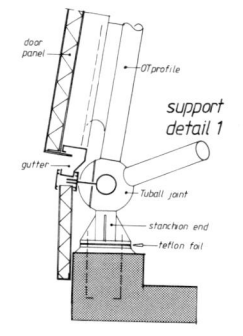

168 Support detail with detail of entrance service door, detailed like hatch back of the car industry.

minum sandwich panels of 1 mm flat aluminum sheet on both sides with an intermediate layer of 50 mm PVC foam glued in between. These panels have overlapping outside skins as an extra security for watertightness. This overlap is sealed off by foamband before the screwstrips are connected to fasten the panels. The integration itself is not structurally, as all panel elements act as secondary cladding elements in their own right; the integration is, like all Tuball-Plus space frames (as will be explained in par 6.3) the integration of the structural and the architectural framing elements into one aluminum extrusion profile. As this system is mainly developed for glass panels with the consequent fine detailing of a completely visible structure, the effect of the panels is worth while mentioning: the two canopies have non-transparent panels in the roof, while the gables are completely glazed. This gives an spatial inside impression of a tunnel or a small-scaled hangar, that is completely different from the glass arcades mentioned in paragraph 4.6 and deserved to be exploited in further future designs. The spatial effect of the dome with glass panels only in the lowest ring is one of a 5-sided helmet, where a basic visual stability is given by 5 triangular base panels containing 4 smoke exits and a service entrance door.

Circus Theater   A last example of integrations between structure and cladding is the proposal by the author in co-design with architect Sjoerd Soeters for the roof over a Post-Modern amusements hall in Zandvoort. The roof was designed and developed in the first alternative as a stretched membrane, and in the second as a single layered space frame in the Tuball-Plus system in saddle shape. The total shape of the roof was conceived as a repetition of 3 elements that were part of a total continuity (See fig 128). As the space frame is not rigid in its own plane because of the pin connected nodes, and the possible deformation of square faces into rhombs, the plywood panels (max size 1.5 x 3 m) were designed to take the shear forces in the roof surface (plate bracing): a certain structural integration. The alternative would have been diagonal bracing and a less structurally acting cladding system.

3   Space Frames and Glass Panels

The visual slenderness of structures is extremely emphasized when using clear glass as covering material. Heavy structures become massive in that case, but lightweight structures are seen in full slenderness. Structures that are lit by daylight are ultimately visible and when they are within a short distance of the observer, they should be detailed in a very refined way. The author has developed a number of ways to combine structural bars of space frames and glazing mullions in one combined aluminium profile, aiming at well designed and detailed slender and elegant glass roof structures.

Tuball-Plus System   The design and development steps that led from the Tuball system to the Tuball-Plus system, have been explained in par 3.7. The result is a frame system composed of spherical nodes in cast aluminium or cast nodular iron , ordinary cylindrical profiles in aluminium or steel, the special so-called O-T profiles and the respective bolts and the necessary auxiliaries. The O-T profiles are called after their primary form, indicating the 'T' for the glass bearing mullion element and the 'O' for the round tube, giving a material translation of the symbiosis between architecture and structure. These O-T profiles have been designed in different shapes, according to structural design and method of application of the glass panels. These profiles are always made in aluminium as this material facilitates the complicated cross-sections. The sizes of the 'O' profiles are basically 40 up to 70 mm and are used according to the required structural action. The width of the upper 'T'-profiles is usually 50 mm as this is a practical minimal width for supporting the glass elements and allowing for expansion. Yet there are three main different 'T'-profiles: in the first one the smooth 'T' used for structurally sealed glass panels with silicon sealant directly on the aluminium upper surface; in the second one a parker screw channel is integrated in the cross section to facilitate the screwing in of the transversal stainless steel screws fixing the outer screw strips with the main O-T profiles; in the third one an additional channel is combined that takes care of internal drainage of leak water and condensation water.

The purpose of combining the two functions 'structure' and 'glazing' is to have instead of 2 separate profiles one combined, stronger and more slender profile. For curved surfaces like domes, cylinders and saddles the manufacturing of these profiles is more simply than of 2 separate profiles. The vertical body of the 'T' can be machined out regularly at wish for an even more airy effect. In the aeroplane industry 90 percent of the aluminium structural material is machined out, so why not in visual architectural structures.

Structurally there are two distinct drawbacks as a result of the immanent struggle of designer and engineer

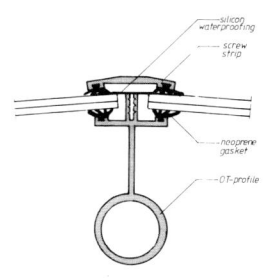

169 Detail joint of the Tuball-Plus system as used in the Haarlem dome, with screw strips.

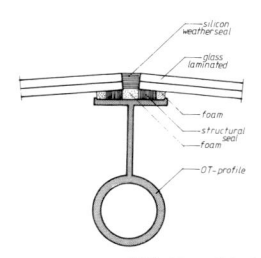

170 Detail joint of structurally sealed Tuball-Plus as used for the Prinsenhof dome in Delft. (see fig. 117) Silicon sealant is used for both adhesion and for watertightness.

during the development of the system. Firstly a vector-active structure in which only normal forces are active is now additionally loaded with bending stresses. This implies certain limitations in span for structures with these profiles, or it means that the structural material cannot be used as optimally as in the case of pure normal stresses. Secondly at the very place where shear forces are maximum, the material is machined away, i.e. directly on top of the nodes.

Load Bearing Spatial Glass Structures   Using heat-strengthened glass panels the author has led fundamental research into the structural use of glass, replacing the structural metal elements of a space frame structure for the major part. This item has initially been designed, developed and researched in 1988 by Rik Grashoff, a civil engineering student from Delft University, as a part of his final studies. This study followed instructions by the author that in itself resulted from writing this book. As the author has assisted Rik Grashoff very closely in the Octatube office, the results of the first attempts to make an initial forward in this theoretical direction, can be given as follows. A growing number of transparently covered Tuball-Plus structures are used for public street furniture: music pavilions, abri's, entrance canopies street coverings etc. As (at least in the Netherlands) street vandalism is a matter of growing concern, the best usable materials for these transparent covering panels are made of glass in laminated and/or heat strengthened panels. The added strength against vandalism of these glass panels is so high that the idea arose to use this additional rigidity also for structural purposes. In the last century glass houses received a certain amount of their overall rigidity by the fact that all glass panels were embedded in hardened putty. Officially in our era we are not allowed to use glass as a structural material, apart from taking wind forces to the supporting structures at the edges of the glass panels. In fundamental research and development the question of official acceptance can be put aside until the last developments have been completed. So the question was put: 'How can we design and develop glass structures mainly with strong glass panels and with only a small number of visual metal components?' Financial relevancy and the building physical behaviour was deliberately not taken as a part of the study, but will be taken into account in further phases of this subject. The following criteria were formulated at the start of the project:

- main structural elements glass or glass-like plates;
- integration of structure and enclosure;
- minimal visual disturbancies;
- applicable in a variety of roof geometries;
- innovating character;
- prototype ready within 3 months of study.

In such a structure there are four different elements to be distinguished:

- Flat transparent panels: primary structural element
- Nodes: structural connecting element
- Joints: sealing element
- Auxilaries: secondary structural elements

The panels are to be made from glass, polycarbonate, acrylate or a combination of these materials in solid materials. The form of the nodes will be dependent on the mode of structural action (of forces between 2 adjacent plates), manufacturing, installation, and final watertightness. The joints are expected to be completely watertight and windtight. This seal is to be solved within the narrow dimensions of the space between two panels. The auxiliary elements like bars, cables, connection elements and bolts to be as minimal as possible. One of the most important considerations was the type of structural action between 2 adjacent plates. The first mode is to bring over tensile forces by means of bows over the adjacent sides of 2 plates, or over the crossing between 4 plates. The mutual movability between 2 plates is not avoided or restricted. The second mode is to bring over the compressive forces by means of distance keepers in the form of small rectangular blocks between the sides, or of octagonal blocks on the crossing. A combination of

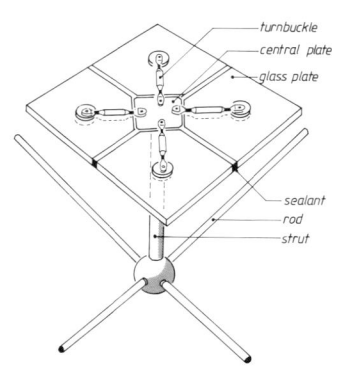

171 Diagram of the first design of the pretensioning joint for the all-glass assembly that resulted in compression forces over the crossing of the glass panels.

172 Mock-up of a first assembly of 9 heat-strengthened glass panels, joined together by pretensioning joints, outriggers and standing rigging.

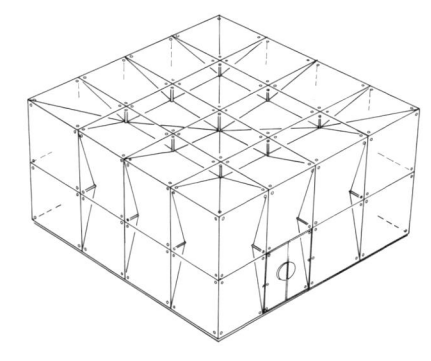

173 Design proposal of a glass exhibition pavilion for the Centraal Museum in Utrecht by architect Wiek Röling and the author, 1988. Size 8 x 8 x 4 m (not realised).

Architecture in Space Structures

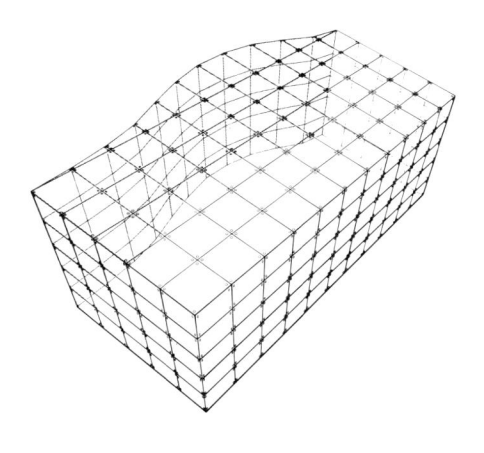

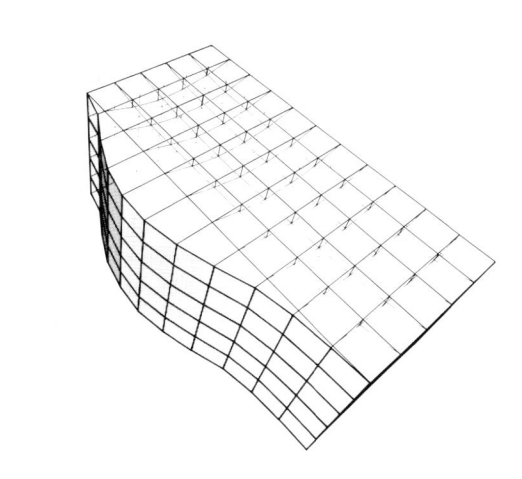

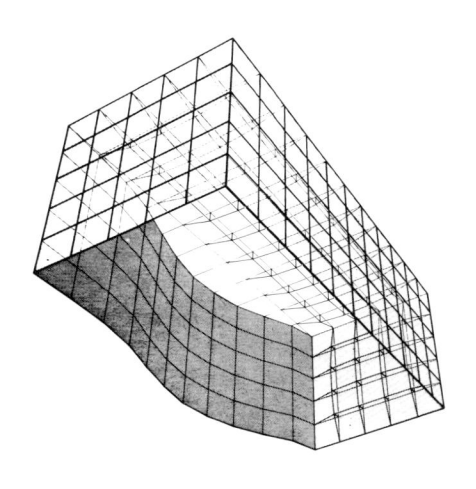

174, 175, 176 Perspective overall view of the glass box to be built as an acoustic envelope for the rehearsal room of the Philharmonic Orchestra in the Exchange of Berlage in Amsterdam. Approximate size 9 x 13 x 22 m in the described structural glass system with internal rigging. Completion Sept 1989. Architect Pieter Zaanen. Structural design and development by the author.

these 2 modes will work structurally. Another mode of bringing over tensile forces is the introduction of a post-tensioning cable in the joint between the 2 adjacent plates. A connection of glued small metal plates on the glass panels will have to be double-sided to get the joint surfaces stressed on shear forces. One of the combinations is a distance keeping block with larger metal plates bolted together. The joint can be made of local sealant material, at the installation of which the conditions of surface plus climate will have a major influence. An alternative joint can be formed by foamband when this can be pressed together during installation. A slender joint only has a size of 10 to 15 mm wide and plate thickness deep (6 to 15 mm). For the first project realised in this system (an expo-pavilion in Osaka) the seams were formed by H-profiled transparent acrylate profiles.

Auxiliaries are mainly dependent on the used structural system, as mentioned in paragraph 2.2 of this book. Flat structures need to be double layered. The second layer can be either glass or open webs of bar elements. Curved structures can be made in a single layer. Linear curved forms have to be reinforced in one direction.

The material investigation proved that glass still is the only appropriate structural transparent material. (See par 2.1). For safety reasons heat-strengthened glass panels will have to be laminated and used as structural plates, although lamination weakens the glass 30% in strength. Single heat-strengthened glass is not safe (depending on vandalism or mechanical loadings and fall height). Duplex strengthened glass has problems with size accuracies. Laminated normal glass is not as safe, but less expensive. The investigation has taken thick heat-strengthened panels as a base that are laminated with thin normal panels for minimal security reasons. As heat-strengthened glass panels are only available in standard thicknesses of 6, 8, 10, 12, 15 and 19 mm, a list was prepared to compare between the maximum compression and tension forces when the plates have sizes of 1.0 to 3.0 m, and are connected in the corners of the plates. A small module 1.0 to 1.5 m has a number of advantages: deadweight and element sizes enable manual installation. Per unit of roof area larger forces can be transferred. But the number of manual connection activities are substantially less in larger elements. The optimal element size is regarded as 1.5 x 1.5 m.

The first mock-up was made of plywood plates with 2 x 4 turnbuckles for post-tensioning. As the result worked quite well in a mechanical way, but was esthetically too crude,(fig 171) a second model was made of 9 glass panels in reduced scale 1:4 and full scale metal joints, which required intensive installation energy, and was presented

Space Frames and Glass Panels

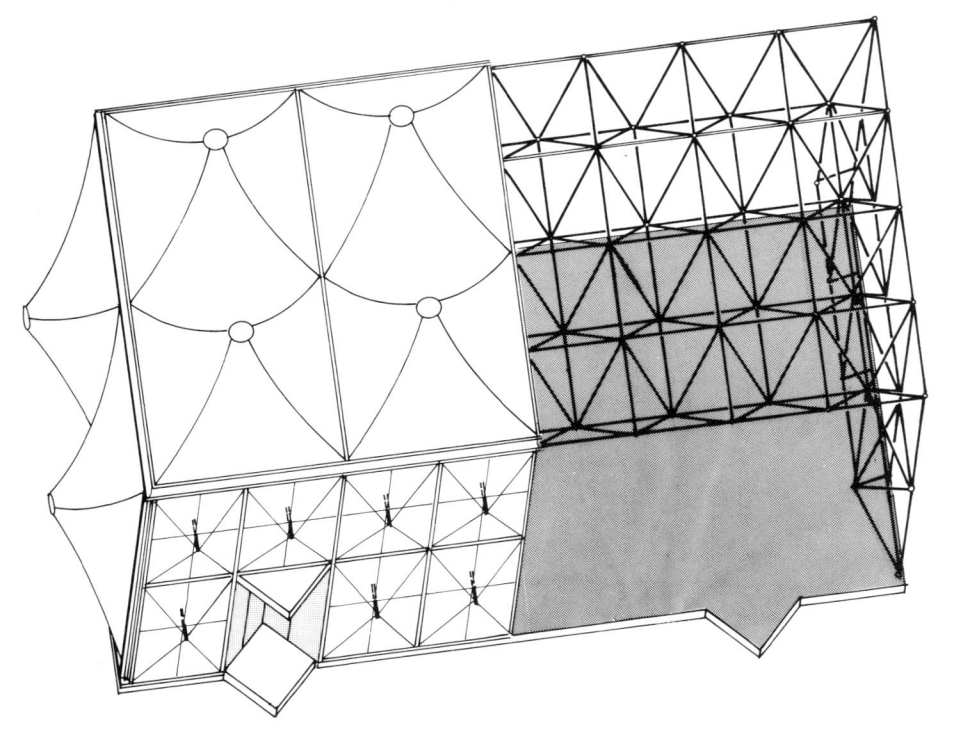

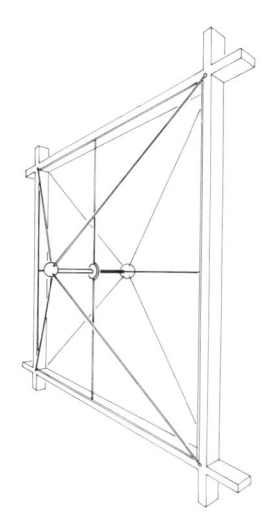

177 Guyed glass fascia elements for a pavilion of the EVD in Osaka, April 1989. The pavilion is composed of a modular aluminium Tuball space frame and modular stretched membranes and is influenced in its design by its rapid erection, the traditional Japanese modular construction methods and the 1970 Osaka pavilion by Renzo Piano. Designed by Frans Prins and the author.

178 Mock-up of the glass elements used in the Osaka pavilion.

180 Isometric view of a proposal for a completely glass pedestrian bridge in the 'House of the Future' in Rosmalen. Architect Cees Dam; bridge designed by the author.

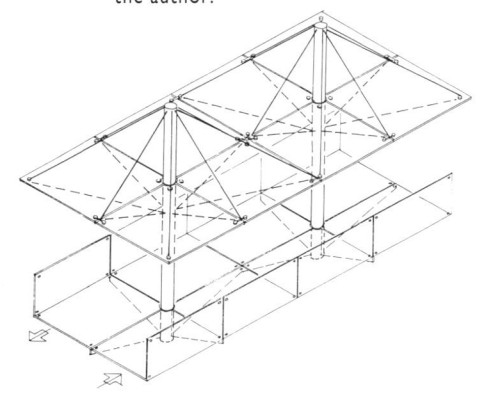

179 Perspective view of the Cool Cat fashion shop, architect Paul Verhey, 1989.

Architecture in Space Structures **128**

as the interim result of the project. (figs 172, 173) The theoretical research part was followed by further designs and developments of three projects: EVD pavilion, Cool Cat glass facade and the Glass Music Box.

The first design was a flat space frame pavilion, covered by membrane elements on three sides and a front wall 4.8 x 19.2 m., composed of elements sized 2.4 x 2.4 m in modules of 1.2 m, using a modification of the corner blocks and post-tensioning procedure to tighten the foamband seals, and applied for a pavilion of the Dutch Ministry of Economic Affairs in Osaka, designed by Frans Prins and the author. (fig 174)

The second design realised is a double stayed glass shop facade for Cool Cat fashion shops in Groningen, and designed by architect Paul Verhey. The glass front on the first floor level, is composed of 6 hardened glass panels 12 mm thick, sized 2 x 2.25 m, suspended within a steel portal frame, and stabilised by a double set of each 3 guying cables plus 4 stuts, giving a total glass area of 6 x 4.5 m.

The third design is a large Glass Music Box in the former Exchange of Berlage in Amsterdam, which is now converted into a cultural centre. The Glass Box serves as a repetition room for the Dutch Philharmonical Orchestra. So primarily the glass thickness was required acoustically as minimal 8 mm thickness. Also the curved wall is an answer on the acoustical design of the box. All glass panels in walls and roof are transparent clear (to experience Berlage's old building around the box, only the curved wall is grey-tinted. Dimensions of the box are: 9 m high, 9 to 13 m wide and 23 m long. The roof structure is formed by a double-layered Tuball space frame, covered by sealed laminated clear glass panels, and surrounded with a (real curtain) suspended glass wall, stabilised on the inside by sets of vertical counterspanning guy cables, spanning between the space frame and the concrete floor. The initial proposal to realise a complete integral glass structure, with the horizontal glass panels under compression, was left in favour of the cheaper space frame table solution. Design of the Glass Music Box by architect Pieter Zaanen and the author; completion in September 1989.

The latest design in a pedestrian bridge for an exhibition house in Rosmalen, designed by architect Cees Dam: the 'House of te Future'. As fig 180 shows, the bridge has an all-glass floor and two equal glass roof structures, stabilised with bar elements on two central masts. The roof glass panels are structurally under compression: really 'structural' glass.

Appendix

Evaluation of the Building Parties

After having presented in par. 3.1 the advantages of the synergetic cooperation of 'architectural, structural and industrial design', and par 3.2 the advantages of combining 'design + production', one could wonder whether this approach is worth while being followed up for other products, by other colleagues. The central question being: 'In what organisation can we expect building component products to be designed, developed and realised optimally in the future?' Our concern is directed towards smaller companies, and from a designer's point of view. Maybe we have to investigate more in the possibility of making temporary joint-ventures between different professions. Which of these professions are most open for design and development of new building products? To evaluate the potential of these joint-ventures an analysis of the competence of the different building parties and their concern towards improvement of quality can be made.

The Master Builder Back in the middle ages the leader of the building process still was the master-builder, descending from a guild or family of strong craftmanship, and guiding his fellow craftsmen to produce a complete building. His responsibility was both for the design, durable stability, the material, personal and on the financial organisation of the building. In more modern times the growing complexity of the building industry and the higher velocity of the building process itself, brought forward the need for specialisation. Not only on the side of the architect, but also around the contractor. The current and common situation in The Netherlands (but probably also abroad) is displaying definite distinctions in professional function between the different building parties:
- the client
- the architect
- the advisor
- the researcher
- the main contractor
- the sub-contractor
- the specialist-producer.

This assemblage of normally ad-hoc cooperating professions may seem a suitable answer on the day-to-day building tasks for most people. It is also based upon getting the lowest costprice for a certain building using established and well-known techniques, but often is performed at the risk of losing quality. When it comes to bringing the quality of the building industry on a higher level, by introducing new materials, new technologies and new applications, the whole set-up all of a sudden seems not to be very suitable for these actions. Or changes introduced in the building process in the established relationships seem only to bear fruits occasionally. Why? For that reason the short functional analysis clarifies why the existing building industry in generally does have a slow technical evolution rather than a quick progression.

Clients   Clients only see as their definitive goal to have a building raised for a reasonable price, in a form and appearance that suits the function of the inhibiting organisation in the short and longer term. Maybe the building will have a certain appeal above the function. But as the client usually is not a building specialist, he only seldomly will aspire to introduce new techniques, maybe only from the point of view of intellectual status, like many of the well-published British 'High-Tech' buildings. Clients who ask for new techniques are very rare: investing large sums of money is an accountable task. Yet they have to be kept informed. History is filled with the deplorable consequences of spending too much money in building: in times of authoritarian regimes impressive and overpowering buildings were realised at the cost of the well-being of the population. The modern industrial variation of over-expenditure leads to instable political situations, for an entire country, and to financial hazards in a private company's life. So the responsibility of clients does certainly not include directly introducing innovations; maybe all the best clients are expected to do in this respect, is to stimulate and support the architect and the building team to produce a building with a recognisable value, a certain over-value, or an inspiration for society.

Architects   Although originally the motor of the building process, architects often find themselves nowadays, willingly or not, in a situation of being functionally devaluated as the designers of the overall conceptual scheme, to give the building an artistic flavour. Needless to say this often coincides with a minimal left-over power and influence in the building process. Buildings are assembled from many smaller components in a large variety of choices. The usual answer of the architect is to have an optimal know-how of the components catalogue. This catalogue know-how is the starting point of many architectural schools: consuming rather than analysing existing building products, or even developing new building products. Building has become an ad-hoc assembly of different components, put into a certain 3-D position with a certain functional aim. Engaged architects see their buildings as an expression of their design philosophy, that often has to be imposed on the other members of the building team with convincing power. The architect has to use all his power for this purpose, offering himself only the way out to use standard products and techniques in his particular design: there will be no other way to have it realised. And, indeed, there are only very few well-known architects who are able to build recognised good architecture, while using improved building techniques. In the Netherlands the small number of architects who continuously try to design and develop new components, illustrates the vast number of architects who feel comfortable with the standard set of techniques on the building market. In the United Kingdom, the number of well known 'High-Tech' architects might be somewhat bigger but also they have been unable to overcome the massive inertia of the total building industry, as one can see driving through the country. Architects have enough trouble maintaining themselves as the leaders of the building teams, to undertake new risks, although they should be the ones with the helicopter vision: combining their experiences from the past with imaginations of future use, giving a more philosophical view over the building industry.

Architects can, however, contribute in two ways to the development of new products:
• in the role of leader of the building team, or as a project-architect requesting new products that fulfil the total brief of functional structural, financial and aesthetic requirements better than existing products;
• in the role of a product-architect receiving his contract from a producer to develop a new product or to improve an existing product. In which case he has to be clear about not mixing functions: not to play a developing and a team-leading role at the same time. In this last set-up the product-architect will work more or less like industrial designers for consumer goods do. The product-architect has the advantage of his extensive knowledge about the situational requirements of building components. Not often these developments might over-ask him in regard to his inventiveness in developing compatible production methods. The mental attitude of architects working with traditional materials like concrete, brickwork and timber, whereby they were used to simply design and detail every building component down to the very nails, (and make extensive working drawings), should now be translated into an equivalent for newer materials. The availability of large number of graduating young architects in the near future is one component in this recipe, an extensive technical know-how on new materials a second component, and the mental attitude to change from project-architect into a product-architect is a third component.

Advisors   Advisors have taken over from the project-architect the responsibility of analysing for example the statical or physical behaviour of the building design. Although they are specialists in this sense, they are sometimes given the freedom to design alternatives within the global overall scheme of the project-architect, or else they have to follow more or less exactly the wishes of the project-architect. Specialisation means possessing more information than others. Some of the structural advisors have given, however, a recognisable extra meaning to their work, and developed new concepts or realised new techniques. Doing so, they inspired their architects: structural engineers like Frei Otto, Felix Candela, Pier Luigi Nervi, Stephane du Chateau and Heinz Isler. (par 1.3.7) These structural designers were mainly specialised in one type of structure. Otto: tents and inflatables, Nervi: prefabricated reinforced concrete curved roofs. Candela: concrete hyparshells. Du Chateau: space frames and polyester shells. Isler: compression shells. For structural designers with a larger scope of work ranging from reinforced concrete to steel and timber structures, it is usually more difficult to profile their succesfulness to the outside world. In that case one of the specialisations of the total structural engineers office might draw attention, like the structural designs of 'High-Tech' structures by Ove Arup, which is only a minor part of their complete oeuvre. The same is valid for ABT in Arnhem: the 'High Tech' structures designed by Arie Krijgsman (Ice scating rink in Heerenveen NL) en Michel van Maarschalkerwaart (Burgers Bush, Arnhem NL) are well-publicised structures, although only a minor part of the projects of ABT. Structural advisors are usually very able to innovate steel structures, concrete structures and timber structures where the techniques are known and the influence of statical analysis coupled with these material properties lead to innovations. In these situ-ations they act as the designers of the structure, sometimes prescribing to the level of shop drawings, and tendering the design afterwards.

This one-directional approach loses its workability when new information has to be integrated: like new material properties, new production techniques or information and attitudes from other disciplines like architecture. Though the specific information can be obtained, the architectural attitude is more difficult: there is a limitation for structural engineers pretending to be architects.

Experiences in the author's practice have shown that structural engineering students informed on the specific architectural applications of a new building product or technique, are quite able to develop a new result. (par 6.3) The introduction of a new skill of advising usually coincides with stripping off one of the functions the architect once had. Starting with the structural engineer, whose tasks are the most finite of all advisors,(depending on country and habits) there was the introduction in the recent past of costing advisors, quantity surveyors, mechanical installation advisors, building physical advisors, organisation advisors, and even advisors on the behaviour of clients.

Product-Architect or Product-Developer
It is the positive opinion of the author that one of the next functions the architect will lose to a separate advisor or specialist is that of building product designer, able to design and develop new building components from new materials and production techniques for the building industry. When architects do not take up this professional field as product-architects, industrial designers will automatically move into this hole in the market. The industrial designer will then pick up a field of interest that the project-architect is not able to cope with anymore. His education gives him the advantage of analytical thinking, starting with function of the design, with materials and production techniques, via a concern for marketing and value of the newly developed product to application. His education is still very material-bound: normally the products he designs are smaller and more consumer-directed, giving him all advantages of knowing all the intrinsic material properties. While architects more or less have lost the intensive feeling of materials: education and practice are far from the actual building site. Architectural schools have lost the smell of the building site. Architectural education is becoming more and more guided in the direction of abstraction of design, and analysing the complexity of the total building process. Also due to the actual immense popularity of industrial design schools, architects will realise in the 1990s in this respect that they have introduced a new and very capable competitor. It will not be very long before industrial design schools, due to their growing popularity and marketing capacities will send their students also into the direction of the building industry, feeding them specific material and technical information usable in architects offices or in specialised companies producing industrialised building components.

Some architects have recognised this future situation to happen, and have indeed moved into the hole in the market: combining their skill as an overall architect and planner with the product development techniques of industrial designers: in the Netherlands both Jan Brouwer Associates and Cepezed Designers have established among colleagues and clients their fame as 'industrial architects' in the architectural world, claiming to incorporate the skills of industrial designers in their regular architects practice. They develop new building components in their function of project-architects, improving the results from project to project. Architect Jan Brouwer is known to have devoted this aspect of his professional interest mainly to the development of the skin of the building: starting in the 1970s with sandwich panels of glassfiber reinforced polyester, followed by glassfiber reinforced cement, complete with windows and air-conditioning elements, followed in the last 15 years subsequently by corrugated steel and profiled aluminium/gypsum board sandwich panels. His last developments concern polycarbonate panels. Cepezed tries to integrate in less depth but more integrally all the composing elements of their buildings like main structure, claddings, floors, internal partitioning walls, ducting etc, using industrialisable materials and components. They have discovered that when working with new materials, the contribution of main contractors can only be that of logistics: they detail completely their buildings in cooperation with possible producers, and work with nominated sub-contractors and specialist-producers, preferably without a main contractor. In the United Kingdom an ever growing group of designers in and around the offices of Richard Rogers, Norman Foster, Nicolas Grimshaw and Michael Hopkins and others produce innovations of industrial components in the growing list of their technical architecture. Architect Alan Brookes (London) is an outstanding example of an architect specialised in claddings of all sorts of techniques and material, gradually acting as a cladding specialist, consulted by his colleague-architects and by producers all over the world.

Researchers Researchers are usually occupied with scientific studies on the behaviour of only one single component of the total building. They are true specialists and work optimally if they can conveniently analyse problems in recognisable aspects. Theirs is more a vision of deepness rather than an overview of wideness. They know everything about (virtually) nothing. The mutual language amongst researchers is one of presenting their research results and trying to understand someone else's results, rather than discuss common problems leading to the development of techniques of a wider influence. Researchers are not very inspiring for architects, and usually try to overwhelm them with an overpower of scientific formulas, schematic models and further abstractions that just do not apply completely with the specific problem to be solved in view of the total complexity of the building to be realised. Researchers who combine a specialist's understanding with a helicopter overview of a wider area of interconnected problems are very rare. Zygmut Makowski is one of them, able to relate research projects on the topic of spatial structures all over the world to interweave connections between the individual researchers, and to explain in single words to architects what is happening.

Main Contractors   Although evolved usually out of the skills of carpenters, bricklayers or concreters, main contractors have developed themselves mainly into an organising and logistic role: their function is to get the building upright in the required time and with the required quality and price. Their actual manual involvement in the building process can mostly said to be reduced to site-supervision, organisation meetings, telephone and paperwork (which due to the complexity of the building process is a fairly complex job already). This situation is displayed at the larger main-contractors firms. Main contractors have a lot of their efforts used to ensure the next project. As this has to be done without a specific skill apart from their organisational and financial skills (but mostly not technical skills), they are not interested in new techniques as these techniques possibly can ruin their time planning : most buildings have to be put up in record time, not giving way to taking time risks. Main contractors could only be interested in new techniques for the same reason they are interested in a high-scoring architect: to enlarge their chances on getting contracts. Like the Dutch HBM has developed a successful building method of jackblock high rise office buildings in the 1960s. HBM and Bredero are known as the only large Dutch contracting companies to be equipped with an extensive R + D department for research in new techniques in traditional materials (e.g. reinforced concrete). The field of power of smaller contractors using traditional techniques is still quite large because of the roots of their craftsmanship. The projects of Cepezed show however the opposite position: the main contractor is not able to master the new techniques. Hence he can be asked to keep only the logistic and organisational function in the building process. In the United Kingdom this type of functioning of main-contractors is now officially entitled 'contract management': there is no pretence to contract for the highest price and sub-contract for a lower price: 'contract management' only means assuring logistics and quality directly to the client. It is such a new form of advising skill, be it with a very high degree of responsibility. Contract management underlines the structure of the modern building industry in another way: building is a joint process of the efforts of sub-contractors and specialist-producers.

Sub-Contractors and Specialist-Producers
Sub-contractors and specialist-producers are the only parties in the building industry regularly forced to innovate their services or products out of necessity to remain in business. The emphasis with sub-contracting is usually more on the supplied labour with a general material while specialist-producers supply (or supply + fix) special building products or building components. Fear of competition often leads to distinction of their products. Developing new products or innovating existing products, however, is mostly guided by a marketing analysis or enquiries received, based upon the existing range of products. So their scope of new products is limited by experiences of current products and also by availability of production equipment. But specialist-producers are usually willing to design their products to fit within the overall concept of the project-architect. Their material experiences are then combined with the more visionary wishes of the project-architects.

Development-Mix   In case of a required development of a new product the Development-Mix of an architect to envisage the fitting-in of a new product in an overall architectural scheme and the mutual influence of this product on the whole, should be enforced with the more material and detail design skills of an industrial designer in order to assist the producer with the right type of product and the right properties of that product. The development of a structural product has to include the structural engineer too: just like the Development Mix of climate installation products need an installation advisor. This Development-Mix connecting the skills of architects, industrial designers and producers is only beginning to be formatted in the Netherlands. The first attempts are stimulative, though the tripartite mistrust for the possible influence of the other parties, reveals that this process of joining forces is quite new to all three parties concerned. As an experiment in this way of thinking, the recently established foundation 'Booosting' (Rotterdam), is aimed at stimulating the mutual co-operation between the three disciplines of architects, industrial designers and production companies in order to

Evaluation of the Building Parties

design and develop new industrial components for the building industry and for architecture. The results of its actions are shown in autumn exhibitions in Rotterdam, the first one in November 1988 titled 'Booosting experiments'. The first 1988 projects of the Booosting foundation were rather ad hoc, the 1989-projects will be more complimentary to each other, larger in number, and the 1990-projects are planned to be more integral, fitting into one integral building project. In this way it is hoped that the attention to the quality of individual building products and to 'product-architecture' will find a wider circle of appreciation, and that specialist producers will be enabled to develop products with over-value. At the end maybe the quality of the built environment will be raised accordingly.

Dutch Summary

1 Ruimtelijke Constructies in het Algemeen

Ruimtelijke constructies zijn belasting dragende constructies toegepast in de architectuur waarbij een werkelijk gebruik wordt gemaakt van de 3-dimensionale krachtsoverdracht. Als ruimtelijk fenomeen hebben ze een grote invloed op de architectuur. Het grootste deel van de studies over ruimtelijke constructies tot nu toe betroffen de rekenkundige aspecten. Maar omdat nu ruimtelijke constructies steeds vaker in de architectuur worden toegepast, en om het gevaar van slechte toepassingen te verkleinen, is de tijd rijp voor de brede visie van een ruimtelijk ontwerper op dit gebied.

Ruimtelijke constructies kunnen op een groot aantal wijzen worden omschreven, van een puur constructieve, architectonische, of een geometrische wijze naar een meer psychologische of overdrachtelijke wijze. Ondanks de in eerste instantie enigszins verwarrende benaming zal toch het begrip 'ruimtelijke constructies' met de constructieve omschrijving gehanteerd worden. Andere omschrijvingen zullen echter ook hun invloed in het boek doen gelden. Onder 'architectuur' wordt in dit boek verstaan het totaal van de ruimtelijke gebouwde omgeving. Het woord is niet opgevat als classificatie van de kwaliteit daarvan, zoals architectuur met een kleine 'a' of een grote 'A'.

Er wordt in het eerste hoofdstuk een aantal hypothesen gegeven betreffende het ontwerpen met ruimtelijke constructies, welke verspreid over de verschillende paragrafen zullen worden onderbouwd.

Ruimtelijke constructies zijn een erkende wijze van construeren in de architectuur geworden in de afgelopen eeuw. Eerdere stappen in deze richting werden gezet door Gustav Eiffel in zijn bruggen en Eiffel-toren. De eerste pogingen om een echt ruimtevakwerk te maken, zijn afkomstig van Alexander Graham Bell in 1907. Desondanks groeide de populariteit van ruimtevakwerken pas na de 50-er jaren, toen deze constructies ook door architecten werden erkend als een voor hen hanteerbare bouwwijze. De grote populariteit van gespannen membranen is door Frei Otto in de 60-er jaren tot stand gebracht, maar door de hoge mate van het benodigd specialisme en door de technische eigenschappen zal dit type constructies nooit de populariteit van ruimtevakwerken benaderen.

Het huidige gebruik van ruimtelijke constructies in de architectuur werd duidelijk gestimuleerd door een aantal ontwikkelingen:

1 De oorspronkelijke uitvinding en verdere ontwikkeling van nieuwe constructieve materialen;
2 Het nastreven van een maximale materiaal benutting van deze constructieve materialen;
3 De ontwikkeling van nieuwe constructieve ruimtelijke schema's;
4 De ontwikkeling van constructieve analyse methoden voor statisch onbepaalde constructies per computer;
5 De functionele eisen naar dakconstructies met grote kolomvrije (enkelvoudige) overspanningen;
6 De vraag naar vierkante in plaats van rechthoekige interne kolomstramienen (meervoudige overspanningen);
7 De persoonlijke inzet en impulsen van de pioniers van de diverse typen ruimtelijke constructies;
8 De toenemende acceptatie en integratie van de diverse typen ruimtelijke constructies in de architectuur.

2 Materialen en Systemen

De drie belangrijkste middelen die de constructief vormgever heeft om er zijn ontwerpconcepten mee te realiseren, zijn: Materialen, Technieken en Systemen. Deze drie middelen worden gebruikt bij de realisatie van het constructieve idee, maar omgekeerd hebben ze ook een grote invloed op ideeën en concepten, voordat deze als definitief worden beschouwd. Gewoonlijk vindt binnen deze wederkerigheid de project-architect een deel van de inspiratie om zijn gebouwconcepten te visualiseren. De product-architect heeft een nog diepere relatie met die materiaal eigenschappen, de productietechnieken en de constructieve systemen die hij gebruikt, omdat deze drie middelen tesamen het product vormen.

Architecten zijn gewoonlijk zeer goed bekend met de traditionele bouwmaterialen zoals hout, metselwerk, gewapend beton en gewalste staalprofielen. In het algemeen is er echter minder kennis van zaken op het gebied van koudgewalst staal, aluminium, gehard glas en kunststoffen. Deze materialen en hun toepassingen in de bouwproducten zijn dan ook voornamelijk ontwikkeld in producerende bedrijven die op een serieuze wijze de verzamelde informatie beschermen of ten minste selecteren. Deze recent verworven informatie is echter van wezenlijk belang voor de architecten om daarmee adequate ontwerpen en toepassingen te realiseren. Soms kan een materiaalstudie de ontwerper een stap naderbij brengen. Materiaalkunde wordt in het algemeen door ontwerpers gezien als een mathematisch en nogal saai onderwerp. Maar bevrijd van de algebraïsche aanpak, kan de werkelijke betekenis van eigenschappen van pure of gecombineerde materialen leiden tot specifieke ontdekkingen.

De mogelijkheden vanuit de productietechnieken die voor metaal, glas en kunststoffen zo verschillend zijn, vormen ook een basis voor het begrip van de ontwerp mogelijkheden. In dit boek zullen geen overzichten worden gegeven van productietechnieken op zich omdat bij Octatube op dat gebied (nog) geen grote ontwikkelingen hebben plaats gevonden. Wel wordt er gerefereerd naar paragraaf 3.2 en 3.6 waar enkele aspecten dienaangaande worden behandeld.

De beschikbaarheid van bepaalde materialen (met geschikte productietechnieken) kan inspireren tot het gebruik van een bepaald type ruimtelijke constructie. De interesse in nieuwe materialen is primair ontstaan door de wens constructieve schema's en vormen te realiseren. Het overzicht van materialen en systemen is zeer beknopt gehouden en moet worden gezien als een zeer persoonlijke keus van inspirerende ontwerpcomponenten.

Een duidelijk gevolg van het gebruik van de genoemde materialen in bouwcomponenten is het 'prefab' karakter waardoor het bouwen verandert van gieten en stapelen op de bouwplaats naar droge assemblage, en eventueel na gebruik, demontage. Alle beschreven materialen kunnen in een werkplaats of fabriek worden vervaardigd, en worden in de vorm van elementen naar de bouwplaats vervoerd, en daar geassembleerd, gemonteerd of geïnstalleerd middels boutverbindingen. Deze prefab elementen hebben vergeleken met de 'bouwplaats' materialen een geheel andere vormgeving tot resultaat.

3 Ontwerpproces van Ruimtelijke Constructies

De wens om onconventionele ruimtelijke constructies te realiseren heeft de auteur gedurende een zevental jaren vanaf 1982 bemoedigd om te experimenteren met een ander proces van het Ontwerpen, Onderzoeken, Ontwikkelen en Toepassen in vergelijking met de gangbare processen. Vanuit die experimenten wordt een aantal observaties onder de aandacht gebracht:

• In het ontwerpproces werken de drie disciplines van Architectonisch, Constructief en Industrieel Ontwerpen onafscheidelijk samen;
• In het ontwerp- en ontwikkelingsproces worden zowel zeer conventionele teken- en modeltechnieken gebruikt, als ook meer geavanceerde computertechnieken;
• De eerste ontwikkeling van nieuwe ontwerpen en systemen wordt effectief gestimuleerd door de aanwezige mogelijkheden van een goed uitgerust laboratorium;
• Door de competenties van Ontwerper en Producent te combineren, is het mogelijk zowel ideeën te presenteren als hun efficiënte realisatie te garanderen voor vaste prijzen tegenover opdrachtgevers;
• Het realiseren geschiedt vanuit hetzelfde bedrijf dat ook zorgt voor het ontwerpen. Dit houdt in dat rijke ervaringen worden opgebouwd, dat snelle terugkoppelingen kunnen worden gemaakt, en dat soms op het laatste moment nog fouten kunnen worden hersteld.
• Gedurende de technische ontwikkeling van een product wordt de marketingontwikkeling gelijktijdig uitgevoerd;
• Als resultaat van de voortdurende inspanningen om de ontwerpen en systemen te verbeteren met behulp van nieuwe materialen, ruimtelijke constructieve concepten, engineering, productie- en assemblage-methoden, en tenslotte de toepassing hiervan in ontwerpen van project-architecten, wordt hopelijk de kwaliteit van de ruimtelijke constructie als product verbeterd. Indien goed toegepast, wordt daarmee een bijdrage aan de verhoging van de kwaliteit van de totale ruimtelijke omgeving gegeven.
• Uit de resultaten van het proces- en het productdeel van dit boek volgt de aanbeveling om studenten op het gebied van ruimtelijke constructies aan te raden tegelijkertijd een gemengd studieprogramma te laten doorlopen van architectonische, constructieve en industriële deelaspecten. Het betekent ook een nauwe samenwerking tussen de verschillende opleidingen. Deze aanbeveling geldt uiteraard ook voor het ontwerpen van andersoortige bouwproducten. In deze gemengde studie moeten 'product-architecten' gevormd worden.
• De introductie van product-architecten op het gebied van onderzoek in de bouw zal gaan resulteren in een meer creatieve benadering van Onderzoek en Ontwikkeling.

4 Ruimtevakwerken

Van de lijst van de diverse ruimtelijke constructies (zie par 2.2), zijn ruimtevakwerken de meest universeel toepasbare. Dit wordt voor een groot deel veroorzaakt door de rechtlijnigheid van de samenstellende elementen. Ze kunnen beter worden aangepast aan de verschillende gebouwontwerpen dan de ruimtelijk gekromde constructies, en passen beter in de huidige stroming van 'ingetogen' architectuur. In dit boek wordt het belang van de architectonische aspecten van ruimtelijke constructies onderstreept, in grotere mate dan de constructieve aspecten zoals grote overspanningen, maar ook meer dan de industriële aspecten zoals productie of de economische aspecten zoals het maximaliseren van de winst uit de onderneming. De totale complexiteit rondom iedere toepassing is meer interessant dan de optimalisering van slechts een of enkele aspecten. In dit opzicht zal het duidelijk zijn dat naast de architectonische begrippen zowel de constructieve als de industriële begrippen moesten worden ontwikkeld, maar altijd in het achterhoofd houdend dat de betreffende ruimtelijke constructie slechts een klein deel uitmaakt van de totale architectuur. Dit betekent dat de ruimtelijke constructie beïnvloed wordt door de complexiteit van de omgevende architectuur. Tevens betekent het dat zij omgekeerd een behoorlijke invloed kan uitoefenen op die architectuur. En als dit soort toepassingen belangrijk zijn, dan is de kunst om een toepasssing van een ruimtevakwerksysteem te ontwerpen in ongeacht welke omstandigheden, en deze toepassing in alle opzichten te optimaliseren, meer van belang dan een nieuw knooppunt uit te vinden of het gewicht van de constructie te laten minimaliseren. In dit alles toont zich de 'bredere' interesse van de ontwerper tegenover de 'diepere' interesse van de onderzoeker.

Alle paragrafen van hoofdstuk 4 zijn geschreven met deze bredere ontwerp-gedachte in het achterhoofd. De behandelde projecten zullen echter alleeen in relatie met de ruimtevakwerken worden behandeld. Een volledige architectonische analyse van het totale gebouw, waarin de constructie wordt toegepast, wordt niet gegeven, omdat het boek zich bewust meer bezig houdt met de ontwerp aspecten van ruimtelijke constructies zelf, dan met de gevolgen voor de architectuur. Het boek behandelt de architectuur in ruimtelijke constructies.

5 Gespannen Constructies

Ruimtevakwerken zijn constructies die in wezen alleen worden belast door normaalkrachten in de staven in druk of in trek. Normaliter worden de elementen van een ruimtevakwerk erop gedimensioneerd om de wisselende belastingen uit verschillende richtingen te kunnen opnemen zoals neerwaardse sneeuwbelasting en opwaardse windzuiging. Alle staafelementen zijn normaliter uitgevoerd in ronde buis- of vierkante kokervorm. Dit is het resultaat van een pragmatische benadering.

Een meer theoretische benadering is het meer extreem onderscheid maken tussen op trek en op druk belaste elementen, en de beide groepen elementen puur op deze functies te dimensioneren. Omdat op druk belaste elementen gewoonlijk een aanzienlijke trekbelasting kunnen opnemen, maar omgekeerd de op trek belaste elementen niet op druk kunnen worden belast, moet er een voorspanning worden geïntroduceerd op plaatsen waar deze tekenomkering in trekelementen toch zou kunnen optreden. Daarmee wordt bereikt dat een passief trek-systeem wordt gewijzigd naar een actief voorspansysteem die door de vermindering van de voorspanning ook in staat is om drukkrachten op te nemen. In dit geval hebben in de neutrale situatie (zonder externe belastingen) alle trekelementen een zekere voorspanning, en door hun verbindingen hebben de drukelementen dan tevens een zekere drukspanning. Externe belastingen kunnen verder resulteren in het verhogen van de trek in trekelementen, waarvoor deze elementen goed zijn uitgerust. Het kan echter omgekeerd ook resulteren in een reductie van de voorspanning. Dit is uiteraard alleen mogelijk tot een bepaalde hoogte, namelijk totdat de totale voorspanning in een element is verdwenen door de geïntroduceerde drukbelasting.

De totale groep gespannen constructies bestaat in wezen uit drie categorieën:
- Tensegrity constructies met een continu en actief voorspansysteem en een discontinu drukstaven systeem, geïntegreerd tot een gesloten constructieve eenheid;
- Gespannen membranen met ruimtelijk gekromde actief voorgespannen kabelnetten of membranen als belangrijkste onderdelen met additionele trek- en drukelementen voor de totale stabilisering van deze open constructieve systemen;
- Ruimtelijke tuiconstructies, waarvan de voornaamste eigenschap is het versterken middels trekelementen van andersoortige constructies. Deze categorie constructies bevat simpele onderspannen masten voor de versterking van balken of balkroosters, en grotere onderspanningen in de vorm van hangende masten onder voorgespannen of hangende daken, verder op druk belaste dakvlakken zoals tensegrity koepels of gebogen dakvlakken, maar tevens onderspannen liggers (zoals Polonçeau spanten) in een ruimtelijke vorm van bijvoorbeeld fietswieldaken. Tot deze groep constructies behoren eveneens de vele soorten 'binnenste buiten gekeerde' constructies (zoals 'High-Tech' constructies ook wel worden aangeduid), in ruimtelijke uitvoering, waarbij verticale of schuine masten worden gestabiliseerd middels tuikabels.

6 Integratie van Constructie en Afdekking

Dit laatste hoofdstuk is gevuld met voorbeelden van diverse combinaties van belasting dragende ruimtelijke constructies en omhullende bekledingen of beglazingen als een sterk persoonlijk specialisme door de auteur geïntroduceerd op het vakgebied van de ruimtelijke constructies in de architectuur. Een architecten opleiding zorgt ervoor dat de ontwerper van een ruimtelijke constructie zich ervan bewust is dat een probleem pas ten dele is opgelost met het globaal ontwerp van de constructie. Vaak betekent de introductie van een ruimtelijke constructie in het ontwerp dat een grotere cirkel van detail problemen moet worden opgelost. Wie is er in staat om een passend omhullend systeem te ontwerpen voor de betreffende ruimtelijke constructie? Met andere woorden: daarmee wordt het ontwerp probleem duidelijker als een aantrekkelijke intellectuele uitdaging. Bij voorkeur moet de ontwerp oplossing gevonden worden in de richting van een speciaal toegesneden of beter nog een geïntegreerde oplossing. De keuze en het ontwerp van de constructie en de bedekking hebben een grote wederzijdse invloed op elkaar omdat bijvoorbeeld de capaciteit van overspanning van de bekleding vaak de moduul van een ruimtevakwerk bepaalt. Maar er zijn nog meer actieve reciproke relaties tussen constructies en afdekkingen behalve deze geometrische relaties. De drie paragrafen tonen een grote verscheidenheid aan typen bekleding, van sculpturele voorgespannen membranen, via de meer conventionele metalen bekledingen en sandwich paneel systemen, naar enkele voorbeelden van geïntegreerde beglazingen, zelfs leidend naar de ontwerp voorstellen van constructies bestaande uit glazen panelen die constructieve normaalkrachten kunnen opnemen (trek en/of druk), en daarmee zowel als dragend constructief element functioneren en tegelijkertijd als klimaatscheiding. Het grensverleggende karakter van deze ontwerpen houdt tevens in dat er nog geruime tijd ontwikkeld moet worden voordat er sprake is van een volwassen product, hoewel tijdens het proces van productontwikkeling voortdurend prototypes in de vorm van projecttoepassingen worden gebouwd.

Buiten deze integraties van constructie en omhulling zijn er ook andere integraties mogelijk: bij voorbeeld de integratie van constructie en elektrische bekabeling voor belichting, of van constructie en verwarming met water of zelfs lucht als medium, of air-conditioning. Deze combinaties kunnen worden vergeleken met de biologische modellen van skelet, huid, zenuwen, hersenen, bloedvatenstelsel en het zenuwstelsel, die weliswaar in het menselijk lichaam niet letterlijk zijn geïntegreerd, maar toch zeer duidelijk en inspirerend gecombineerd optreden in de eenheid van het lichaam.

Bibliography

1 Wachsmann, Konrad. *Wendepunkt im Bauen* Wiesbaden 1959

2 Chant, Christofer. *Aviation, an illustrated history* London 1986

3 Kaplicky, Jan and David Nixon. *Skin* in: Architectural Review July 1983

4 Kaplicky, Jan and David Nixon. *Aerospace Technology as a Resourse for New Lightweight Structures Concepts* in proceeding First International Conference on Lightweight Structures in Architecture Sydney 1986 pp 118 - 122

5 Otto, Frei. *Das Hängende Dach* Berlin 1952

6 Otto, Frei. *Zugbeanspruchte Konstruktionen band 1 + 2* Stuttgart 1965 / 1967

7 Glase, Ludwig. *The work of Frei Otto* the Museum of Modern Art New York 1972

8 Eekhout, Mick. *Frei Otto and the Munich Olympic Games* in: Zodiac nr 21 Dec 1972 pp 12 to 74 1971

9 Donin, Gianpiero. *Renzo Piano, Pezzo per Pezzo* Rome 1982

10 Faber, Colin. *Candela: the Shell Builder* New York 1965

11 Huber, Benedikt Jean-Claude Steinegger. *Jean Prouvé* Zurich 1971

12 Beeren, Wim. *Constructeur Jean Prouvé* catalogue Museum Boymans - Van Beuningen Rotterdam 1981

13 Fuller, Richard Buckminster. *Ideas and Integreties* Toronto 1969

14 Makowski, Zygmunt. *Räumliche Tragwerke aus Stahl* Düsseldorf 1963

15 Makowski, Zygmunt. *Analysis, Design and Construction of Double Layer Grids* London 1983

16 Makowski, Zygmunt. *Analysis, Design and Construction of Braced Domes* London 1984

17 Makowski, Zygmunt. *Analysis, Design and Construction of Braced Barrel Vaults* London 1985

18 Mengeringhausen, Max. *Mero-Raumtragwerke* Wurzburg 1985

19 Emde, Helmut. *Geometrie der Knoten-Stab-Tragwerken* Würzburg 1977

20 Kato, Arinori. *Pier Luigi Nervi* in: Progress nr 23 pp 6 to 163

21 Oosterhoff, Jaap. *Constructies* Delft 1980

22 Aluminium Zentrale. *Aluminium Taschenbuch* Dusseldorf 1984

23 Gordon, James. *Structures, or Why Things Don't Fall Down* Harmondsworth UK 1983

24 Gordon, James. *The New Science of Strong Materials, or Why You Don't Fall Through the Floor* Harmondsworth UK 1983

25 Morse, S.P. *Marketing in de Praktijk* Deventer 1970

26 Leduc, R. *Marketing van Nieuwe Producten* Alphen aan de Rijn 1973

27 Meerendonk, H. van de. *Netwerkplanning* Deventer 1969

28 Peter, Laurence. *Why Things Go Wrong, or the Peter Principle Revisited* New York 1985

29 Polónyi, Stefan. *Mit Zaghafter Konsequenz* Braunschweig 1987

Publications

- Eekhout, Mick ea. *Kabelconstructies* Kenniskapsule TU Delft 1970

- Eekhout, Mick. *Frei Otto and the Munich Olympic Games* in: Zodiac nr 21 Dec 1971 pp 12 — 74

- Eekhout, Mick, Alfons Holslag, Suzan van Westenbrugge *Pneus* Kenniskapsule TU Delft 1972

- Dicke, Dick, Mick Eekhout, Hans Mekel, Gernot Minke ea. *Tensegrity* Seminar TU Delft 1972

- Eekhout, Mick. *Air-mattress for education and for rehabilitation* in: Conference 'Pneumatics and Education' Columbia, Maryland USA May 1973

- Eekhout, Mick, Ron Nieuwenhuis, Thieu Ponsen. *Pneus in de gebouwde omgeving* in: Plan nr 5 1973 pp 17-37

- Niesten, Joop. *Octatube, een ruimtevakwerk met architectonische kwaliteiten* in: De Architect nr 10 1979 pp 120 - 125

- Eekhout, Mick. *Ruimtevakwerken, Het Dak van München, Houten Schaaldaken* in: De Architect Themanr 'Daken' 1981 pp 17 - 20 pp 21 - 23 pp 25 - 27

- Eekhout, Mick. *Metalen Ruimtevakwerken met Ondergehangen Kunststof Huid* in: H2O nr 11 1982 pp 256 - 273

- Eekhout, Mick. *Tenten, Kabelnetten en Pneus in Nederland* in: De Architect nr 12 1982 pp 66 - 73

- Eekhout, Mick. *Ontwerpen met Ruimtevakwerken* in: De Architect nr 4 1983 pp 74 - 81

- Eekhout, Mick. *Ruimtevakwerken* in: NBD catalogus level 2 Deventer 1983/1984 pp 1 - 8

- Eekhout, Mick. *Constructief Vormgeven met Aluminium* in: PATO TU Delft 'Aluminium Constructies' Nov 1984 pp 1 - 14

- Eekhout, Mick. *De Ontwikkeling van Octatube en Tuball* in: PATO TU Delft 'Konstruktief Vormgeven met Ruimtevakwerken 1' Jan 1985 pp 1 - 36

- Eekhout, Mick. *Ontwerpen met Ruimtevakwerken* in: PATO TU Delft 'Konstruktief Vormgeven met Ruimtevakwerken 2' March 1985 pp 1 - 31

- Eekhout, Mick. *Ruimtelijke Constructies van Octatube* in: Thermisch Verzinken nr 14 1985 June 1985 pp 27 - 31
translated:
in: Feuerverzinken nr 14 1985 pp 27 - 31

- Asselbergs, Thijs. *Jongleren met Constructies* in NRC-Handelsblad 2 Febr 1985 p 11

- Niesten, Joop. *Ruimte voor Ruimtevakwerken* in: De Architect June 1986 pp 78 - 81

- Eekhout, Mick. *Nieuwbouw Octatube in Delft* in Bouwen met Staal nr 76 June 1986 pp 56 - 59

- Eekhout, Mick. *Architectural Design of Space Frames* Octatube seminar Kuala Lumpur June 1986 Singapore Nov 1986 pp 1 - 17

- Eekhout, Mick. *An Architectural Generation of Space Structures* in: Proceedings 'First International Conference on Lightweight Structures in Architecture' Sydney 1986 pp 96 - 103

- Eekhout, Mieke en Mick. *Ruimtelijke Constructies in de Architectuur, overpeinzingen na een Congres in Australie* in: De Architect Oct 1986 pp 85 - 93
(translated:)
Reflections on a Conference in Australia, a Personal View in: Space Structures vol 2 nr 4 1986/1987 pp 251 — 255

- Makowski, Zygmunt. *Profile, Ir Mick Eekhout - A Dutch Designer of Space Structures* in: Space Structures vol 2 nr 4 1986/1987 pp 262 - 269

- Eekhout, Mick. *Jongleren met Ruimtelijke Constructies* in: Proceedings PATO TU Delft 'De Invloed van Constructies in de Architectuur' May 1987 pp 173 — 205

- Eekhout, Mick. *De inpassing van Ruimtelijke Constructies in de Architectuur* in: Proceedings PATO TU Delft 'De Invloed van Constructies in de Architectuur' May 1987 pp 147 - 171

- Eekhout, Mick. *Integratie tussen Architectonisch, Constructief en Industrieel Ontwerpen* TU Eindhoven April 1987

- Eekhout, Mick. *Inside-Out Structures or How to Arrive at High-Tech* in: Proceedings International Conference on Non-Conventional Structures London Dec 1987 pp 11 - 19
(translation:)
Binnenste-Buiten Constructies, of wat het etiket 'High-Tech' inhoudt in: Bouwen met Staal nr 84 pp 35 — 39 and nr 85 1988 pp 19 - 24

- Eekhout, Mick. *Generaliseren of Specialiseren, over een creatieve O3 formule in de Architectuur* Gemeentelijk Symposium Jonge Bedrijven Delft Nov 1987 pp 1 - 14

- Eekhout, Mick. *Het vormgeven van Aluminium tot Ruimtelijke Constructies* in: Symposium Alutech 88 Utrecht Febr 1988 pp 2 - 13

- Eekhout, Mick. *De Elegance van Staalconstructies* in: Staaldag 88 / Bouwen met Staal nr 86 1988 pp 29 - 33

- Eekhout, Mick. *De Specialist-producent in de Bouw* in: Proceedings symposium Boosting, Rotterdam Nov 1988 pp 1 - 9

- Eekhout, Mick. *The origin of Partitioning Walls* at: opening exhibition Interfinish ION Rotterdam Nov 1988

- Eekhout, Mick. *De Product-Architect Organiseert.* in: Bouw 27 jan 1989 pp 31 - 34

- Eekhout, Mick. *Constructieve Beglazingen* in: De Architect, themanummer Glas 1989

Biography

Adrianus Cornelis Jozef 'Mick' Eekhout, 1950

Education
Highschool (HBS-b) St. Stanislas College, Delft 1962-1968
University of Technology in Delft, at the faculty of
Architecture 1968 - 1973
Practical works
Institut für leichte Flächentragwerke/Frei Otto Stuttgart 1970
Renzo Piano, Genova 1970
Student assistant TH Delft 1971-1973
Graduation
1973 cum laude (Prof Jaap Oosterhoff/Prof Carel Weeber)
Doctor's degree
1989 (Promotors Prof Jaap Oosterhoff/Prof Moshe Zwarts)

Profession
1973 computer analysis space frames, TU Delft
1973 architect at Groosman Partners Total Planning, Rotterdam
1973/1974 architect at Thunnissen, Van Kranendonk, Becka, The Hague
Architect
Independent office from Jan 1976 - Jan 1982
Engineer
Start Octatube Engineering bv April 1978
Producer
Start Octatube Space Structures bv Dec 1983 (General Director)
The Octatube Group has several daughter companies in Delft and abroad.
In 1988 Octatube had 50 employees in Delft.
Rotterdamseweg 200, 2628 AS Delft.

Lectures
From 1972 - 1988 regular lectures on space structures / structures in architecture etc at TU Delft, TU Eindhoven, at Academies of Architecture in Rotterdam, in Tilburg, in Amsterdam, and NHIBS in Antwerp. Lectures given for professionals in the Netherlands and in Antwerp, London, Sydney, Singapore, Kuala Lumpur, and in Baltimore.
Conducted several post-academical courses on structural design/architecture at the TU Delft.
Co-starter of Delft Design, Delft, 1987
Co-starter of Booosting, Rotterdam, 1988

This book has been written as a dissertation at the
University of Technology in Delft, the Netherlands.
Promotors were Prof.ir. J. Oosterhoff and Prof.ir. M. Zwarts.